Degrees of Freedom

Degrees of Freedom

American Women Poets and the Women's College, 1905–1955

Bethany Hicok

Lewisburg
Bucknell University Press

©2008 by Rosemont Publishing & Printing Corp.

All rights reserved. Authorization to photocopy items for internal or personal use, or the internal or personal use of specific clients, is granted by the copyright owner, provided that a base fee of $10.00, plus eight cents per page, per copy is paid directly to the Copyright Clearance Center, 222 Rosewood Drive, Danvers, Massachusetts 01923. [978-0-8387-5693-5/08 $10.00 + 8¢ pp, pc.]

Associated University Presses
2010 Eastpark Boulevard
Cranbury, NJ 08512

The paper used in this publication meets the requirements of the American National Standard for Permanence of Paper for Printed Library Materials Z39.48-1984.

Library of Congress Cataloging-in-Publication Data

Hicok, Bethany, 1958-
  Degrees of fredom : American women poets and the women's college, 1905-1955 / Bethany Hicok
    p. cm.
  Includes bibliographical references (p.   ) and index
  ISBN 978-0-8387-5693-5 (alk paper)
1. American poetry—Women authors—History and criticism. 2. College verse, American—History and criticism. 3. American poetry—20th century—History and criticism. 4. Moore, Marianne, 1887-1972—Knowledge and learning. 5. Bishop, Elizabeth, 1911-1979—Knowledge and learning. 6. Plath, Sylvia—Knowledge and learning. 7. Women poets, American—Education (Higher) 8. Women's colleges—United States. I. Title.

PS151.H53 2008
811'52099287—dc22

2008000100

PRINTED IN THE UNITED STATES OF AMERICA

*For Jonathan
and Sam*

> . . . . With knowledge as
> with wolves' surliness,
> the student studies
> voluntarily, refusing to be less
>
> than individual.
>
> —Marianne Moore,
> "The Student"

Contents

Acknowledgments	11
Abbreviations	15
Introduction: Degrees of Freedom	19
1. To Work "Lovingly": Marianne Moore at Bryn Mawr, 1905–1909	29
2. Serpents in Paradise: Marianne Moore and "Marriage"	57
3. Elizabeth Bishop's "Queer Birds": Vassar, *Con Spirito*, and the Romance of Female Community	84
4. *Con Spirito*, Improvisation, and the Poetry of the 1930s	107
5. Sylvia Plath's Brave New World at Smith, 1950–1955	131
6. "Order[ing] a Box of Maniacs": Questions of Power in the Bee Poems	155
Coda	175
Notes	179
Bibliography	201
Index	210

Acknowledgments

IT IS A PLEASURE TO THANK THOSE FRIENDS AND COLLEAGUES WHO HAVE provided insight and support throughout this project. I would first like to thank James Longenbach whose lively seminars in modern poetry at the University of Rochester and generous criticism and guidance started me down the road to this book. Charles Berger has been a good friend and tough critic throughout the drafting and revising stages. Our conversations about poetry have inspired me over the past few years.

Many others have contributed to the process. Robin Schulze provided enthusiastic support and excellent criticism. Mary Chapman, Thomas Travisano, Jeredith Merrin, Angus Cleghorn, Bette London, Mark Betz, Amanda Howell, and John Palatella, all read and commented on my work at various stages. I thank them for their generosity and their stimulating conversation. Camille Roman organized a wonderful panel for the Society for the Study of American Women Writers, which allowed me to try out ideas for chapter 4. I am grateful to my editors, particularly Christine Retz, managing editor of Associated University Presses, and Greg Clingham at Bucknell University Press.

The argument of this book depends on the unpublished writing of Moore, Bishop and Plath, and so I owe a debt to the scholars and librarians who work with those papers. Karen Kukil has been enormously helpful in directing me through the Plath material at Smith, as well as in reading and commenting on drafts of the Plath chapters. Evelyn Feldman, who was formerly with the Rosenbach Museum and Library, and Patricia Willis, were generous in sharing their knowledge of the Moore papers in the early stages. Nancy MacKechnie at Vassar helped me find my way through the Bishop papers. I would also like to express gratitude to the Lilly Library at Indiana University for the use of its resources in my work on Plath.

This project focuses on the undergraduate experiences of poets in the first half of the twentieth century and how it shaped their later development. Such a project has benefited from my own undergraduate students at Westminster College. Two in particular have worked as my research assistants: Lindsay Onufer worked alongside me on the Sylvia Plath Papers in the Lilly Library at Indiana University and offered insight in her reading of Plath's undergraduate experience; and Julie Tvaruzek helped with the final editing and preparation of the manuscript. She also designed the jacket cover for the book. The students in my Sylvia Plath seminar at Westminster contributed in lively and stimulating ways to my thinking about Plath's poetry.

My research has been supported by a number of research and travel grants. Westminster College has been generous in its support with travel, research, and conference funds, and, most recently, the McCandless Scholar award. I would especially like to thank Frederick Horn and Sandra Webster for their tireless efforts as faculty development officers of Westminster College to encourage, support and create a culture of scholarship on campus. Mount St. Clare College also provided research funding, and the Susan B. Anthony Center at the University of Rochester awarded a travel grant for work on the Moore and Bishop papers in the very early stages of the project.

My friends and colleagues at Westminster College inspired me in many ways during the course of finishing this book with good conversation, food, wine and a model for productive scholarship. I want to especially thank Jeffrey Kripal, James Perkins, Russell Martin, Carol Bové, Betsy Ford, and Deborah Mitchell. I would also like to thank Connie Davis, Westminster College Interlibrary Loan, for tracking down a variety of materials.

Most of all, I would like to thank my husband, Jonathan Miller, to whom (along with our son) this book is dedicated. His generous support, professional knowledge, and love have sustained me in both my life and work for many years.

Grateful acknowledgment is made to the following publishers and individuals for permission to reprint materials from copyrighted sources.

Permission for quotations from Marianne Moore's unpublished works granted by Marianne Craig Moore, Literary Executor for the Estate of Marianne Moore. All rights reserved.

Unpublished letters and materials by Marianne Moore and others from the Marianne Moore Collection, reproduced by permission of the Rosenbach Museum and Library, Philadelphia, Pennsylvania.

From *Observations* by Marianne Moore, copyright © by the Dial Press. Reprinted by permission of Faber and Faber Limited.

Excerpts from *The Complete Poems: 1927–1979* by Elizabeth Bishop (copyright ©1979, 1983 by Alice Helen Methfessel); excerpts from *The Collected Prose* by Elizabeth Bishop (copyright ©1984 by Alice Helen Methfessel); excerpts from *One Art: Letters* by Elizabeth Bishop, selected and edited by Robert Giroux (copyright ©1994 by Alice Helen Methfessel; introduction and compilation copyright ©1994 by Robert Giroux). Reprinted by permission of Farrar, Straus and Giroux, LLC.

Excerpts from unpublished notebooks and unpublished letters written by Elizabeth Bishop (copyright ©2008 by Alice Helen Methfessel). Printed by permission of Farrar, Straus and Giroux, LLC on behalf of the Elizabeth Bishop Estate.

From *The Collected Poems of Sylvia Plath* (copyright ©1960, 1965, 1971, 1981 by the Estate of Sylvia Plath). Editorial material copyright ©1981 by Ted Hughes. Reprinted by permission of Faber and Faber Limited and HarperCollins.

From "The Bee God" by Ted Hughes (copyright ©1998 by Ted Hughes). Reprinted by permission of Faber and Faber Limited.

From *The Selected Letters of Marianne Moore* by Marianne Moore (copyright ©1997 by the Estate of Marianne Moore). Introduction, annotations, and additional editorial material (copyright ©1997 by Bonnie Costello). Used by permission of Alfred A. Knopf, a division of Random House, Inc.

From "Marianne, My Mother, and Me" by Maxine Kumin (copyright ©1989). Reprinted by permission of Maxine Kumin.

An earlier version of chapter 1 was published under the same title, "To Work 'Lovingly': Marianne Moore at Bryn Mawr, 1905-1909," in *The Journal of Modern Literature* 23, nos. 3/4 (Summer 2000): 483-501, and is reprinted here with permission of Indiana University Press.

An earlier version of chapter 3 was published under the same title, "Elizabeth Bishop's 'Queer Birds': Vassar, Con Spirito, and the Romance of Female Community," in *Contemporary Literature* 40, no. 2 (Summer 1999): 286–310, and is reprinted here with permission of The University of Wisconsin Press.

Abbreviations

Moore Chapters

BMM — *Becoming Marianne Moore: The Early Poems, 1907–1924.* Edited by Robin G. Schulze. Berkeley: University of California Press, 2002.

CPo — *The Complete Poems of Marianne Moore.* Revised edition, New York: Macmillan/Viking, 1981

CPr — *The Complete Prose of Marianne Moore.* Edited by Patricia C. Willis. New York: Viking, 1986.

SL — *The Selected Letters of Marianne Moore.* Edited by Bonnie Costello, Celeste Goodridge, and Cristanne Miller. New York: Knopf, 1997.

RML — Marianne Moore Collection, Rosenbach Musuem and Library, Philadelphia, Pennsylvania.

PMM — *The Poems of Marianne Moore.* Edited by Grace Schulman. New York: Viking, 2003.

Bishop Chapters

CP — *Elizabeth Bishop: The Complete Poems.* New York: Farrar, Straus and Giroux, 1991.

CPr — *Elizabeth Bishop: The Collected Prose.* Edited by Robert Giroux. New York: Farrar, Straus and Giroux, 1984.

SL — *One Art: Elizabeth Bishop Letters.* Edited by Robert Giroux. New York: Farrar, Straus and Giroux, 1994.

VC	Elizabeth Bishop Collection, Vassar College Library, Poughkeepsie, New York.

Plath Chapters

BJ	*The Bell Jar,* New York: Perennial, 1996.
CP	*The Collected Poems of Sylvia Plath.* Edited by Ted Hughes. New York: HarperPerennial, 1981.
LH	*Letters Home, Correspondence 1950–1963.* Edited by Aurelia Schober Plath. New York: Harper, 1975.
UJ	*The Unabridged Journals of Sylvia Plath,* 1950–1962. Edited by Karen V. Kukil. New York: Anchor Books, 2000.
BJ	*The Bell Jar.* New York: HarperPerennial, 1999.
LL	Sylvia Plath Collection, Lilly Library, Indiana University, Bloomington.

Degrees of Freedom

Introduction:
Degrees of Freedom

> "In America," began
> the lecturer, "everyone must have a
> degree...."
> —Marianne Moore, "The Student"

MY EPIGRAPH IS TAKEN FROM MARIANNE MOORE'S 1932 POEM "THE Student" and underscores a major point in my study of American women poets and the women's college. As my title for this book suggests, for many Americans in the first half of the twentieth century, college degrees were considered synonymous with freedom, particularly for disenfranchised groups, such as African Americans and women. As Moore's poem tells us, "school . . . / is both a tree of knowledge / and of liberty,— / seen in the unanimity of college // mottoes . . . "[1] Moore entered college in 1905, among the second generation of college women to earn degrees in this country, and her understanding of the student as "a variety / of hero" emerges from her own experience as a student. Moore tells us that the student must be "'patient / of neglect and of reproach,'—who can 'hold by // himself'" (*CPo*, 102). While this may be true of all serious students, the statement is particularly resonant for women who attended women's colleges in the first half of the twentieth century.

Women's colleges provided an important cultural and critical space for American women poets and played a central role in their poetic development. Many of our major modern poets attended northeastern elite women's colleges, primarily the Seven Sisters, including Marianne Moore and H. D. (Bryn Mawr), Edna St. Vincent Millay,

Elizabeth Bishop, and Muriel Rukeyser (Vassar), Sylvia Plath (Smith), and Adrienne Rich (Radcliffe). Despite the dominance of this experience for women poets in America, there has been no full-scale investigation of its impact on shaping women's poetic production.[2] Yet as Gail McDonald's work on Pound and Eliot suggests, a focus on a poet's education can illuminate how that poet defines self and work.[3]

But women's colleges were distinct from the male institutions that Pound and Eliot attended, not in their lack of academic rigor, but in the intense scrutiny paid them by the outside world. Women's college presidents had to justify not only their curriculums but also how and why they were educating women at all and for what purpose. Consequently, the question of a writing career for women poets in same-sex institutions became inseparable from questions about women's sexuality, marriage, and motherhood, which was simply not the case for male poets.

The women's college experience often provided women poets with a framework for study and work that allowed them to insert themselves into a poetic tradition (or make a new one). However, particularly in the 1950s, it might just as easily hold them back, discourage them, and make them feel that their expensive educations only led to the chance of better educating their sons. While Moore's Bryn Mawr supported its female students' rights to an equal education in opposition to the larger culture with its activist, feminist agenda, Plath's Smith joined the larger postwar culture in its relentless push of women back into the home. By midcentury, the modern women's college had moved from the Progressive Era to the McCarthy Era.

It is this historical arc—from activism to conformity—that my book traces as I reconsider the cultural history of women's poetic production as emerging from the women's college experience. In tracing this arc, I will examine the impact of the women's college experience on the careers of three poets—Marianne Moore, who graduated from Bryn Mawr in 1909; Elizabeth Bishop, who graduated from Vassar in 1934; and Sylvia Plath, who graduated from Smith in 1955. These poets not only exemplify what we have come to value in twentieth century American poetry, but their experience (and, I believe, their work) also reflects what happened in higher education for women from the beginning of the century to the 1950s, allowing us to learn a lot about poetic production and literary history through them.

During this fifty-year period, the Seven Sisters colleges changed dramatically. Moore's was a unique period in the history of the women's college, as the values of American progressivism, women's education, and the ideology of separate spheres came together in a kind of perfect storm that created a climate for cultural change. The college experience at this time, Lynn Gordon notes, "expanded many students' social consciousness and desire for change."[4] Colleges and universities during the Progressive Era, from 1890 to 1920, acted as "intellectual laboratories for reformers and their programs," making them "an important arm of American progressivism."[5] Bryn Mawr during Moore's time was a leader in Progressive Era reform movements. In her biography of Bryn Mawr's radical feminist president M. Carey Thomas, Helen Lefkowitz Horowitz refers to the years 1904 to 1911 (almost exactly corresponding to Moore's years at Bryn Mawr) as "the high tide" of Thomas's leadership.[6] She had become not only a nationally recognized leader in higher education but, according to Horowitz, also a leader who "lent the educated women's voice to the suffrage movement."[7]

Moore and her mother were actively involved in suffrage, and according to Moore's letters home, Thomas often held forth on suffrage in both her weekly chapel talks and during dinners at the Deanery where select students were invited. She had also become a formidable figure in the educational community, often publicly chastising Charles Eliot, president of Harvard, over issues of educational reform and women's higher education. Thomas once criticized Eliot for his notion that women should be educated differently from men, and in her response to Eliot, she asserted—as Virginia Woolf would do a few years later in *A Room of One's Own*—that "the life of the mind had no sex."[8]

Here was a powerful woman who was willing to go head-to-head with any man, a formidable figure for Moore to learn from and emulate. Just before Moore entered Bryn Mawr, John Singer Sargent had painted Thomas's portrait, which hung in the Deanery and that Moore undoubtedly saw when she was invited there from time to time during her undergraduate years. The portrait aligns Thomas in many ways with the ruling families of the Renaissance, the Medicis of Florence. Posed in the Mannerist style of the popular Medici painter Bronzino, Thomas looks straight out at the spectator. It is a calm, self-assured, and powerful portrait. Thomas in person and in portrait wielded a power and authority from which Moore would learn a great deal.⁹

The wave of reform that Moore rode during her Bryn Mawr days and that led to real political change for women during the Progressive Era disappeared after women won the vote in 1920. Not surprisingly, as Gordon notes, as "women's progress and influence reached its height, a cultural backlash appeared," which manifested itself in, among other things, an embrace of a more aggressive masculinity and "quotas for female admissions to colleges and graduate schools."[10] Moreover, as a result of the medical-scientific discourse that began to permeate the debates over women and higher education, women's communities began to be associated with social disorder, sexual perversion, and disease. In this discourse, women's colleges became possible "breeding grounds" for the lesbian. By the time Elizabeth Bishop entered Vassar College in 1930, women could be expelled for showing too close an attachment to another woman.[11] The result of this change in attitude was that "women students," according to Gordon, "began to view their unmarried teachers as unfulfilled or even sexually deviant old maids."[12]

While such a definition of female community tended to discourage women from turning to each other for support, it also, in Michel Foucault's words, became "a starting point for an opposing strategy."[13] Bishop's little community of writers at Vassar is a good example of how this works. It might even be said that these women embraced the "sexually deviant old maid" label in their brilliant parody of *The American Spectator*, the aggressively male literary magazine begun in the 1930s. They actually launched the publication of their own avant-garde literary magazine *Con Spirito* by going head-to-head with *The American Spectator*, employing that magazine's language of biological determinism in order to challenge its notion that Smith and Vassar women were unnatural and their professors "dessicated old maids."[14]

Sylvia Plath's college experience at Smith in the 1950s followed another aggressive backlash against women in education.[15] Educators were placed under a great deal of pressure to uphold the postwar homemaker ideal that dominated American culture by preparing their undergraduate women to assume domestic roles. Women were told it was their "democratic duty" to serve husband and children. Women who went to college in the late 1940s and early 1950s "must want, above all, to be married."[16] As Barbara Solomon has argued of Vassar women, "a diamond ring on the fourth finger was the sign of success most valued in one's senior year at Vassar in 1949."[17] Smith's college newspaper, *The Sophian*, then called *Scan*, joined this chorus in 1951 when it reported on Smith's "annual marriage and engagement poll," sounding more like the clubhouse of the Kentucky Derby than a women's college. "Inter-house competition shows close results," the story blares. "Hopkins leads with seven rings. Second place is held in a four-way tie—by Gillett, Capen, Lawrence and Wilder. A large number of other houses have five students with fiancées or husbands."[18] Hence, women's colleges "too often . . . resembled a marriage market," Solomon argues, "with peers and professors reinforcing the public mood of conformity."[19]

On the one hand the women's college curriculum continued to educate women in preparation for a career. On the other, women's colleges were debating whether to transform their curriculums, but this time not to foster political change that would help women gain a greater voice in the marketplace, but rather to reflect the postwar move of women back into the home by offering courses in marriage and motherhood. One stunning example of the change can be seen in the difference between M. Carey Thomas and her niece, Millicent McIntosh, who gave into conservative pressure in the early 1950s. As president of Barnard College, she joined with the presidents of Vassar and Wellesley "to 'caution that [a woman's] first duty is to [her] children,'" according to a *New York Times* headline.[20] Moreover, the U.S. Cold War policy of "control and containment" that pertained to both lesbians and communists, according to Lillian Faderman, was also reflected in the discourse on the 1950s women's college campus, making it "perhaps the worst time in history for women to love women."[21]

Although sometimes run by male administrators with a good proportion of male faculty, women's colleges were primarily female-dominated communities that served as sites of negotiation and renegotiation for women writers over questions and definitions of literary authority, women's economic independence, motherhood, marriage, friendship, feminism, and female sexuality. As a space of female community—"a social microcosm," as Barbara Solomon has called it[22]—women's colleges provided the opportunity for these women to consider a writing career a possibility and fostered ideas of work that helped them develop that career. As Katherine Adams has argued in her study of women's writing groups and higher education, the curriculum developed by women's colleges encouraged women to see themselves as part of a "community of writers" and helped them prepare for professional writing careers.[23] Moore, Bishop, and Plath all experienced the women's college as a "community of writers," as a workshop for their developing writing aesthetic and careers.

In these colleges, women were encouraged to compete against each other, not against men, for scholarships and awards. As college women, Moore, Bishop, and Plath defined themselves and their place in the literary world not only within and against a male-dominated literary tradition but also against and in dialogue with other women. Their experience represents the kind of "historical struggles and differences among, between, and within writing women" that Betsy Erkkila has suggested is an important part of women's experience.[24] In her work on women's literary history, Erkkila suggests that feminist scholars begin to look not only at women's relationships in terms of their potential for sisterhood but also in terms of the differences and struggles between women. Women's literary history, then, becomes more of "a field of cultural struggle."[25] It is possible to see the women's college as such "a field," as well, to understand that the women's college was centrally important to the developing poetic practice of Moore, Bishop, and Plath because of its contradictions and because it was a site of contestation, struggle and change.

Bryn Mawr, I argue in my opening chapters, taught Marianne Moore how to be modern, and her major modernist collection, the 1924 *Observations*, grew out of Bryn Mawr's progressive educational environment, fostered by its radical feminist M. Carey Thomas. Drawing on the significant body of letters Moore wrote home to her family, drafts of early poems, college reading notebooks, and prose and poetry written in college, I chart Moore's development as a writer and identify a link between the educated New Woman—those strong, independent young professional women who were emerging from women's colleges at the turn of the century—and Moore's modernist aesthetic. The women's college of Moore's day also fostered close ties between women coupled with an academically rigorous and competitive curriculum that allowed many college educated women of Moore's generation to reject marriage and establish themselves in successful writing and editing careers. I also identify a new theoretical concept for understanding the educated woman's relationship to her work, the "romance of scholarship," which I find in Moore's work as well as in fictionalized accounts of college women written by Bryn Mawr faculty and alumnae at the turn of the century.

As a student at Vassar in the 1930s, Elizabeth Bishop "discovered" Moore, but it is not this much-discussed relationship that will form the focus of my two chapters on Bishop. Rather, I argue, that the group Bishop formed at Vassar in the 1930s was at least as important to Bishop's development of style and response to modernism as her relationship with Moore. My two Bishop chapters look at Bishop's collaboration with a brilliant coterie of writers, including Mary McCarthy, Eleanor and Eunice Clark, Muriel Rukeyser, and others, who started their own avant-garde literary magazine, *Con Spirito*, to rival the college's "traditional" literary magazine. But *Con Spirito* was also a response to masculinist notions of female writers and the women's college put forward in the pages of *The American Spectator*, and so it involved a dual challenge to the boundaries of literary and sexual convention both inside and outside the Vassar community.

The spirit of experimentalism the group fostered in its criteria for publishing in *Con Spirito* allowed Bishop to try out different kinds of writing and even to explore her "deviant" sexuality, however covertly. Within this circle, she was allowed a greater degree of artistic freedom than the college's established literary magazine fostered. I look at how Bishop and her rebel sisters negotiate questions of literary production, lesbian identity, and female community and how they help Bishop define the next wave of modern poetry and her place in it. Finally, the experience of *Con Spirito* operates as a kind of fantasy of community I trace throughout Bishop's poetic career, from the 1936 poem "The Man-Moth" to the 1971 "Crusoe in England." This fantasy, which I most closely identify with Bishop in this book, nevertheless runs through representations of female community in writers throughout the twentieth century. The phrase that most captures what this might mean comes from Bishop herself in a 1948 essay on Marianne Moore's animal poetry, which, she writes, sometimes makes one think of "some realm of reciprocity."[26] Given its origins in Bishop's reading of Moore, I also take it as a metaphor for the solidarity that women had lost.

Historically, the women's college has been a site where women could gain authority from other women, at least in part because it was a site of struggle, disputation, and power. But it has also been invested at various points with a utopian desire for an ideal female community, a "realm of reciprocity," to borrow Bishop's phrase. Some women, according to Patricia Palmieri's study of women faculty at Wellesley, described the women's college environment in the early part of the century as an "Adamless Eden,"[27] a phrase that resonates in Moore's work. It is certainly not the case that the women's college in reality was "some realm of reciprocity" that provided a space for the supposedly natural bonds of sisterhood between women to flourish, nor would it be a realistic or desirable goal to expect that of women's colleges now. The comparative approach I take here between poets who each experienced this environment twenty years apart challenges the idea that the bonds of sisterhood are a natural rather than a social and cultural arrangement.

Yet the desire for that "realm" glimpsed on occasion in Moore's, Bishop's, and even Plath's work represents a utopian desire that runs through the history of the feminist movement. Sometimes that desire is even attached to the work itself, as in the "romance of scholarship" I discuss in connection with Moore. Tracing this desire through the work of these poets begins to get at a little-discussed aspect of modern poetry—that is, its creation of an eroticized and shared space of intimacy where the poet meets others like herself but also the reader. I would even say with Roland Barthes that this space allows the poet to "cruise" the reader.[28] In this sense, Barthes tells us, "a site of bliss is . . . created," opening up "the possibility of a dialectics of desire, of an *unpredictability* of bliss."[29] Much of Bishop's work can be seen anew if one considers it in the light of the possibility of "cruising" the reader. The implications of cruising the reader in the 1930s amounts to nothing less than "subversive intent," to adopt Susan Suleiman's phrase, if Bishop's work is considered in the context of the paranoia that had come to be associated with the women's college environment over same-sex relationships at the time.[30] In discussing these various fantasies, I want to emphasize a psychoanalytic understanding of the word in that it has a structural and structuring element, that allows the reader, the poet, and others within the fantasy to take a variety of subject positions within it, subject positions that can cross many boundaries, including those of gender and sexual orientation. But, as I will argue, these fantasies are not universal. They emerge from a specific time and place and take different forms, depending on the women's college culture that produces or contributes to them.

In the final chapters of the book, I focus on Sylvia Plath at Smith from 1950 to 1955. The college newspaper at Smith and Plath's journals, notebooks, letters, and literary essays set the stage for examining Plath's ambivalence toward other women, marriage, and motherhood during one of the most aggressive backlashes against independent women in the history of the women's college, as well as one of the most homophobic periods. Contrary to much Plath scholarship, which is obsessed with her marriage to the poet Ted Hughes and her breakdown and suicide, my work focuses on Plath as a serious artist who had already established herself as a professional writer before meeting Hughes. Her method of working and her intellectual life were already well established in college and formed the foundation of her developing poetic style. For instance, a series of critical essays that Plath wrote in college reveal a sophisticated understanding of power relationships at the level of the individual and the community that not only reflect the emphasis on the interconnectedness of her liberal arts education, but that also would become the foundation of Plath's best poetry, particularly the bee poems where Plath investigates the overlapping issues of poetic production, reproduction, female community, and power that make her bee poem sequence one of the most powerful poetic statements in midcentury poetry.

In my analysis of Moore's, Bishop's, and Plath's development within the context of women's colleges, the female relationships formed there, and the wider poetry community, I want to shift the focus away from individual psychological histories to a wider cultural field. I am interested particularly in how their writing was involved in—to borrow Joan Wallach Scott's words—the "production of cultural knowledge" about female relationships, female sexuality, and literary production.[31] My study is concerned with how women writers negotiated their position within a predominantly female-defined community, but also how they established poetic authority in relationship to the major currents of poetry in their time. Moore, Bishop, and Plath defined their work, as other feminist scholars have argued, in terms of a then male-dominated profession, but they also responded, read, and revised each other's work. I focus on the emergence of a feminist practice at various times in literary history, on hierarchical structures within all-female communities, such as women's colleges, on poetic responses and challenges to these structures, and on the centrally important establishment and simultaneous critical erasure of a female genealogy in literary modernism. Women's experience of relationships with each other has historically been one of both solidarity and struggle, as have the fantasies of those same relationships. But I also see these struggles within the larger context of women's communities and feminist activism and find that for these women poets, all of whom were involved in critiquing polarized gender categories, the absence of a political structure for transformation in Bishop's and Plath's experience meant turning to a different set of strategies in the struggle for creative power and authority.

Finally, Moore, Bishop, and Plath exemplify for me the kind of passionate student who can absorb all that a liberal arts college education potentially offers. With this point in mind, I turn again to Moore's poem "The Student" where the exemplary student becomes "a variety / of hero." She is not merely an "undergraduate," but a student who understands that "knowledge" is not "just opinions." She is a student, rather, who "studies / voluntarily, refusing to be less / than individual" (*CPo,* 102). The poetic careers of Moore, Bishop, and Plath all took their significant shapes within the walls of elite women's colleges in the first half of the twentieth century, but each one, in her turn, was a student, in Moore's sense of the word, "refusing to be less / than individual."

1
To Work "Lovingly": Marianne Moore at Bryn Mawr, 1905–1909

> At Bryn Mawr the students are allowed to develop with as little interference as is compatible with any kind of academic order . . .
> —Marianne Moore, Letter to Bryher[1]

IN AN AUGUST 1921 LETTER TO HER FRIEND BRYHER, MARIANNE MOORE wrote that her experience at Bryn Mawr gave her "security in my determination to have what I want."[2] She described to Bryher the "intellectual wealth" she had received at Bryn Mawr as not something that could be "superimposed," but something that must be "appropriated" (*SL*, 178). This statement is perhaps Moore's strongest and most direct declaration of literary ambition and points to the central role that Bryn Mawr played in her career. Further inquiry into Moore's experience at Bryn Mawr provides a fruitful starting point for new readings of Moore's poetry that emphasize her strong feminist voice and offer ways in which we might reconsider the cultural history of women's poetic production.

Moore, who graduated from Bryn Mawr in 1909, was among the second generation of women to enter college in America.[3] This generation was particularly interesting, according to Lynn Gordon, as it represented a "transitional" one between Victorian and modern America.[4] Moore's letters home during this time reveal that Bryn Mawr combined what Carroll Smith-Rosenberg has called a "female world of love and ritual," a nineteenth-century concept, with twentieth-century ideas of the New Woman, the strong, independent young professional women who were emerging from women's colleges at the turn of the century.[5] The college campus of Moore's years at Bryn Mawr was a place where "female separatism, social activism, and belief in a special mission for educated women characterized [the students'] activities."[6]

Bryn Mawr's radical feminist president M. Carey Thomas fostered close ties between women, because she felt they gave women support in their pursuit of professional careers. Ritual practices, such as tea ceremonies and May Day celebrations, according to Virginia Wolf Briscoe, helped women create a sense of community on the Bryn Mawr campus.[7] These close relationships were combined with an emphasis on academic rigor and individual achievement. By encouraging women to consider their lives in terms of "purposeful social, civic, and professional activity," Bryn Mawr brought "women's culture into the public sphere."[8] Moore's letters home and the writing she published at Bryn Mawr during these years indicate that she benefited from Victorian female culture even as she rejected those aspects of the culture that warned women about the dangers of going to college.

Moore's early writing also demonstrates that her sense of herself as a modern professional woman developed at Bryn Mawr, and it was there where Moore tried out new kinds of writing, published, and began to establish herself within an avant-garde tradition. In short, it was at Bryn Mawr where Moore—to borrow Gail McDonald's phrase—"learned to be modern."[9] Learning to be modern meant that Moore must create space for the female artist within the male-dominated avant-garde, which is what she set out to do in her Bryn Mawr writing. It was the crucial mapping of this territory in her Bryn Mawr work and beyond that paved the way for the stunning poetry of Moore's 1924 *Observations* with such poems of the late teens as "Black Earth" and "Peter."[10] Moore's *Observations* stands as a pivotal achievement of modernism's first wave, along with T. S. Eliot's *The Waste Land* (1922), Wallace Stevens's *Harmonium* (1923), William Carlos Williams's *Spring and All* (1923), and Ezra Pound's *A Draft of XVI Cantos* (1925). But while Moore's volume shares many characteristics with these male poets, it is fundamentally different because her experience and art emerge from a very different environment: an intellectually rigorous, mutually supportive, and loving female community at home that was reinforced in the women's college of Bryn Mawr from 1905 to 1909, an environment that actively shaped Moore's feminism and artistic development.

Letters Home

Moore's letters home to her family during her Bryn Mawr years represent a detailed cultural document of this period in the history of the women's college and provide insight into the important role family members played in supporting college women. The story they tell, as Patricia Willis has suggested in her reading of the letters, is that at Bryn Mawr, Moore "became wise in the ways of success and adversity, praise and criticism, hard work and the private consolation of having done one's best."[11] They also tell a larger story of how Bryn Mawr helped to shape a major modernist writer and how the women's college, in turn, contributed to Moore's aesthetic response to key issues of modernity, a response that was stylistically similar but different in vision to that of other modernists of Moore's group, particularly Pound and Eliot.

When Moore entered Bryn Mawr in 1905, she sent letters to her family several times a week. The letters would be passed round robin among the family members—Mrs. Moore, Marianne, and Marianne's brother Warner, who was already at Yale. While communication was not as fast as electronic mail, postal delivery was much quicker than it is today. So if Moore posted a letter to her mother from Bryn Mawr in the morning, she could expect Mrs. Moore to receive the letter 140 miles away in Carlisle by the afternoon post. Moore could count on a fairly immediate response from her mother when she solicited her advice about college life, which she often did. The effect of this immediacy when reading through the Bryn Mawr letters is to be privy to a lively conversation between mother and daughter that seems at times to be taking place in the same room.

Moore's mother, Mary Warner Moore, provided constant encouragement while her daughter was away at college. Discussions of this relationship have focused almost exclusively on the mother-daughter bond, while ignoring its cultural context. Such an approach tends either to treat the relationship sentimentally or see it as oppressive or limiting to Moore's life and work.[12] But as Patricia Ann Palmieri has argued, supportive families and extremely close mother-daughter relationships were important to a woman's academic success at this time. As she writes of Wellesley, "academic women . . . came predominantly from close-knit, middle class families noted for the love and support they gave their bright daughters."[13]

Certainly this was true of the Moore household. Moore's mother had separated from her husband (who had suffered a nervous breakdown) and moved back into the home of her father, a Presbyterian minister in Kirkwood, Missouri. Marianne was born at the manse on November 15, 1887. When John Riddle Warner died seven years later, Mrs. Moore moved her family to Carlisle, Pennsylvania, and began teaching English at the Metzger Institute for Girls and raising her children alone. The family became intensely close during these years and remained so even after Warner married. The four years Moore spent at Bryn Mawr were the only prolonged period she spent apart from her mother. Mrs. Moore encouraged her daughter, counseled her, gently criticized her work, steadied her flightier tendencies, and provided a strong moral framework for her life and work. Most of all, she encouraged her daughter to cultivate her intellect. She surrounded both her children with books and intelligent conversation and set an example of female independence for Marianne.

Moore became part of an extended female family in Carlisle after they met the Norcross family. The Reverend George Norcross was pastor of the Presbyterian Church the Moore family regularly attended. His wife, Louise Norcross, and their four daughters (three of whom had graduated from Bryn Mawr) formed a kind of enchanted circle in the lives of Mary Warner Moore and her daughter.[14] Moore writes of them in her 1963 essay "Education of a Poet," "We were constantly discussing authors. When I entered Bryn Mawr, the College seemed to me in disappointing contrast—almost benighted."[15] Mary Norcross, a graduate of Bryn Mawr, tutored Moore in the fifteen difficult Bryn Mawr entrance examinations in mathematics, ancient history, physiology, Latin, English, French, and German.[16] When Moore passed them all, Mrs. Moore wrote exuberantly to "Uncle Fangs"[17] (one of Marianne Moore's pet names), "I am rich—oh so rich no one can estimate the amount of our riches!"[18] As had Moore in her letter to Bryher, Mrs. Moore equates intellect with "wealth." Moore experienced this kind of self-affirming and exuberant support for academic achievement from women on all sides.

This family support followed her to Bryn Mawr, and despite her claim that college seemed initially "benighted," reinforced her drive toward excellence.

M. Carey Thomas had argued that women, like men, "find their greatest happiness in congenial work."[19] Moore's mother shared in a similar discourse when she admonished her daughter in an April 1907 letter for not working "lovingly enough."[20] Mrs. Moore's advice to her daughter about work in this letter reinforces the college's philosophy that women, like men, should find their life's purpose in a profession that they love. Moreover, such an activity could be an act of love: "Your work, writing,—and I fear studying—you don't do lovingly enough; as Tina did with her kittens, you turn them all off too early. One who works lovingly doesn't work by the clock, but looks only to see if there be not yet one thing more that he can do."[21] Moore responds to her mother's letter a few days later with renewed energy to work hard, "feeling once more *prime*," as she puts it.[22] And Mrs. Moore follows up the next day with further encouragement: "Don't think your writing was but a spurt and then out forever. It would be queer if it should gush continually. Your first story was ripening many months before it fell; and if you just drudge away, Petty, at dull lessons, unconscious cerebration will work for you all the while and bring you forth a golden apple every now and again."[23]

Mrs. Moore's metaphors offer more than just reassurance. They are part of a language between mother and daughter that expands Moore's perception of her place as a woman in the world. The dominant view of women outside Bryn Mawr's walls was that study was bad for women, who had limited energy that should be used for reproduction; if they used up this energy, they would damage their "female apparatus," in the words of one prominent physician.[24] In January 1908, Moore wrote that her friend Marcet Haldeman had left college on the advice of S. Weir Mitchell, the Philadelphia society physician whose prescriptions for "nervous" women Charlotte Perkins Gilman had criticized in "The Yellow Wallpaper." Moore reported that Dr. Mitchell had told her friend that "college was a great nervous strain on her and not as good for her as quiet un-college-populated spots."[25]

Moore had received similar advice when she had sought the help of a chiropractor during her first year at Bryn Mawr: "Dr. Pennock riles me almost beyond endurance attributing every ill quirk and turn to college work. At all times, my blood is being used for the brain and therefore cannot be distributed."[26] A month earlier, she had written: "Dr. Pennock is very much opposed to college for women for she thinks they are not strong enough and that there's too much strain. I took great satisfaction therefore in giving her the statistics in regard to the Freshman class's health. I also said that Miss Thomas had told us; that the health of classes had in every case been better when they left than when they had entered."[27]

Such medical opinions, adopted here by a female doctor, reinforced the classic oppositions that were typical of Victorian constructions of masculinity and femininity. Smith-Rosenberg states that Victorian doctors believed the human body was "a closed energy system, [which] allocated scarce energy resources governed by rigid, biologically determined and gender-linked priorities."[28] According to this theory, women were ruled by their reproductive organs, men by their heart and brain. "The woman who favored her mind at the expense of her ovaries," Smith-Rosenberg writes, "would disorder a delicate physiological balance. Her overstimulated brain would become morbidly introspective. Neurasthenia, hysteria, insanity would follow. Her ovaries, robbed of energy rightfully theirs, would shrivel, and sterility and cancer ensue."[29] Mrs. Moore's metaphors for her own daughter's creative processes upset the binary divisions of this medical discourse that aligned women with reproductivity and men with productivity. Mrs. Moore equates creativity with mothering, an intellectual and creative process, rather than with childbirth, a biological process. Women can mother children—or, in the case of Tina, kittens—but they can also mother texts, lovingly bringing them to maturity. Moore can produce works of art with the same love, attention, and care as she can produce children, not out of her body, but out of her mind. The language of Moore's mother and Thomas's statistics (that Moore takes delight in repeating to Dr. Pennock) establish women as a source of authority, an authority that allows Moore to counter medical "wisdom" and push forward, "feeling once more prime" and, as she put it in her letter, "willing to work like a horse for a year and a day."[30] Here the authority that passed from mothers to daughters—or for that matter from female college presidents to female students—counters Victorian notions of femininity and motherhood.

In "Adamless Eden"

But there were other Victorian attitudes that prevailed into the women's college of the early twentieth century that actually protected these women from undue scrutiny over their intense same-sex relationships. Victorians cast women as passionless and passive, incapable of initiating sex without a male partner, which meant that intense relationships between women were not defined as threatening to the social order. These relationships were not only tolerated, they were encouraged by educational leaders, such as Thomas, who were wise in knowing what women needed to compete in the professional world. As Solomon has argued, women's colleges in this part of the century allowed for a broad range of close relationships between women.[31] Alternative families, such as the one M. Carey Thomas shared at "the Deanery" with Mamie Gwinn and then with Mary Garrett, were widely known and much commented on relationships, and they were common at the time among all-female communities, such as women's colleges and settlement houses.[32] The archival record suggests that Mrs. Moore enjoyed a similar relationship with Mary Norcross. This was the world of Marianne Moore at Bryn Mawr, truly a kind of "Adamless Eden," as one Wellesley student had called her experience of a women's college.[33]

The open expression of love between women was common during this period, and Moore's letters home during her years at Bryn Mawr are full of detailed accounts of various "crushes"—or "smashes" as they were sometimes called—she had while in college. "I have what sad to say corresponds to a crush," she writes in one unpublished letter home just before Valentine's Day in 1906.[34] In a 1907 letter she writes, "It's April now and I've given Margie up. I fear me she is a branch of blossoms which it is possible to bend down but not break neatly off."[35] In May of that year she had taken up with someone else. "3 p.m. I've just been out walking with Frances (B). She is 'it' for me" (*SL*, 26). And by February 1908, Moore is marking the end of her relationship with Peggy. "Peggy James has thrown me down—she is a sweet 'piece of fur' but I am too rough I guess."[36] There was actually a paper on campus called "The Bird News," which Moore describes in a letter home to her family. It "comes out daily on the bulletin board," she writes, and features news on "all college crushes" (*SL*, 27). Although there were certainly male teachers at Bryn Mawr during Moore's time, women had very little social interaction with men on campus. Even for formal dances at the college, the young women would invite other Bryn Mawr women as their guests and present them with flowers.[37]

Often these friendships intertwined with strong competition among women for powerful positions on campus. Moore seems to have had a crush at one time on Margaret Morison, who was an editor on the "Typ." Morison had acted for a brief time as a mentor for Moore, criticizing and encouraging her work. But the competition seems to have ended when Morison resigned from the magazine and Moore took her place as an editor, an event that Moore relates triumphantly in a letter home. "I am on Typ! . . . (Margie has resigned and I suppose in a manner I have her vacant spot.) She will moreover write for me."[38]

But it is Moore's relationship with Peggy James, as Linda Leavell has suggested, that most brings together Moore's ambition as a writer and her intense involvement with another woman. Leavell links Moore's "infatuation" with Peggy, who was William James's daughter and Henry's niece, to "her emerging writer's identity" between 1907 and 1908 at Bryn Mawr.[39] Leavell writes, "[Moore's] obsession with Peggy seems virtually a distillation of her obsession with writing, and her letters often veer between the two passions."[40] Such a convergence of passions (and, indeed, fascination with the James family) seems to come together in "Pym," written in her junior year and published in *Tipyn o'Bob*, Bryn Mawr's undergraduate literary magazine.[41] The story, which Moore claimed in one letter was "full of Peggyisms,"[42] involves the struggle of the main character, Alexander, to express his own individual "style," as Moore had said of herself in her letter to her mother, in the face of criticism and "requirements," which he cannot seem to meet.

Patricia Willis has also suggested that Moore enacts the writing struggles of her Bryn Mawr career in this story.[43] Written in the form of diary entries, "Pym" relates several days in the life of Alexander Pym, who wants to be a writer against the wishes of his Uncle Stanford who would like him to read law. When the story begins, Alexander is working for his friend Cob, who is also an editor. Cob is the one who pressures Alexander to write to certain "requirements," a task that Alexander finally finds impossible. The story also seems to be Moore's first clear statement of modernist purpose, or at least one that could be read as such in retrospect: "I feel that I may have been a little stubborn," Alexander thinks. And then, "one must be pertinaciously ingenious as well as genuinely a little blind, to follow long a course which insists upon maintaining its original, experimental character" (*CPr*, 15). Moore defended just such stubbornness throughout the early phases of her career.

Moore, like her character Alexander, struggled mightily with her writing in college. Moore's Bryn Mawr teachers and sometimes her peers complained of her obscurity. As one professor told her with exasperation, "Please a little lucidity! Your obscurity becomes greater and greater."[44] And just before Moore wrote "Pym," an editor of the *Tipyn o'Bob* mentioned that a recent story "showed that she was afraid of making her point and that she should 'be obvious rather than too subtle, to be understood.'"[45] On October 24, Moore wrote to her mother to express her frustration and desire: "Between lectures I scratch, in the hope that every 'little bit helps'—and I have written, what I like better than anything I have ever writ before, a thing called *The Nature of a Literary Man*—Perhaps, 'Pym'—It expresses nothing but a series of individual impressions in 'my latest style' and is crystal-clear—If it doesn't come out, I shall not know what to think—It is what James calls the record of 'a generation of nervous mood' but has a satisfactory solution—"[46]

The words and phrases "impressions" and "my latest style" link Moore to Henry James whom she mentions at the end of the letter, a writer Moore greatly admired. As Willis has noted, James was very much a presence on the Bryn Mawr campus, having lectured there on Balzac in 1905 and given the commencement address in June of that year. In October 1907, William Morton Fullerton, who later became Edith Wharton's lover, gave a lecture on James, which Moore attended. Bryn Mawr students read and discussed James's work for pleasure.[47] The words "crystal-clear" seem to have come from a remark M. Carey Thomas made after Fullerton's talk about James in which she said that James's "earlier books were 'absolutely crystal-clear.' But that in his later style his ideas were the obstacle, that the complicated nature and the vast amount of what he had to communicate made lucidity impossible." Moore repeated Thomas's comments in her October 17 letter to her family, and by October 24, she had adopted Thomas's phrase to describe her own writing in order, perhaps, to explain her difficulty with lucidity and elevate her dilemma to the realm of literary drama. As she said in an April 1908 letter: "Writing is all I care for, or for what I care most, and writing is such a puling profession, if it is not a great one, that I occasionally give up. You ought I think to be *didactic* like Ibsen or poetic like 'Sheats' [Shelley/Keats?], or pathetic like [J. M.] Barrie or witty like Meredith to justify your embarking as selfconfidently as the concentrated young egoist who is a writer, must" (*SL,* 45-46).

With the inclusion of Peggy James in the story and the link to Uncle Henry, Moore's literary ambitions overlap with her personal "crush" on Peggy. Moore literally inscribes her professional ambitions onto the figure of Peggy James, or rather the painting that stands in for James in the story. At the beginning of the story, Alexander, while trying to write the required work for Cob, gazes at a painting he has in his rooms: "I rest my eye fixedly upon my portrait of the unknown lady in the green dress. I watch an occasional diagonal of firelight splash a path across her dark slippery hair, across the zig-zag light parts in her dress, and over her hands. My words, I realize, are coming unusually well . . . ." (*CPr,* 12). According to Willis, Moore had in mind John White Alexander's painting *A Quiet Hour,* which she had admired at the Pennsylvania Academy of Fine Arts in 1905.[48] This painting, in turn, reminded Moore of Peggy James's dark "slippery hair."[49]

"A Quiet Hour," painted in 1901, might be said to represent the dominant nineteenth-century view of women. There is so little tension in the woman's body she resembles the drapery that covers her. The painting might even be used to illustrate how ill-suited women are for study. The woman in the painting is dozing over her book, eyes closed, one arm lying languidly at her side, another falling over the open book, which is, suggestively, blank. The mossy green drapery falls off her arm, exposing one shoulder. She kneels submissively before a bed or divan, draped in the same mossy green, a perfect Victorian representation of female passivity. Despite the woman's passivity, or perhaps because of it, the painting acts as an inspiration for the writer, and the unknown woman becomes a kind of muse, spurring Alexander on to produce words that "are coming unusually well" (*CPr,* 12). In her description of the painting, that muse has a certain sensual, if not erotic, quality, a quality the woman shares with Moore's description of Peggy James in an October 1907 letter home. "She is such a fascinating (in the real sense) darkling garnet of a person, I wonder she isn't affronted with 'birds.'"[50]

At the end of the story, Alexander leaves Cob to return to Uncle Stanford and the law, but there is no indication that he has given up on his ambition to write. But what is significant here is that he describes his career decision in exactly the same terms as he had noted the light patterns on the dress in the portrait, which inspired his writing and suggested Moore's relationship with Peggy James. The pattern becomes a sort of homoerotic inscription, as Alexander wonders how to explain his "crazy zig-zag course to Uncle Stanford" (*CPr*, 15). The intersection between this passionate female friendship and professional "work" for women becomes fairly transparent at this point in Moore's story and is reinforced by Alexander's decision at the end of the story to take only two things with him from his rented rooms—his rug and the portrait of the unknown lady in green. Both objects have personal referents for Moore. The portrait reminded Moore of Peggy James, and Leavell notes, the rug is a "private tribute" to a close family friend, Mary Norcross, an artist of the Arts and Crafts movement who had woven a rug for Moore's college room.[51]

The decision that Alexander makes at the end of this story to take only these two personal possessions with him are a powerful testament to a concept of friendship that nurtured the emotional life and professional ambitions of the New Woman. In the context of Moore's story, they provide a powerful antidote to what Alexander calls Cob's "harshness and materialism" (*CPr*, 13). Presumably what Moore means here is that Cob is an editor and must meet the requirements of his readers and, ultimately, make money. When Alexander leaves Cob, he takes the only two things that have meaning for him precisely because of their personal connections, not because of their monetary worth. Moore's mother encouraged Moore to think of each close friend as "one of [her] flesh and blood belongings,"[52] thereby echoing a concept of friendship that we find in Ralph Waldo Emerson's account of male friendship in his essay titled "Friendship," which, interestingly enough, Peggy James had recommended to Moore in a letter the summer before "Pym" appeared.[53] In Emerson's view, which shares characteristics with the "female world of love and ritual," friends are described as being "a delicious torment" to each other:[54] "The moment we indulge our affections, the earth is metamorphosed: there is no winter and no night: all tragedies, all ennuis vanish,—all duties even; nothing fills the proceeding eternity but the forms all radiant of beloved persons."[55] And a few lines later, Emerson describes this union in terms of possession. "Who hears me, who understands me, becomes mine,—a possession for all time."[56]

These early musings on painting, friendship (as possession and, perhaps, obsession), and inspiration that form the core of Moore's "Pym" share some of the illumination of similar contemplative moments in Moore's later poetry, most notably in Moore's 1921 "When I Buy Pictures" but also in her 1923 "Marriage" during the speaker's contemplation of Eve. "When I Buy Pictures" is not about literal ownership of a painting that gives pleasure, but one in which the viewer becomes "imaginary possessor." It is a temporary arrangement, and the viewer decides ultimately to "fix upon what would give me pleasure in my average moments" (*BMM*, 101).

The speaker goes on to delineate what those images might be: "the mediaeval decorated / hat-box, / in which there are hounds with waists diminishing like the / waist of the hourglass," or "the silver fence protecting Adam's grave, or Michael taking / Adam by the wrist" (*BMM*, 101). She cautions the reader not to put "too stern an intellectual emphasis upon this quality or that," which "detracts from one's enjoyment" (*BMM*, 101). What is most important is that the picture "must be 'lit with piercing glances into the life of things'; / it must acknowledge the spiritual forces which have made it" (*BMM*, 101). These are the final lines of the *Observations* version of the poem, but in the first published version in *The Dial*, the last three lines read:

> it must acknowledge the forces which have made it;
> it must be "lit with piercing glances into the life of things;"
> then I "take it in hand as a savage would take a looking-glass."
> (*BMM*, 255)

The *Observations* version, to my mind, is the best of the three known variants of the poem,[57] but the last line here leaves a stronger trace of what I have been talking about with regard to friendship and possession. Moore was right aesthetically to eliminate this last line, which seems overly fierce given the control of the rest of the poem, and yet its very "savagery" is provocative. It certainly echoes the kind of concentrated intensity that pervades the rest of the poem in the speaker's examination of pictures she likes; it suggests the possibility (through the eyes of the "savage") of seeing things anew, as if one has never seen anything like it before, mimicking the wonderment of the child; and it is in this moment, the line suggests, when the poet comes closest to inspiration, of seeing herself in the mirror of art, and discovers as well the uncanny experience of the double. Although the moment here seems ungendered, it is not in "Pym," nor in the speaker's contemplation of Eve, which I will discuss in the next chapter. Nevertheless, "When I Buy Pictures" alludes to a nineteenth century concept of friendship as possession that seems to be central to the significant spiritual forces that Moore argues must shape the artist's imagination that lights up the art.

Friendship, in the context of the intellectual environment of the women's college, was also closely aligned with ideas of work, so that it was believed that friendships could sustain one in the hard work of the world. Mrs. Moore expresses just such an idea in a January 1908 letter:

> When you turn missionary to the outside world, then maybe those you love will go in with you shoulder to shoulder comrade fashion, and you and they co-operate, in big things and little . . . . Those who press forward in the fight together, never thinking about the impression they are making on each other, and speak right out the feelings that are uppermost, oftentimes find out when peace and quiet come, that love sprang up with each for the other, all unconsciously to either, and lo! They are bound together forever.[58]

Mrs. Moore's language suggests the boundaries between the public sphere of work and the private sphere of friendship and love are permeable, easily crossed by those who were engaged in important work, who were "comrades" together. Her language also suggests that female friends, when engaged in useful work in the world, can form an edenic community, bound together through love and work.

Although at first glance "Pym" seems a rather conventional story, staying as it does safely within the confines of Victorian fiction, if we read it alongside Moore's exchange of ideas with her mother about ambition and friendship, it seems rather to be testing the boundaries of literary ambition and the range of relationships Moore experienced within the female community of Bryn Mawr. Women acted all things to each other within this community—they were competitors, lovers, and friends. There were no men at the dance.

"Learning to be Modern"

"Pym" was one of many stories Moore published in the college's literary magazine that explored the nature of ambition, friendship, and work, but as she began to write verse, similar concerns dominated the images she chose. One poem in particular, which Moore published in her senior year in *The Lantern,* seems to distill Moore's immensity of desire in the image of the jellyfish.[59] "A Jelly-Fish" marks the beginning of Moore's mature work. It is altogether different from any of the occasional verse she wrote before this, and she included a shorter version of it among her *Complete Poems*:

> Visible, invisible,
> A fluctuating charm,
> An amber-coloured amethyst
> Inhabits it; your arm
> Approaches, and
> It opens and
> It closes;
> You have meant
> To catch it,
> And it shrivels;
> You abandon
> Your intent—
> It opens, and it
> Closes and you
> Reach for it—
> The blue
> Surrounding it
> Grows cloudy, and
> It floats away
> From you.
>   (*BMM*, 342)

The hand reaches for something that remains out of range, out of reach, elusive, even dangerous. In her junior year, in her comparative anatomy notebook, Moore drew a detailed jellyfish.[60] She had studied these creatures and knew that jellyfish sting and paralyze the prey that wander into their tentacles. This knowledge would not have been lost on Moore, since the precise observation of animals became a hallmark of her poetry.[61] Jellyfish are dangerous objects for which to reach. That Moore was aware of her desire as a social taboo—women should not want too much—may have been behind the object choice of the stinging jellyfish in her poem.

"A Jelly-Fish" was not published again until Moore's book *O to Be a Dragon* in 1959. And the title poem of that volume returns fleetingly to the tone of passionate desire struck in her early poems:

> If I, like Solomon, ...
> could have my wish—
>
> my wish ... O to be a dragon,
> a symbol of the power of Heaven—of silkworm
> size or immense; at times invisible.
>   Felicitous phenomenon!
>
> (*CPo*, 177)

In the 1959 version of the jellyfish poem, she ends halfway through with the two lines "You abandon / Your intent—"[62] In the 1959 version, the grasping hand, as if unable to accept another defeat, withdraws immediately; the effort is quickly taken up but quickly abandoned as well. In the 1909 version, the hand is undaunted by the object shriveling away from it and tries a second time. This time the jellyfish floats away, clouding the water with its defensive ink, but the repetition of the attempt suggests that the hand may keep reaching for the desired object indefinitely.

It is significant that one of Moore's first identifiably modern poems was begun in a lecture notebook she kept for the Imitative Writing course taught by Georgina Goddard King at Bryn Mawr. Willis calls King's class "probably the setting for the most significant literary development at college for Marianne."[63] As her course notebook shows, Moore studied intensively the work of seventeenth century writers in King's class. On one notebook page she lists some of these writers on the far left-hand corner of the page—Andrews, Howell, Hooker, Milton, Raleigh, Taylor, Traherne. On the right, she lists characteristics of style—grand style, irony, and imagery. Pages are devoted to the study of Milton's *Paradise Lost*, which became the basis for Moore's long poem "Marriage." We also see statements of what would become some of the hallmarks of Moore's own style. She writes on February 25, 1909, presumably quoting King, that "the indispensible thing is *restraint.*"[64] She underlines the word "restraint" twice, a value that Moore would emphasize in her 1924 poem "Silence" in which she writes, "the deepest feeling always shows itself in silence; / not in silence, but restraint" (*BMM*, 124, 309).

In her emphasis on seventeenth century prose style in her course, King was ahead of modernist public statements on the subject, according to Willis.[65] Willis speculates that King may also have introduced Moore to modern writers, such as Pound, and King "knew Gertrude Stein and Alfred Stieglitz."[66] Moore had certainly discovered Pound by the summer of 1909, because she wrote in her reading notebook, "Ezra Pound and Ernest Dowson—at all costs."[67]

The first reference that indicates she was reading Pound's poetry comes in the summer of 1911 in this same notebook where she indicates that she bought Pound's *Personae* and *Exultations* at Elkin Mathews's bookstore in London during her trip to Europe with her mother that year. At any rate, as early as 1909, it seems, Moore knew that her identity as a poet was tied up with what was modern in poetry. Moore wrote home to her family in February 1909, calling King "the best teacher I have had here (for my hobby—). She reads the best things and criticizes with tremendous point and acuteness and gets you in a fever of enthusiasm which is no small achievement in as inert and 'wise' a community as this."[68] During that spring, in addition to "A Jelly-Fish," Moore turned out several poems that seem distinctly modern. First, "To a Screen-Maker" in the January 1909 issue of *Tipyn o'Bob* and then again in *The Lantern*, the college's alumnae magazine. "Ennui" in the March 1909 issue of *Tipyn o'Bob*, a poem inspired by the movements of Caliban in the Ben Greet Players performance of Shakespeare's *Tempest* at Bryn Mawr. Finally, "Progress" appeared in June 1909 (*BMM*, 337–43). These poems differ from the light, rhyming verse she produced earlier in her college career. "Ennui," for instance, which begins "He often expressed / A curious wish, / To be interchangeably / Man and fish," shares with Moore's later poetry a fluidity and freshness of image, and in its choice of subject, an interest in the adaptations of the marginalized and despised—in this case, Caliban. These poems really show that by the end of her Bryn Mawr career, Moore had begun to develop a "modern" style in her poetry that she would continue to work with and refine in the years after Bryn Mawr.

The New Woman

It is in 1909, too, that Moore makes the link in prose between the figure of the New Woman and modern style, a connection that she would begin making in her poetry a bit later. Between 1883 and 1900, the New Woman appeared in more than a hundred novels, and "her status was fiercely debated in prose and parlours," according to Angelique Richardson and Chris Willis in their introduction to a recent edited volume on the subject.[69] But although the term New Woman was "contested" and subject to "competing definitions," Richardson and Willis point out that representations of the New Woman shared many characteristics: "her perceived newness, her autonomous self-definition and her determination to set her own agenda in developing an alternative vision of the future."[70] It is not hard to see, with this definition, how much Moore's feminist agenda overlapped with Pound's manifesto for modern poets to "make it new." Carroll Smith-Rosenberg has most closely associated the New Woman with the independent, professionally trained women emerging from women's colleges during this period.[71] Moore began to represent the New Woman in her fiction toward the end of her college career. Her short story "Wisdom and Virtue," published in the June 1909 issue of *Tipyn o'Bob*, considers for the first time the role of the female artist as a professional woman, a woman who can take charge of her life and support herself financially. The story concerns a meeting between the painter, Miss Duckworth, and her uncle, a smugly satisfied man who owns a publishing concern. Mr. Duckworth visits his niece in her apartment and studio. The place is probably New York, since there are many references to "Bohemian" lifestyles and customs. In January, Moore had just taken her first trip to New York City, a city that was to become the focus of Moore's desire until she and her mother moved to their apartment at 14 St. Luke's Place, Greenwich Village, in 1918 to be closer to the artistic community that would help advance her career. If New York was "the savage's romance," as the first line of her 1921 poem "New York" suggests, it was also "accessibility to experience," in Henry James's words, which Moore quotes in the last line of that same poem (*BMM*, 107, 267).

Moore explicitly addresses the marginality of the female artist in "Wisdom and Virtue," perhaps in anticipation of what she would find when she left Bryn Mawr in search of work. First, we find out that Mr. Duckworth has visited his niece only when "the fact of his niece's existence had occurred to him" (*CPr,* 26). In Mr. Duckworth's world, "pious women, clever men, and obedient children, were the order of things" (*CPr,* 27). Yet Moore asserts the possibility of rethinking this world to include professional women and, particularly, the female artist. Miss Duckworth's apartment is comfortable and even elegant. She has a maid, who brings in fresh flowers. There is a drawing room with a Turkish rug, and the apartment overlooks the "smoky" city on one side and the river on the other. The curtains on the windows are "silky." The furnishings of the apartment and the quiet assuredness of Miss Duckworth suggest the life of a relatively successful, single, professional woman. In many ways, the description of the apartment, at least in terms of the comfort and success it conveys, matches Moore's description of Thomas's Deanery at Bryn Mawr, which at one point she describes as "an Elysian garden" (*SL,* 65). Against her uncle's smugness, Miss Duckworth defends the life she has chosen.

Clearly, "feminine professionalism" and success mystify her uncle. He must criticize and trivialize Miss Duckworth's achievements. About one of her paintings he comments, "Rather a puddle, I should say. It takes art to get art *out* of things like that" (*CPr,* 29). Even when one painting of a man particularly interests Mr. Duckworth, he must end his praise with a criticism that connects stylistic quirks to Miss Duckworth's gender. "His hands sag down on his pockets too much and his elbows stick out," Mr. Duckworth says. "It's like a woman to construct the thing that way" (*CPr,* 29).

The significance of Mr. Duckworth's implied insult that women can't create good art is reflected in Miss Duckworth's anxiety about her own signature on a painting:

> "What is that?" [Mr. Duckworth asks.]
> "That?" Miss Duckworth bent down. "That is my signature." A small reddish device lay scrawled against a purple oblong. "It's an earthworm, rather like one, don't you think? Suppose we go." Her eyes reverted to the worm and a settled gloom appeared to descend upon her. (*CPr,* 29)

Miss Duckworth has signed her painting, claiming it as her own, but she has to "ben[d] down" to see the signature. What's more, it is rather like an earthworm, a silent, primitive, and earthbound creature. Miss Duckworth seems to sense the significance of the earthworm and its relationship to the representation of the female artist, for she experiences a gloom that "descend[s]" upon her. The words "bent down," "reverted," and "descend upon" all work to pull the artist down to the level of the earthworm. However, Moore recuperates some of Miss Duckworth's power by the end of "Wisdom and Virtue." As the door closes on her uncle, she says, "Gloomy, Janus-headed man. Wisdom palls upon him" (*CPr*, 30). Miss Duckworth stands alone in her apartment after the door closes, a defiant smile flashing across her face. The reader is left with the surety that "wisdom" cannot be applied to Mr. Duckworth. It is Miss Duckworth who combines both wisdom and virtue, radiating a strength of character associated with the New Woman. Miss Duckworth's clash with her uncle is simultaneously a comment on gender and modernity. Duckworth represents the old order, while his niece stands in for the new. Miss Duckworth's defiance suggests the "stance" that Cristanne Miller argues is characteristic of Moore's early years, one "more belligerent than modest."[72]

Moore's 1919 poem "Radical," for instance, is about a carrot that survives " . . . with ambition, im- / agination, outgrowth, // nutriment, / with everything crammed belligerent- / ly inside itself" (*BMM*, 90). The carrot stuffed with all these things might be compared to Moore's description of her studying at Bryn Mawr in an amusing letter she wrote to her brother on January 1908. "Gadzooks!" she wrote, "How I am pouring 'learning' into myself!"[73] Linda Leavell has suggested that "Radical" might be read as a "self-portrait," since the carrot's color is described as "fused with intensive heat to / color of the set- / ting sun . . . ," and Moore was a redhead.[74] In addition, as Leavell points out, she was "at the time emerging as a 'radical' artist."[75] Moore undoubtedly meant radical in the sense of rooted or from the root, as well. Such a sense is suggested at the end of the poem, when the voice of the carrot tells the farmer to, "dismiss / agrarian lore," and in the final two lines states a new wisdom as: "that which it is impossible to force, it is impossible / to hinder." The carrot, in other words, stays rooted, determined that its own way of growing will take it to the source—to what is important. One is tempted to compare this wisdom about the carrot to Moore's letter to Bryher that defines her growth at Bryn Mawr in similar terms: "At

Bryn Mawr the students are allowed to develop with as little interference as is compatible with any kind of academic order and the more I see of other women's colleges, the more I feel that Bryn Mawr was peculiarly adapted to my special requirements" (*SL*, 178). The voice at the end of "Radical" is a modern one, able to dismiss the body of traditional information about a subject, the "lore," and substitute a different knowledge, the knowledge, perhaps, of the New Woman.

But how did Moore get to this point in her poetry? By her senior year in college as I have suggested, Moore had become a serious student of style via King's course, as well as a serious student of the modern. But one would need to take a closer look at how she achieved this fusion of the modern with the New Woman as she further developed her poetry from graduation in 1909 to 1918 when she produced what I see as two of the strongest representations of the strong, defiant, and independent modern woman—her two animal poems "Peter" and "Black Earth,"[76] placed just before "Radical" in the *Observations* edition.

A good example of Moore's process of "learning to be modern" during her years of poetic apprenticeship and an early use of the New Woman can be seen in a study of the various versions of what was eventually published in the July 1916 issue of *The Chimaera* as "To Be Liked by You Would Be a Calamity" (*BMM*, 218–19). The final version of the poem conveys the feistiness of the New Woman and focuses on a contentious sparring between men and women that is certainly a feature of Moore's poetry between about 1912 and 1923. Many of these early poems between 1909 and 1915 feature lines and subject matter that would later be employed in "Marriage." "To Be Liked By You" begins with a quotation from Thomas Hardy's *A Pair of Blue Eyes*: "Attack is more piquant than concord." Moore quotes the lines in her reading notebook of this period. The quotation refers to the attraction that the book's heroine, Elfride Swancourt, feels for Harry Knight, the intellectual who criticizes her writing. Elfride writes medieval romances that become the subject of Knight's harsh criticism. Tragically, Elfride is already engaged to another man, the mild-mannered Stephen Smith, the son of a mason. In some senses, Moore's reading of Hardy concentrates Moore's desire and dilemma. "Writing is all I care for," she had written in one letter home, but to be modern, she had to cast off the medieval trappings that clung to her own poetry. Medieval imagery often appeared in

Moore's early poetry and prose, a result probably of both the Bryn Mawr curriculum, as well as the ritual May Day celebrations, according to Willis.[77] Such imagery dominates an early version of "To Be Liked by You," called "My Lantern," published in the 1910 Bryn Mawr *Lantern*:

> The banners unfurled by the warden
> Float
> Up high in the air and sink down; the
> Moat
> Is black as a plume on a casque; my
> Light,
> Like a patch of high light on a flask, makes
> Night
> A gibbering goblin that bars the way—
> So noisy, familiar, and safe by day.[78]

The manuscript version of this poem shows Moore working it over to produce a second poem the title of which—"Elfride, Making Epigrams"—now makes clear the reference to Hardy. The two poems are contained in the same folder at the Rosenbach. Still featuring medieval (and late Victorian) imagery of "moats" and "casques," the poem now begins to get at the attraction and conflict between men and women that the final poem addresses. Moore indicates on the manuscript that she considered using the alternate title "The Tentative Critic." This poem, also published in *The Lantern*, begins in almost the same way, but then continues with slight variations:

> Devices as slender as pennons float
> Up high in the air and sink down; the moat
>   Encases her head like a casque;
>   Her light
> Sorties, like highlights on a flash,
>   Requite
> Men with torrents of toads from lips of lead
> And then grind up her bones to make their bread.[79]

It should be noted that Elfride's penchant for epigrams also resonates with Moore's own developing epigrammatic style at this point, yet another reference to the seventeenth-century prose style she studied with King. Her Imitative Writing notebook is full of pithy statements by Bacon, Milton, Dryden, and many others. In addition, her reading notebook of these years shows that she was reading Emily Dickinson, another master of the epigram. By 1916, "Elfride" had taken on the language, imagery, and subject matter of the fully modern poem in "To Be Liked by You Would Be a Calamity":

> "Attack is more piquant than concord," but when
>   You tell me frankly that you would like to feel
> My flesh beneath your feet,
>   I'm all abroad; I can but put my weapon up, and
>   Bow you out.
> Gesticulation—it is half the language.
>   Let unsheathed gesticulation be the steel
>   Your courtesy must meet,
>   Since in your hearing words are mute, which to my
>   senses
> Are a shout.
>
> (*BMM*, 79)

Moore manages to keep the medieval imagery, like Pound in "Sestina: Altaforte"—"I have no life save when the swords clash,"[80] but here she employs that imagery to play out a more modern ritual between men and women where women themselves have the upper hand in their ability to refuse. The Elfride of Moore's poem does not live out the tragedy of Hardy's heroine, but rather, like Miss Duckworth in "Wisdom and Virtue," bows the critic out of her life. Moore continued to write epigrammatic poems, but by 1915 she was also developing a syllabic style and long poetic line that would characterize some of her most stunning poetry.

By 1918, Moore would claim the full power of the New Woman in two animal poems that take sensual delight in the "natural" characteristics of their subjects—the elephant of "Black Earth" and the cat of "Peter." "Black Earth" opens with these powerful lines:

> Openly, yes,
>   with the naturalness
> of the hippopotamus or the alligator
> when it climbs out on the bank to experience the
>
> sun, I do these
> things which I do, which please

> no one but myself. Now I breathe and now I am sub-
> merged; the blemishes stand up and shout when the object
>
> in view was a
> renaissance; shall I say
>   the contrary?
>
> (*BMM*, 87)

In these opening lines, the poem's speaker, an elephant, takes sensual pleasure in its own independence. Kirstin Hotelling Zona notes the "sensual immediacy" of this poem, an example of what she has called Moore's "strategic selfhood," a poetic strategy that "deconstructs the lyric 'I'" and understands subjectivity "by sensual response rather than sexual convention."[81] John Slatin suggests that Moore's reference to the hippopotamus is to T. S. Eliot's poem "The Hippopotamus," in which case Moore may be claiming the same authority for herself to write as Eliot claims.[82] Slatin has argued that in this early phase of her career, Moore seeks to establish an identity as a poet by setting herself apart from other modern poets.[83]

Throughout the poem, the speaker holds in tension seemingly contradictory or "contrary" attitudes—"Now I breathe and now I am sub- / merged." But Moore characteristically complicates the line by breaking the word *submerged* into its components by breaking the line. The prefix *sub-* means under, beneath, or below, while *merge* can mean to join or unite but also to lose or cause to lose identity by being absorbed, swallowed up, or combined. By splitting the word, Moore is perhaps doubly emphasizing the sense of drowning and losing one's identity. As a woman poet, this would be a particularly resonant theme for Moore. Women writers were lumped together and their art devalued as Miss Duckworth's encounter with her uncle in Moore's "Wisdom and Virtue" proves. Even though Ezra Pound encouraged, nurtured, and was instrumental in getting Moore published, he could as easily succumb to relegating Moore to the margins. When grouped with Mina Loy in one review, for example, Moore became one of "these girls."[84]

But in "Black Earth" the elephant takes pleasure in its own individuality and difference:

> . . . .The sediment of the river which
> encrusts my joints, makes me very gray but I am used

> to it, it may
> remain there; do away
>   with it and I am myself done away with, for the
>   patina of circumstance can but enrich what was
>
> there to begin
> with. This elephant skin
>   which I inhabit, fibred over like the shell of
>   the cocoanut, this piece of black glass through which no
>   light
>
> can filter—cut
> into checkers by rut
>   upon rut of unpreventable experience—
>   it is a manual for the peanut-tongued and the
>
> hairy toed. Black
> but beautiful, my back
>   is full of the history of power. Of power? What
>   is powerful and what is not? My soul shall never
>
> be cut into
> by a wooden spear; . . .
>
> <div align="right">(<i>BMM</i>, 87–88)</div>

The elephant's "patina of circumstance," which it wears on the skin it inhabits, makes clear that the subject of the poem is both an individual subject and an historical one, a subject who can both act and be acted on by historical circumstance. Such a sense of self was very much a part of the politically charged environment of Bryn Mawr in the early part of the century. As a subject of history, then, the elephant embodies power struggles of all kinds by those who faced persecution because of gender, race, or religious faith. The African references in the section that begins "Black / but beautiful, my back / is full of the history of power" were not lost on Pound who asked Moore in a letter whether she was "a jet black Ethiopian Othello-hued, or was that line in one of your *Egoist* poems but part of your general elaboration and allegory and designed to differentiate your colour from that of the surrounding menageria?"[85] Pound is baiting Moore here. Are you one of us, he seems to be asking. Moore rises to the bait in her reply. "'Black Earth,' the poem to which I think you refer, was written about an elephant that I have, named Melanchthon; and contrary to your impression, I am altogether a blond and have red hair" (*SL,* 122). Yes, I am one of you, Moore seems to reply.

The racial overtones that Pound reads in "Black Earth," however, are more complex. Cristanne Miller has noted that Moore's "efforts to overturn racial stereotypes" are an important part "of the politics of her poetry," as were her efforts to resist gender stereotypes.[86] Miller argues that, "Moore marks race and gender in two ways" in her work: "Through a directly political attempt to overthrow widespread hierarchical stereotypes (generally through negation: 'The Negro is not brutal'), or through an indirectly political (occasionally romanticized) attempt to create new space or recognition for stigmatized people and qualities (a maternal black male hero, or unmaterialistic African desert tribe)."[87]

Her use of the African reference in "Black Earth" might be considered in terms of Miller's second category, an "attempt to create new space." Moore recognizes that in the history of power there have been those who have had less access to it, but it is important to remember that she used this category, as Pound suggests, as a "general elaboration and allegory" in order to "differentiate [her] colour from that of the surrounding menageria"—that is, other poets. In "Black Earth," Moore uses color to identify her difference and signal the arrival of some new entity, one that emerges out of history.

A further layer is added to the poem's historical connections in Moore's reference to Melanchthon. Moore had a small, carved elephant that she had named Melanchthon after the Reformation leader Philipp Melanchthon, who, as Leavell has pointed out, "was Martin Luther's collaborator, friend, and humbler, more diplomatic complement."[88] As usual with Moore, there are several layers of reference associated with this name. This Reformation leader had taken the Greek name, Melanchthon, in place of his original name, Schwarzerd, which is "German for 'black earth'" (*SL,* 122; note 1). Melanchthon's involvement in educational reform was probably of significance to Moore, as well. By using the name, Moore may also be suggesting that the lesser-known reformation leader had his role in the "history of power," and so too might Moore have her place within her chosen field.

Like the elephant in "Black Earth," the cat in "Peter," revels in his own individuality and sensuality, creating space simply by being himself. Peter is "strong and slippery," and he does as he pleases:

>   .... Springing about with
> froglike ac-
>
> curacy, emitting jerky cries when taken in the hand, he is
>   himself
> again; to sit caged by the rungs of a domestic chair would
>   be unprofit-
> able—human. What is the good of hypocrisy? It
>   is permissible to choose one's employment, to abandon
>   the wire nail, the
>   roly-poly, when it shows signs of being no longer
>   a pleas-
>
> ure, to score the adjacent magazine with a double line of
>   strokes. He can
>   talk, but insolently says nothing ....
>
> <div align="right">(<i>BMM</i>, 94)</div>

Moore's choice of words participates in the feminist discourse that she heard at Bryn Mawr. It is "human" to allow oneself to be "caged" by a "domestic" life, and it is distinctly "unprofitable" for women, as Moore argued in many letters home to her family. But it is not the life for Peter. He takes such pleasure in what he does that one might ask if this is what it means to "work lovingly." What is significant for Peter is that, "It / is permissible to choose one's employment," not something that could be said of most women of the period, nor even of the four percent of women who attended women's colleges at the time, who faced many restrictions on what an educated woman could do.

Peter has a "dispo- / sition" that "affront[s]," because, as the speaker tells us, "an animal with claws wants to have / to use / them." That Moore associates "claws" with ambition, and uses it as a metaphor for her own work and chosen profession, is evident in a letter she wrote to her brother on October 18, 1915. Other writers and artists that Moore had met in New York were encouraging her to move there, including Alfred Kreymborg who had already been publishing Moore in his radical little magazine *Others*. Kreymborg had instructed Moore to, in her words, "direct my claws to New York."[89]

In the version of "Peter" that appears in the *Complete Poems*, Moore has changed the line to "an animal with claws should have an opportunity to use them" (*CPo*, 44). Although the change suggests a phrase common to educational reform—opportunities for women—it alters the meaning and power of the line. In the earlier version, Peter's claws are not a question of opportunities. The emphasis is on desire. He "wants / to have / to use / them." Notice the line breaks, how the verb "wants" can be combined with both the infinitive "to have" and the infinitive "to use." In other words, Peter wants to have those claws, *and* he wants to use them. No "pair of ragged claws / Scuttling across the floors of silent seas" for Peter.[90] He boldly makes his mark, and so, in a sense, becomes the opposite of Prufrock. "*Prufrock*" came out in 1917, and Moore wrote "Peter" in 1918, so it could very well have been a response to Eliot's disaffected persona. The originality and startling look of "Peter" on the page in the *Observations* version seems to fit its subject extremely well, in a way that the more regularized free-verse form of the *Complete Poems* version does not at all. Although "Peter" is not strictly syllabic, the syllabic method that Moore was adopting at this time in many of her poems, such as "Black Earth," certainly influenced the look of the early "Peter."[91]

"Peter" in its early version is powerful. We have the spirit of the cat, leaping about with "froglike ac- / curacy, emitting jerky cries when taken in the hand." Peter even seems a fair representation of Moore's own work as she described it in a letter to Pound. "My work jerks and rears and I cannot get up enthusiasm for embalming what I myself, accept conditionally" (*SL,* 123). Moore was discouraged at this point about her ability to publish her work, and so she had retreated into a stance of appearing to want it less, although, as Cyrena Pondrom has argued, this stance was probably more a disguise than a reality.[92] Although the description of her work seems somewhat negative here in her letter to Pound, in "Peter" Moore turns it into a strength. Peter, like Moore's poetry, is playful, hard to pin down.

The poem ends with a final celebration of Peter's fierce independence:

> . . . . To
> leap, to lengthen out, divide the air—to purloin, to pursue.
>   to tell the hen: fly over the fence, go in the wrong way
>   —in your perturba-
>   tion—this is life; to do less would be nothing but
>   dishonesty.
>
>   (*BMM,* 94)

Something of Peter's defiance, his independence, the suggestion that to be less than he is would be dishonest, can be seen in a letter to Marianne from her mother dated October 20, 1905. Moore had written to ask advice about some difficulties she was having with a friend at school. Mrs. Moore wrote back, reminding her daughter to "study your subject, and, looking on High for grace to use your power lovingly and generously, command those who intrude upon you."[93] These are powerful words. Mrs. Moore counsels her daughter to "command" her subjects. It is not an easy path, she reminds her daughter, "but be patient[;] you are only winding around to a higher point."

Mrs. Moore suggests a path for her daughter that can turn around, subtly, a position of disadvantage to one that comes out in the end to "a higher plane." That path is the one that Peter follows in Moore's poem. Far from the Victorian ideal of true womanhood, where a woman might be expected "to sit caged by the rungs of a domestic chair," Peter does not accept such "hypocrisy." He "command[s]" his subjects and in so doing shares some of the characteristics of life and work that Moore had learned at Bryn Mawr. Her experience there taught her that to work lovingly and "to use [one's] power lovingly" meant that one must take time, one must be true to one's principles, and, when one has claws, one "wants to have / to use / them."

2
Serpents in Paradise: Marianne Moore and "Marriage"

> Men do not yet understand that women, like themselves, find their greatest happiness in congenial work.
> —M. Carey Thomas

ON THE EVE OF THE TWENTIETH CENTURY, M. CAREY THOMAS GAVE a speech to the Bryn Mawr community that earned her international fame as a leader in women's education.[1] Given in 1899, several years before Moore came to Bryn Mawr, Thomas criticized Harvard's president Charles Eliot for his stance on women's education. Eliot felt that women should be educated differently from men to prepare them to fulfill their biological destiny as wives and mothers. Thomas challenged Eliot's notion that women's only role in life was a biologically fixed one by calling for a complete refashioning of the educated woman. Thomas told her audience that what she wanted at Bryn Mawr was to create an intellectual and social atmosphere where, by "mutual association," women would be "fashioned and perfected" into "the type of Bryn Mawr women which will, we hope, become as well known and universally admired a type as the Oxford and Cambridge man or as the graduate of the great English public schools."[2] Not content to take on just Eliot, Thomas proceeded to lambaste President Carter of Williams who had suggested that the "ideal" women's college should foster both the intellect and the "sweetness" of its female students. Thomas scoffed. "Sweet sixteen," she told her audience, "has the charm of childhood and ignorance that will shortly be relegated to the harems of the east."[3]

Two years after Thomas's speech, *A Book of Bryn Mawr Stories* appeared, seemingly to take up Thomas's challenge to refashion the Bryn Mawr woman.[4] Many of the stories focus on the promising lives educated women could create for themselves outside of marriage and suggest that choosing marriage meant giving up an autonomous, fulfilling life. These stories, while conventional in their narrative structure, are not stereotypical in their representation of women. They focus on serious women actively applying for scholarships and prestigious graduate fellowships, giving important speeches, convincing male audiences of the need to support women's colleges, and agonizing over whether to give up their careers for marriage. What is striking about these stories is that most reject marriage as a viable option, reflecting the trend of women's college graduates at the time. According to Carroll Smith-Rosenberg, nearly 60 percent of the women of Moore's generation of Bryn Mawr graduates did not marry.[5] The Bryn Mawr of Moore's day, with its emphasis on same-sex bonds, created a workable alternative to marriage. At the beginning of the century for most women, marriage could never be an equal partnership and, as Moore's letters home from Bryn Mawr suggest, under Victorian laws were akin to a kind of slavery and servitude.

A Book of Bryn Mawr Stories, written by Bryn Mawr graduates and faculty and published in 1901, provides a starting point for imagining the forces that shaped Moore's world and her views on marriage. The stories are but one way I will consider the radical refashioning of the female subject that was going on at Bryn Mawr during Moore's years, a refashioning that would shape Moore's views on the subject of marriage and contribute to the creation of the New Woman. Since Moore was to write her longest poem and perhaps one of her most powerful modernist statements and feminist critiques on the subject of marriage, a more thorough consideration of the considerable influence of her education on both her attitudes toward the subject and the style she developed to best convey her critique is long overdue. Although she does not discuss "Marriage," Rachel Blau DuPlessis has argued that Moore wrote much of her early poetry from the subject position of the New Woman, a position that allowed her to develop a kind of "analytic lyric" that adapted the "social analysis" of the "prose tradition to poetic form."[6] Moore's "Marriage" is an example of this adaptation, which, I will argue, was initially fashioned out of her Bryn Mawr study of seventeenth-century prose in Georgina Goddard King's class; her major program of history, economics, and politics; and her adoption of the suffrage arguments of the period. These are lessons she revisited in the 1920s when she became involved in the marriage debates that were raging among her Greenwich Village friends and fellow artists.

But before turning to an examination of Moore's "analytic critique" of the institution of marriage, it is important to consider once again Moore's world at Bryn Mawr, which provided women with a variety of alternatives to marriage if they wanted to pursue careers. At the time, it was almost impossible to have both. Women were expected to give up the few careers open to them if they married, so it was clear to women of Moore's generation that they must *choose*, as at least one story in *A Book of Bryn Mawr Stories* suggests. In "Catherine's Career," although the heroine, Catherine Neville, originally rejects marriage—she says she is not going to be happy with a domestic life and supports her case by telling the young man who visits her that "only 17 percent" of her fellow college students will marry—she ends by quitting college and agreeing to marry. The story sums up her decision with this observation: "Catherine had decided upon her career. She had found her purpose in life."[7]

The heroine of Georgina Goddard King's story "Free Among the Dead" makes quite a different decision. Although I can't prove that Moore read this story or any others in the collection, she was part of their world, and King, as I noted at some length in my last chapter, was a crucial teacher for her. The title of King's story underscores its major point—that the heroine's freedom comes with choosing scholarly pursuits over domestic ones. Moreover, "Free Among the Dead" emphasizes the importance of close female relationships in supporting scholarly women and so brings us closer to why so many college-educated women were able to reject marriage. King's story focuses on a group of women who are waiting for the faculty to decide on a scholarship that will determine their future. At the center of the story is the romance of the story's heroine, Esther, and her partner, the ambiguously named Sydney, both of whom are competing for the scholarship. Esther wins it, which essentially ends her relationship with Sydney, who later announces her engagement. Esther's friend Hilda responds to this announcement by saying, "Oh, dear! . . . I'm rather sorry. I always believed in her, you know. She might have done things."[8] King's story—and others in the collection—make clear that one had to reject marriage in order to "do things" and that romance resided elsewhere, not in heterosexual marriages but in close and intimate relationships with other women and in the romance of college and scholarship itself. At the end of King's story, Esther takes Hilda as her companion to share in her scholarly life.

Esther's world at Bryn Mawr was also Moore's, whose letters home, as I have suggested, were full of enthusiastic accounts of "crushes" she had on other women. The network of female friendships that sustained her at Bryn Mawr continued to nurture her as she committed herself to a life of writing and, for a short period, editing. These relationships, coupled with the pleasure that "congenial work" could offer the scholar, undoubtedly helped Moore to choose her career over marriage. Even as late as 1963, in a brief memoir she wrote for *Writer's Digest*, the "Education of a Poet," she suggested that she learned to do her work "lovingly" at Bryn Mawr (*CPr*, 571–73). In her focus on the significance of her Bryn Mawr experience, she mentions several Bryn Mawr professors and then a Miss Randolph, who Moore describes as "a demonstrator" who "made biology and its toil, a pleasure and like poetry, 'a quest'" (*CPr*, 572). At the end of King's Bryn Mawr story, Esther makes knowledge her quest. "Curiosity . . . is the only insatiable emotion," she thinks. "There were tracts of knowledge infinite and unfathomable where one would never tire."[9] In both Moore's comment and in Esther's final thought, scholarly work itself becomes a kind of romance, a romance of scholarship.

King's story turns into fiction what was foundational to the Bryn Mawr experience under Thomas's leadership, the nurturance of scholarly excellence and achievement. In a 1908 article she published in the *Educational Review*, Thomas charged that women's colleges must maintain graduate schools in philosophy "to discover and foster imaginative and constructive genius."[10] Women's colleges, she argued, are particularly suited to nurture the intellect through the assistance of other women scholars who could mentor their efforts and "tide over the first discouragements of a life of intellectual renunciation."[11] Such pursuits required sacrifice on the scholars' part, since women at the time found it almost impossible to combine marriage and a career, but, as Lynn Gordon has argued, college-educated women "did not necessarily lead lonely lives."[12] As they graduated from college and moved into professional careers, "they carried [their college] friendships with them, maintaining lifelong partnerships and family ties" that sustained them.[13]

Thomas emphasized the whole of the Bryn Mawr experience—the life and community of Bryn Mawr—to provide sustenance for women scholars. Marian MacIntosh's "Her Masterpiece," another story in the Bryn Mawr collection, captures the essence of the experience, again through the idea of "romance." In "Her Masterpiece," the successful Ellen Blake, "a leader among progressive women," we are told, is charged with telling "the women's Congress the value of life in a woman's college," and she's having trouble figuring out what to say.[14] When she finally does give her speech, which is brilliant, she is stopped afterwards by an old friend of her father's, Ned Cartwright, who shares his own college experiences with her and tells her how much Ellen's sounded like his own. He'll "send every girl to college if it's like that," he tells her. "It's romance, that's what it is, and they've a right to their romance; for I'm an old man, my dear, and perhaps you'll take my word for it, it's the romance of life that counts,—for the girls as well as the boys."[15]

Although it is unclear whether Moore ever read the stories in this collection, she was immersed in the scholarly world that produced them. In her 1923 poem "Marriage," she makes a relatively clear announcement at the beginning of the poem, albeit through layers of literary allusion, that Esther's choice to pursue her scholarship with Hilda as her companion was the best one for Moore as well. Moore, after all, chose to live at home with her mother as companion after she graduated from college. And, like Esther, she makes the pursuit of knowledge her "province," not marriage. The announcement in "Marriage" comes via a passage from Sir Francis Bacon. She refers to the wedding band at the beginning of the poem as "this firegilt steel / alive with goldenness; / how bright it shows— / 'of circular traditions and impostures, / committing many spoils,' / requiring all one's criminal ingenuity / to avoid!" (*BMM*, 115). The quotation "of circular traditions and impostures, / committing many spoils," is a slight misquotation of Bacon.

With her appropriation of Bacon's words, Moore provides for the poem's first radical reversal of the expected. She turns the legal institution of marriage into a fraudulent enterprise that will leave you behind bars. I am reminded again of "Peter" refusing to be "caged by the rungs of a domestic chair." Bacon's word "spoils" in this context further emphasizes the criminal behavior that might be found within this legal institution. Since women were essentially defined as property within the Victorian marriage contract, a point Moore makes crystal clear in a suffrage letter she wrote from college, the taking of "spoils" through violent force is certainly suggested here, a fact of marriage that then requires "all one's criminal ingenuity / to avoid." Charles Berger has argued that Moore "foreground[s] her own celibate status" in the phrase "criminal ingenuity."[16] In a brilliant etymological reading of the word *ingenuity*, Berger uncovers a rich "palimpsest" of meaning, finding the words "ingenuity' (skill)," as well as "'ingenuous' (from *gen—beget), meaning 'free, frank, free-born,'" and "hiding in the word shadows," as he puts it, "'*ingénue*,' whose refusal to taste experience, prolonged beyond a certain age, becomes criminal in the eyes of some."[17] Finally, he notes that, "lodged in all these words is the root *gens*, and all the issues it raises involving generation."[18] The cumulative effect of all this word play, Berger argues, is to drive home the following stunning point: "The real crime in avoiding marriage might well be the placing of one's own procreative imagination above the imperative to reproduce biologically."[19] In this way, Moore neatly sets up the logic that will dominate the entire poem.

In avoiding marriage, the speaker of Moore's poem suggests an alternate route, also via the same quotation from Bacon, but also drawing on what Moore learned at Bryn Mawr. In a notebook she kept during the drafting of "Marriage," Moore copied out passages from an *Encyclopaedia Brittanica* entry on Bacon. It is from these passages that she lifts the "Marriage" quotation. In this section of her notebook, Moore writes, "I confess that I have as vast contemplative ends as I have moderate civil ends." And then she quotes Bacon to explain "for I have taken all knowledge to be my province." Bacon had been writing about science, which he said must be "purge[d]" of "2 sorts of rovers." He describes these "rovers" as one of "frivolous disputation, confutations and verbosities" and the other of "blind experiments and *circular traditions and impostures [which] hath committed so many spoils*" (emphasis mine).[20] By getting rid of these "rovers" in science, Bacon writes, he hopes, "I shall bring in industrious observations and grounded conclusions and profitable inventions and discoveries." The quotation is more than a little suggestive, since Moore named the first volume of her poetry over which she had editorial control *Observations*.

Moore misquoted the passage to read errors, instead of rovers, and the poem shifts the subject from science to marriage.[21] In misquoting the Bacon passage after raising the subject of marriage, Moore establishes that the pursuit of knowledge is vastly more important than marriage, "a civil end," as Moore tells us, and that this pursuit must be "purge[d]" of the "error" of marriage to allow her to attend to her own "industrious observations." Margaret Holley argues this passage is about as clear evidence as we're going to get that Moore thought marriage would be a detriment to her work.[22] I would argue there is quite a bit of evidence for this view.

Moore wrote a number of poems, for instance, that remained unpublished until recently with Grace Schulman's edition of *The Poems of Marianne Moore*, that "tried out" the ideas that would eventually form the core of "Marriage."[23] These poems, probably written between 1910 and 1915, reject marriage on the grounds that it would hinder the artist. In "'And Shall Life Pass an Old Maid By?'" the last line of the poem's first stanza reads, "Convention's face misleads the artist's feet."[24] And in "Piningly," the speaker of the poem rejects multiple suitors, all of whom "looked piningly on her." Just after graduating from college, Moore, it seems, was plagued by suitors. She mentions seven of them in one letter home that she wrote during the few months that she worked as a stenographer at Melvil Dewey's Lake Placid Club in upstate New York (*SL*, 82; 73). She also mentions the unfortunate Mr. Walker who "took a fancy to me," whom she says made her "fidget and gnash with indignation" (*SL*, 80). She writes that a Mrs. Heston had tried to act as a matchmaker. "If there is a more odious institution in modern society than a matchmaker I should like to see it" (*SL*, 80). Finally, she complains that, "Mrs. Heston felt sorry for Mr. Walker and thought she could sacrifice *me*, a nice tidy little quail" (*SL*, 80). While one of the problems that Moore defines in "Marriage" is that women must become a kind of sacrifice to men within the marriage contract, in "Piningly" the suitors are sacrificed. The last lines of the poem read, "They were left like food: they were the inevitable mere / Residue—scattered negligently. 'They were left like crumbs from a lion's / Meal—a couple of shins and the bit of an ear'" (*PMM*, 30). Moore is quoting from the Biblical prophet Amos 3:12, a passage that she uses again in "Marriage" to suggest Eve's bondage in the married state, calling attention to *her* sacrifice, a point I will return to in more detail later.

In defining marriage as a fraudulent institution, Moore was probably thinking also of her friend Bryher's marriage of convenience to the editor and writer Robert McAlmon in 1921, which, as Robin Schulze has pointed out, was the immediate impetus for the poem. Her lively exchange of letters with Bryher and with Bryher's companion and lover, H. D., during this period expose much of Moore's thinking on the subject. Moore was clearly distressed by Bryher's decision to marry McAlmon for appearances rather than love.[25] The whole affair prompted her to write in one March 1921 letter to H. D. that "there is no such thing as a prudent marriage . . . marriage is a Crusade; there is always tragedy in it" (*SL,* 149).

But while Bryher's imprudent marriage appears to have created a kind of catalyst for the poem, the poem's feminist critique of marriage was formed by Moore's intellectual and political training at Bryn Mawr. Moore's sensitivity to exactly what the contract of marriage meant for women is clear in a letter she wrote home to her mother on Valentine's Day 1909 while she was a student at Bryn Mawr. She wrote of her attempts to persuade her friend Elsie, who was "on the fence" about suffrage, that the vote was essential to equality for all women, and she makes the point that when women are economically dependent on their husbands—when they cannot own property, when their husbands essentially own them and all the clothes on their backs—then democracy is not possible. Moore borrowed her argumentative strategies and ideas from suffragist Anna Howard Shaw who had just spoken at the college on the "Modern Democratic Ideal."[26] She begins by pointing out to Elsie that her luxuries are had at the expense of the labor and exploitation of others. " 'If you want to oppose women's voting' I said, 'you merely say you are willing to tramp over people's bodies to get all these luxuries you take so calmly.' I said, 'If women are going to support children and perhaps unproductive adults they ought to have as much pay as men and ought to work eight hours if men work eight hours, and not work ten.' I delivered a cruel flow on the score of men" (*SL,* 64). Moore goes on to make a wonderful and witty argument over the absurdity of women's property rights (or lack thereof). She ends by telling Elsie that by the logic of these rights a woman "would have to be buried before she was dead" to "get any use out of" her husband's cemetery lot (*SL,* 64).

Moore tells her mother in the letter that she really "wasn't as rabid as I sound here, but I was pretty bulldoggy" (*SL,* 64). Her final strategy is to remind Elsie to look beyond her own privileged status: "Of course woman suffrage doesn't mean much to you, because you're petted and have money lavished on you and you wouldn't think what a slum looks like and wouldn't think of touching an infected horsehide or dangerous machinery for anything, but a lot of girls that haven't quite your chances could see why it might help some" (*SL*, 64). The letter demonstrates Moore's awareness of class issues and women's economic dependence in marriage. She uses Shaw's arguments to point out logical fallacies in the marriage laws, such as the inheritance of property and cemetery lots, arguments that come into play in "Marriage."

Like Moore's entire poem, this letter engages in the kind of "reverse" discourse, or discourses of resistance, that marked the feminist language of suffrage discussed by Susan Kingsley Kent in her book on sex and suffrage in Britain. Although Kent focuses on the British suffrage movement, her arguments are relevant to American suffrage discourse as well. As part of the suffrage movement, Kent argues, suffragists challenged the separate sphere ideology that aligned women with the domestic sphere by appropriating the language of the marketplace. The dominant metaphors of their critique were borrowed from the public sphere—words such as "contract," "production," "labor," and "class."[27] Like suffragist discourse, Moore here "challeng[es] the prevalent ideas about marriage as 'connubial bliss,'" by appropriating the language of the public sphere.[28] Moore's poem, after all, begins with these lines: "This institution, / perhaps one should say enterprise / out of respect for which / one says one need not change one's mind / about a thing one has believed in, / requiring public promises / of one's intention / to fulfill a private obligation." Marriage requires "public promises," Moore's poem argues, and therefore cannot be considered a private matter, far from the concerns of the public domain of business and commerce. Moore shows how the two spheres cannot be considered separately, since marriage requires "public promises / of one's intention / to fulfill a private obligation" (*BMM*, 115). In establishing marriage as an institution, Moore opens it to the possibility of critique and reform, which is precisely what the poem does.

Another of the poem's reversals offers a revisionary portrait of Eve, Moore's own Bryn Mawr "type," who arrives first in paradise before Adam. Eve shares more than a few characteristics with Peter and the elephant of "Black Earth," as well as Miss Duckworth in

Moore's college story "Wisdom and Virtue," all of which I have read as various representations of the New Woman. The New Woman reappears in the 1930s in an androgynous form as Ambrose, "the college student," who "sits on the hillside / with his not-native books" in "The Steeple-Jack." And, like Eve, appreciates "an elegance of which / the source is not bravado" (*CPo,* 6). The section on Eve begins:

> Eve: beautiful woman—
> I have seen her
> when she was so handsome
> she gave me a start,
> able to write simultaneously
> in three languages—
> English, German and French
> and talk in the meantime;
> equally positive in demanding a commotion
> and in stipulating quiet:
> "I should like to be alone";
> to which the visitor replies,
> "I should like to be alone;
> why not be alone together?"
> Below the incandescent stars
> below the incandescent fruit,
> the strange experience of beauty;
> its existence is too much;
> it tears one to pieces
> and each fresh wave of consciousness
> is poison.
>
> (*BMM,* 115–16).

Punctuation slows down the line—the colon, the dash in one line—and Eve is frozen in a tableau vivant—"Below the incandescent stars / below the incandescent fruit"—that calls attention to her status as an object of desire in marriage. The insertion of the line "I have seen her" introduces the speaker and even perhaps the reader as mutual spectators in the contemplation of Eve. Moore almost never uses the first person in her work. Oddly enough, the speaker's claim also puts the "I" of the poem in the position of Satan, the voyeur, who in Book IX of *Paradise Lost* nearly gives up his attempt to beguile Eve when he is momentarily stunned into being "stupidly good" by her beauty and innocence. Milton's epic, reportedly read to

Moore when she was only eight, held the special status in the Moore household that only childhood books can have, calling forth, as they certainly would in Moore's case, the maternal scene of instruction. A further scene of instruction is evoked in the knowledge that Moore quoted *Paradise Lost* at length in her study of style in King's class. *Paradise Lost* is behind much of Moore's poem, which several critics have read as a feminist revision of Milton's patriarchal text.[29] The echo here also calls forth its sublimity, to bring us closer to the speaker's and our mutual admiration of Eve, an important moment that focuses desire in the poem, a desire that Charles Berger has identified as "Moore's guarded, ambiguous, self-identification as a lesbian."[30] In a shrewd move that dismantles traditional readings of the poem that take "the visitor" to be Adam, Berger argues that "the visitor" is more likely to offer a kind of marriage proposal between same-sex partners here. As Berger has pointed out, "nothing in the poem authorizes the gender of this visitor as masculine, other than the traditional heterosexual marriage plot."[31] Such a reading gains further support if considered alongside the range of same-sex partnerships offered to readers of *A Book of Bryn Mawr Stories*. Both Eve and the visitor would like to be alone, and so why not propose this shared aloneness? Such a reading is also consistent with King's representation of scholarly helpmates.

Moreover, the listing of Eve's intellectual accomplishments jostles with her beauty for equal status. Eve is "able to write simultaneously / in three languages— / English, German and French / and talk in the meantime" (*BMM,* 115). As we know from Moore's notes on these lines, they come from a story on multiple consciousness that appeared in *Scientific American* in 1922 (*BMM,* 144). The lines point to the performative aspects of the poem. Eve is performing for a public audience. She is demonstrating her skills as if it were an examination. But what is interesting is that this performance emphasizes Eve's college education, since English, German, and French are associated with scholarly learning in the Western tradition. These lines anticipate Eve's role as orator later in the poem and, as Cristanne Miller has argued, demonstrate her linguistic mastery.[32] To put Eve's learning on display instead of her body is to begin to undermine the status of woman as commodity within the marriage contract. She is no longer simply a beautiful object; she speaks as well, and what's more, she speaks in a learned way.

But the *Scientific American* connection also makes Eve a bit of a freak, since the article Moore quotes from analyzes this case of multiple consciousness as if in a scientific investigation, an allusion perhaps to the scrutiny and pseudoscientific discourse attached to women in higher education who were treated as freaks of "nature." These lines describing Eve are also reminiscent of "Roses Only," another *Observations* poem that, like "Marriage," takes apart the traditions associated with the rose—beauty and romantic love. "Roses Only" begins with the lines "You do not seem to realise that beauty is a liability / rather than / an asset" (*BMM*, 83). Beauty, the speaker tells us ("in view of the fact that spirit creates form") "must have brains." Again, Moore borrows her vocabulary from economics, emphasizing the woman's status as property, and "Roses Only" refers us to that same passage in Book IX of *Paradise Lost* when Satan, who finds Eve in the garden propping up drooping roses with myrtle, calls the roses "her best prop so farr."[33] The lines in "Marriage" tell us Eve's beauty is also a "liability": "its existence is too much; / it tears one to pieces." Originally, Moore's Eve was closer to the *Vogue* cover girl illustrated by Moore's Carlisle neighbor George Plank that might have been the subject of "Those Various Scalpels."[34] In an earlier version, Eve's gown is encrusted with jewels, and the line read "Eve: beautiful woman—stiff with jewels / her dress embroidered all over with / snakes of Venice gold and silver. . . ."[35] The "snakes of Venice gold" subsequently show up in the Virgin Mary's robe in Moore's 1924 fanciful poem "Sea Unicorns and Land Unicorns." The change Moore makes here moves the attention from Eve's clothing, which would have been a distraction, to her conversation and, therefore, her "brains," at least temporarily.

In many respects, Eve is a kind of chaste, intellectual Diana in Moore's portrait of her, and in that respect she is able to confer the authority of the New Woman. In reflecting in 1958 on her own experience as a young person, Moore wrote that chastity "confers a particular strength."[36] Although Moore's comment was published at the height of midcentury conservatism and could have been used to support a conservative agenda for women, such a choice at the beginning of the century had an entirely different valence. Such a view of chastity at that time would have been in line with the New Woman's desire to maintain her independence and, as we shall see later, became a mark of resistance to what marriage had to offer.

While Eve is set down first in an "Adamless Eden," whose analogue might be thought of as the women's college of Moore's generation, she cannot remain there, and so the rest of the poem concerns itself with what happens when Adam arrives and Eve chooses marriage, although the sense that she has much of a choice is called into question. The first thing that happens to Eve with Adam's arrival is that her speech is restricted. She is "constrained in speaking of the serpent— / that shed snakeskin in the history of politeness / not to be returned to again— / that invaluable accident / exonerating Adam" (*BMM,* 116). Adam, on the other hand, in the next section of the poem "goes on speaking" (*BMM,* 117). Adam's speech not only takes on the high lyric mode of apostrophe, which Moore's own poetry resists (he is the "O / thou to whom, from whom, / without whom nothing—Adam"), his speech is "the speedy stream / which violently bears all before it, / at one time silent as the air / and now as powerful as the wind" (*BMM,* 116–17). Moore's quotation represents yet another reversal since, as Elizabeth Joyce has pointed out, these quotations, which according to Moore's notes are from Richard Baxter's *The Saints' Everlasting Rest,* are actually used to critique marriage.[37] While the purpose of Baxter's 1650 Calvinist text was to provide readers with a "prescription for passage to heaven,"[38] Moore's usage reverses Baxter's purpose and perhaps even critiques such Protestant prescriptions by suggesting that Adam's speechifying, indeed his preachiness, mows down everything in its path, while claiming to contain "everything convenient / to promote one's joy" (*BMM,* 117).

But Adam, as one might expect of a man who speaks in the high lyric mode, is "plagued by the nightingale," and here begins yet another complicated set of reversals in Moore's poem (*BMM,* 118). With the nightingale's entrance, Moore introduces the central theme and problem of "Marriage"—that is, Adam's desire and the "illusion" that marriage will quench that desire. "It clothes me with a shirt of fire," he says of the nightingale; he is "impelled by 'the illusion of a fire / effectual to extinguish fire'" (*BMM,* 118). And so Adam "stumbles over marriage, / 'a very trivial object indeed.'" The words are William Godwin's, and following Moore's logic here is crucial to understanding the poem. Moore quotes Godwin in full in her notebook. "Marriage is a law and the worst of all laws. . . . If two men happen to feel preference for the same woman, let them both enjoy her *conversation* and be wise enough to consider sexual intercourse 'a very trivial object indeed.'"[39] The substitution of marriage for sexual intercourse is the crucial metonymy on which the logic of the entire poem turns. Men do not enjoy women's conversation in Moore's poem; they either silence it, or they talk over it, as in the section of the poem when Adam and Eve argue.

Thomas conveyed a similar message to Godwin's when she wrote in an article published in the *Educational Review* in 1908 that men and women must "subordinat[e] the distracting instincts of sex to the simple human fellowship of similar education and similar intellectual and social ideas."[40] Thomas was responding to the "horrible oversexuality" and "pseudo-scientific" theories that male educators and physicians were using to "degrade" the female scholar.[41] These theories had made women's biology their destiny and turned them into "the sex" by reducing them to a collection of reproductive organs, Thomas argued. Thomas had reassured Bryn Mawr women that same year, according to a letter Moore wrote home to her family, about their overall good health in the face of physicians' dire warnings that they would turn themselves into invalids if they studied too much. Later, after Moore and her mother had moved to Greenwich Village in 1918 and Moore had become actively involved in avant-garde artistic circles, she, too, suggested that enjoying conversation and intellectual pursuits was a reasonable response to the newly sexualized environment of the teens when Freud's theories took hold. In a notebook entry from August 2, 1923, for instance, Moore "records a conversation" at a tea given by her friend, fellow feminist and *Dial* editor, Alyse Gregory. As Linda Leavell notes, "The topic [of the conversation] was 'marriage as a Freudian necessity.'"[42] Moore, now called on to defend her choice of not marrying and her own "domestic arrangements," apparently countered the argument with a list of what J. Sibley Watson would dub "blameless bachelors," including "Traherne, Beethoven, Sir Isaac Newton, Washington Irving, Charles Lamb, [and] Henry James."[43] Moore later adopted, according to Leavell, the "blameless bachelor" as a "model of resistance."[44] She had actually referred to herself as a "bachelor" in 1914.[45]

Moore, always one to make use of the arguments of others for her own resistant purposes no matter what their original context, had actually marshaled Freud's theories in an earlier instance to make a case for not marrying. "The physical is important as well as the spiritual," Moore wrote in one letter to Bryher in 1921 when she was objecting to Bryher's marriage. But, as she points out, "Freud says . . . our capacity for transferring energy from one field to another is almost infinite and the adjustments of one need to another, involve so many things that it is no easy matter to be absolute as to what course of action we are compelled to adopt for our all round best good" (*SL,* 153).[46] Moore's statement makes a case for the "sublimation" of sex, while resisting "absolute" solutions. In a sense, Moore's statement might be said to emphasize the range of "adjustments" that her own generation of college-educated women could make, thereby rendering marriage a nonnecessity. Moore's sustained critique of "Marriage" makes clear why that was not, for her, a "course of action" for a college-educated woman's "all round best good."

Gregory's own views on the subject of marriage reflect the newly sexualized environment that greeted Moore on her arrival to New York. Her essay "The Dilemma of Marriage" was published in *The New Republic,* the same year as the Manikin edition of "Marriage" appeared, and it identifies sex as the "dilemma" of the essay's title. Charles Molesworth, in his brief mention of Gregory's article, suggests that Moore probably discussed it with Gregory before it came out, and Moore may have responded to a draft of it during the composing process of "Marriage."[47] Her reading notebooks at the Rosenbach show that she was very interested in the article and copied out long passages of it. Moreover, a comment that Moore's mother made about Gregory and her daughter provocatively alludes to their roles as radical agitators as female editors of *The Dial.* Moore replaced Gregory as managing editor. Mrs. Moore refers to them as the "'serken' [serpent] in *The Dial's* 'Man Paradise' of ease."[48]

Gregory's article was a response to D. H. Lawrence, the "latest string" of men, Gregory argues, who have written about marriage and women from an "anti-feminist perspective."[49] Lawrence's writing was, of course, heavily influenced by Freud's theories. According to Gregory in a passage Moore quotes in her notebook, Lawrence advocates "a new kind of mystical subjugation" for women where "man may enter or escape the enchanted circle of sex," while "woman must remain forever engirdled within it."[50] Moore uses this quotation, interestingly enough, to lead into the Bacon quotation that describes marriage as an institution of "circular traditions and impostures," thereby emphasizing that Moore had been thinking at the time that

Marianne Moore and Alyse Gregory at *The Dial*. Photograph by Doris Ulmann, n.d. Yale Collection of American Literature, Beinecke Rare Book and Manuscript Library.

it was sex that entrapped women in marriage. Gregory had written, "The pure sex instinct is always explorative, destructive, aberrant. It is stimulated only through new, and ever newer adventures. In practice it is a game in which each is seeking covertly for advantage, like animals stalking their prey, so that a culmination of the pursuit means a cessation of excitement. The game is over, and with a capture, where no ambushed reserves are suspected, comes a sense of satisfied power to one and humiliation to the other, ending in ennui and misery."[51]

Gregory goes on to say, "Men and women are drawn together in the entangling net of sex, drawn together in the glamour of an illusion. They marry. The explorative impulse, always inconstant in its very nature, is soon satisfied and veers away—perhaps in months, perhaps in years. Some couples, thwarted, dismayed, each angrily blaming the other for what is inevitable, drift rapidly into enmity and separation."[52]

In "Marriage," Moore's partners follow a similar progression from passion to enmity. As in Gregory's example, the animals stalk their prey:

> The blue panther with black eyes,
> the basalt panther with blue eyes,
> entirely graceful—
> one must give them the path—
> (*BMM,* 119)

The sensuality of this passage is also reminiscent of the "Circe" section of H. D.'s *Hymen,* which Moore reviewed for *Broom* in January 1923 and may have had in mind:

> Panther and panther,
> then a black leopard
> follows close—
> black panther and red
> and a great hound,
> a god-like beast,
> cut the sand in a clear ring
> and shut me from the earth . . . .[53]

In both passages, the speaker of the poem is outside the ring of circling beasts, but in "Circe," the speaker is shut out, "shut . . . from the earth" without choice, whereas in "Marriage," the speaker "give[s] them the path," willingly. H. D.'s poem ends with Circe willing to give up "my power and magic / for your glance."[54] Moore's speaker makes no such concession, for the poem continues chillingly with the onset of jealousy and anger:

> the spiked hand
> that has an affection for one
> and proves it to the bone,
> impatient to assure you
> that impatience is the mark of independence
> not of bondage.
>
> (*BMM*, 119)

The suggestion here is that there really is no escape from bondage for women within the marriage contract as it is defined in Western culture in the early twentieth century. One must, then, "give them the path." The speaker of Moore's poem is not prepared to give up her "power and magic" for anyone's "glance."

In her *Broom* review of H. D.'s *Hymen*, Moore subtly critiques the types of women in H. D.'s poetry:

> Talk of weapons and the tendency to match one's intellectual and emotional vigor with the violence of nature, give a martial, an apparently *masculine* tone to such writing as H. D.'s, the more so that women are regarded as belonging necessarily to either of two classes —that of the intellectual freelance or that of the eternally sleeping beauty, effortless yet effective in the indestructable limestone keep of domesticity. Woman tends unconsciously to be the aesthetic norm of intellectual home life and preeminently in the case of H. D., we have the intellectual, social woman, non-public and "*feminine.*" (emphasis mine; *CPr*, 82)

If we pay close attention to how Moore uses the terms *masculine* and *feminine* in the review, we see that the word masculine forms an associative chain with the terms "weapons," "violence of nature," "martial," and "intellectual and emotional vigor," a connection that Moore disassociates in her own poetry, so that "intellectual and emotional vigor" does not "naturally" go hand in hand with violence. In "He 'Digesteth Harde Yron,'" for instance, the camel-sparrow "watches *his* chicks with / a maternal concentration," while in "Those

Various Scalpels" Moore aligns hyperfemininity with weaponry, a combination that she may have borrowed from Pope's *Rape of the Lock* (*CPo,* 99). Moore had written a parody of Pope's mock epic in college with her friend Mary Nearing, lines of which she incorporated into "Marriage." Moore dissociates herself in this review from the first two categories of woman she finds in H. D.'s poetry, according to Rachel Blau DuPlessis, but favors a third category: "the intellectual, social woman, non-public and 'feminine,'" which for Moore fuses "the best of New Woman and old."[55]

While DuPlessis does not focus on "Marriage" specifically, her discussion of Moore's poetry as written from the subject position of the New Woman is relevant to my argument. Following Carolyn Burke's insights on the New Woman, DuPlessis argues that Ezra Pound's category "logopoeia" can be used to analyze Moore's feminist strategies. Pound applied the term to Mina Loy and Moore in a 1918 review of their work. DuPlessis describes logopoeia via Pound as follows: "One of three ways of creating meaning—by visual imagery (phanopoeia), by sound (melopoeia), or in logopoeia, by using the word in some special relation to 'usage,' playing ironically with the contexts in which one expects it. This is something like what Bakhtin (1981) calls heteroglossia—the deploying of different social registers and jargons to create, in a phrase retooled from 1918, " 'the dance of the intellect among words.'"[56]

Historically "formed in opposition to the romantic lyric," logopoeia has as "its most radical effect . . . a resistance to normal poetic pleasures," DuPlessis argues.[57] A kind of "analytic lyric," DuPlessis notes that logopoeia has often been interpreted "as the desire to bring into poetry the density of social analysis in the 'prose tradition.'"[58] For Loy and Moore, she argues, logopoeia "began . . . as an attack on the gender narratives of lyric poetry: femininity, beauty, a certain gaze on female objects, unironic sexual yearning, the underlying lyric narrative of romance. It is, as Burke argues, a poetry written from the subject position of the New Woman."[59] In "Marriage," Moore deploys all of these strategies to destabilize our romantic notions of marriage.

Moore brings Gregory's social analysis, which itself is influenced by the arguments of feminist social critique, to bear on her "analytic lyric." When a woman, as in Lawrence's novels, "must cede to the male assertion," Gregory writes, her reward is a "tranced peace, a sub-life of strange untroubled beauty, far from the hard, fleeting world, where cold intellectual concepts like hailstones driven on a relentless wind, sting between the eyes to thought."[60] Compare Gregory's "tranced peace" to what happens to Eve after Adam arrives. Moore emphasizes "the strange experience of beauty" and then describes "the heart rising / in its estate of peace" (*BMM*, 116). With Gregory's critique in mind when considering Eve, Moore's words take on quite a different valence. And Moore, like Gregory, traces the trajectory of marriage from passion to enmity as Moore reminds her reader at the end of this section that "experience attests / that men have power / and sometimes one is made to feel it" (*BMM*, 120).

In speaking of Lawrence, Gregory reminds her readers that "every generation" will have its "anti-feminist" until "women themselves, less acquiescently entrapped, rapacious and thought-dulled, are freed from economic servitude in their relations with men."[61] In Moore's poem, the reality of marriage as "economic servitude" hits home in all its violence at the end of the final section of Adam and Eve's "conversation" when they break into full-scale argument, and illusions of "connubial bliss" are shattered on both sides. As Heather Cass White points out, Adam and Eve's "'conversation' is really an alternation of incompatible perspectives from people too distant from each other to actually converse."[62] In the first exchange, Adam resorts to the lowest form of insult by calling Eve's beauty into question. Adam says,

> . . . "What monarch would not blush
> to have a wife
> with hair like a shaving-brush?"
> The fact of woman
> is not "the sound of the flute
> but very poison."
>
> (*BMM*, 120)

Adam's insult vibrates with a series of allusions that leads back not only to Moore's college career but also to a satire of another patriarchal text, Pope's *Rape of the Lock*, which according to her notes, Moore helped write with her Bryn Mawr friend Mary Nearing (*BMM*, 146). She had studied the text in her Imitative Writing course.[63] Adam's insult also closely parallels the kinds of insults Moore encountered frequently in work by male writers whom she reviewed for

The Dial and other little magazines of the period. To take just one example (and there are many), in her review of Maxwell Bodenheim's *Against this Age* and *Crazy Man,* which appeared in *The Dial* in 1924, Moore writes, "This author's concept of woman puzzles one. Surely there is false perspicacity in an analysis which results always in the exhibiting of woman's 'enticing inferiority'; which finds her an embarrassing adjunct, 'cooing and crawling for your money,' a creature of perfumed effeteness, of 'interminable evasions,' 'waving surrender in the foreground,' never other than a receiver of 'men's ornaments and poverties'" (*CPr,* 104). Moore goes on to say, "The writer's attitude of pronouncement reaches its apex in the statement made by one of his *dramatis personae,* that there is zest in bagging a woman who is one's equal in wits." Moore acidly adds, "The possibility of bagging a *superior* in wits not being allowed to confuse the issue" (my emphasis; *CPr,* 104).

Eve demonstrates her superior wit in her reply to Adam, and Moore adds weight and feminist authority to Eve's response by quoting Thomas, thereby raising Eve's status to that of an orator, a role usually reserved for Adam:

> She says, "'Men are monopolists
> of stars, garters, buttons
> and other shining baubles'—
> unfit to be the guardians
> of another person's happiness."
> (*BMM,* 120)

This quotation could serve as an epigraph for the poem, bringing to bear as it does the full weight of Thomas's feminist calls for reform in women's education and her views on marriage.

Thomas was an impressive orator, and her words here, placed in Eve's mouth, make her a crucial orator in the poem. To represent women as compelling speakers is not at all unusual for Moore since she had many examples at Bryn Mawr from which to choose. Many well-known feminists came to speak, including Shaw, who was president of the National American Woman Suffrage Association (NAWSA), and Jane Addams, and Moore heard Thomas weekly in chapel. Thomas herself formed and then became president of the National College Equal Suffrage League in 1908, providing a national platform from which she could now speak. The suffrage campaign produced compelling female orators. Moore gives the full quotation of Thomas's speech in her notes to the poem: "Men practically reserve for themselves stately funerals, splendid monuments, memorial statues, membership in academies, medals, titles, honorary degrees, stars, garters, ribbons, buttons and other shining baubles, so valueless in themselves and yet so infinitely desirable because they are symbols of recognition by their fellow craftsmen of difficult work well done" (*BMM*, 146). In short, men were accustomed to receiving recognition, while women were not, which raises a major concern of Moore's in these early stages of her career as she worked to publish her poetry. In a later speech, Thomas linked this type of recognition to "the next advance in women's education," which, for Thomas, was "to throw open to the competition of women scholars the rewards and prizes of a scholar's life and to allow women professors like men professors to marry, or not, as they see fit."[64]

Adam's insulting reply to Eve's demand for recognition emphasizes the idea that marriage, women, and domesticity are a kind of living death for the man and a kind of childlike subservience and slavery for the woman, a toxic brew, Moore suggests, that even leads to the woman in her role as wife personifying death itself:

> He says, "These mummies
> must be handled carefully—
> 'the crumbs from a lion's meal,
> a couple of shins and the bit of an ear';
> turn to the letter M
> and you will find
> that 'a wife is a coffin'
> that severe object
> with the pleasing geometry
> stipulating space and not people,
> refusing to be buried
> and uniquely disappointing,
> revengefully wrought in the attitude
> of an adoring child
> to a distinguished parent."
> (*BMM*, 120–21)

Here is the Amos quotation again. In Moore's earlier poem, "Piningly," as I suggested, the line is used to indicate the rejection of suitors. Here the "mummies" are actually compared to what is left over after the lion's meal, which, if you follow Moore's logic, is actually quite a wicked joke. With the word "mummies," Moore brings in an Egyptian reference that would be in keeping with the subject matter of Amos, since his message from God to the people of Israel is that their sins—specifically their oppression of others—pain God even more because he chose to deliver them from slavery out of Egypt. Again, Moore draws on references to slavery to help define what the state of marriage means for women. Moreover, the direct quotation from Amos refers to the Lord's threat that when he punishes the people of Israel, only a few will survive, just as the shepherd recovers only a couple of legs or a bit of an ear from the lion's mouth after his meal. Is Moore suggesting here that only a few will survive the oppressive world of marriage? Are these body parts suggesting what women are reduced to in marriage—their reproductive organs? The joke, it seems, is that "mummies," are in fact what *is* left over after the lion's meal, or in this case, Adam's meal of Eve—since "mummies" are, after all, a British term for mothers.

The double meaning of "mummies" with its suggestion of both motherhood and Egyptian tombs leads into Adam's statement that "a wife is a coffin," which Moore in her notes attributes to her fellow modernist Ezra Pound. The argumentative section of the poem duplicates the rhetorical logic of Amos, as each statement by Amos to the people of Israel is prefaced by a reminder that he is speaking the word of the Lord, rendered as "The Lord says" in some translations. Each section of the argument between Adam and Eve begins with either "He says" or "She says." That would, in a sense, make the speaker of the poem a kind of cipher for the prophet, who passes on the word of Adam and Eve as almost a kind of warning.

In this section of the poem, the ideas of Moore's letter on suffrage quoted above also suggest the context of Adam's insult. While the quotation from Pound implies that a wife will bury a man alive (or at least the way Moore uses it here), Moore turns it around when she suggests that this wife is "refusing to be buried." However, she is ultimately "disappointing," since she is totally dependent, "*revengefully* wrought [by society] in the attitude / of an adoring child / to a distinguished parent" (emphasis mine; *BMM,* 121). Women, it would seem, have been turned into children from beginning to end, from the cute child's term for mother at the beginning of the section to the adoring, childlike wife at the end.

Moore identifies exactly the role that women took on in marriage, and she points to how women are molded to this role, not born that way, again suggesting that the role is constructed, peculiar to the institution of marriage, not, as the dominant argument went, a natural one. In Adam's language, Moore also echoes Thomas again, as we can see from another letter she wrote home dated April 15, 1909. In a speech where Thomas urged Bryn Mawr women to read Charlotte Perkins Gilman's book on children (probably the 1898 *Women and Economics*), Thomas "said how women were dead weights (financially)! hanging about their husband's necks, as things are now and we ought to try to break up the superstition that it is indecent for women to work until their husbands have got well established—."[65] Moore echoes an earlier feminist as well in this section, Mary Wollstonecraft, who argues in *A Vindication of the Rights of Woman* that men were not doing women any favors by bringing them up to be "overgrown child[ren]."[66] Adam's voice speaks in the voice of a long history of men's oppression of women, grinding down women, as Moore suggests in her suffrage letter, and contributing to their continuing state of inferiority.

At the end of the argument, Moore reminds the reader once again of the inequality of a relationship where "'some have merely rights / while some have obligations.'" The section ends:

> he loves himself so much,
> he can permit himself
> no rival in that love.
> She loves herself so much,
> she cannot see herself enough—
> a statuette of ivory on ivory,
> the logical last touch
> to an expansive splendor
> earned as wages for work done:
> (*BMM*, 121)

Here we return with chilling force to exactly what Eve's role is in this relationship. She is splendid, because this is the "logical last touch" that she has "earned," for what?

Kent argues that the suffrage movement used resistant discursive strategies to "challenge and overturn cultural constructions of femininity and female sexuality":[67] "Challenging the prevalent ideas about marriage as 'connubial bliss,' feminists posited that marriage resembled nothing more closely than a commercial contract, in which women exchanged themselves—their legal rights, their property, their bodies, and the fruits of their labor—for a wage paid in the form of material subsistence."[68] Moore makes clear here that the price Eve pays for her splendor is that she is Adam's sex slave. Moore points out exactly what sex could become within the bonds of marriage, hence shattering any illusion that this is a romantic arrangement.

Gregory had argued, "Women must find in sex that old unity which for so long has been spun out of the desires of human beings." But as she notes, "There is no unity in sex. There is no unity in life. At the very best, there is only an identification of interests, at times an armed neutrality, and rarely a glowing comradeship."[69] In Moore's poem, "One sees that it is rare— / that striking grasp of opposites / opposed to each other, not to unity" (*BMM*, 122). In bringing these two texts together, we begin to see marriage as, indeed, the subject of both Gregory's article and Moore's poem, but sex (never actually mentioned in Moore's poem except via metonymy) becomes their shared object. Gregory and Moore herself show that sex (as a means to dominance) is the problem and "dilemma" of marriage, the real problem for the desiring subject, who must direct her desire elsewhere if she is to escape "the enchanted circle."

Moore's long poem ends with an image that essentially compares marriage itself to a dramatically violent moment in America's history involving slavery—the Civil War. Moore's final words on marriage come from an inscription on a statue, the statue of "an archaic Daniel Webster" that stands in Central Park. The words are the famous lines "Liberty and union / now and forever." Moore knew that Webster's strong stance for American nationalism in the face of southern secession helped to preserve and expand slavery, and she knew that his position was to preserve the union at all costs, even if it meant that one group of people would remain enslaved. Moore alongside Gregory calls attention to the irony of the statue presented in this context. Moore calls into question unequal power relations, not only between men and women in marriage but also in any relationship built on an unequal balance of power. Her final words on marriage, in other words, are ones that belong, as does discussion of marriage, in the public domain. Marriage is perhaps left standing at the end of the poem like the statue of Daniel Webster, but it has been "treated with acid," as William Carlos Williams noted of Moore's method, "washed, dried and placed right side up on a clean surface."[70] Or perhaps we should consider the statue of Daniel Webster in light of what Moore said about statues in a 1937 review of Wallace Stevens's *Owl's Clover* where she wrote that there was only hope for the world if we are ashamed of statues and what they have come to stand for—"marble victories—horses or men—which will break unless they are first broken by us" (*CPr*, 349).

Women's colleges, like Bryn Mawr, provided a structure that helped women collectively break these patriarchal statues. Under the leadership of female educational reformers, such as M. Carey Thomas, "college education became an agency for social change rather than social cohesion," according to Carroll Smith-Rosenberg.[71] If, as Patricia Ann Palmieri has suggested, women's colleges in Moore's time were an "Adamless Eden," Moore's experience at Bryn Mawr and her later experience as editor of *The Dial* show that women who banded together could indeed become serpents in paradise.[72] Moore found her "greatest happiness in congenial work." She was supported in her decision by a network of close female relationships and her choice of lifelong companion, her own mother. She appears to have chosen the path of chastity, because it seems to have been what she needed for her "all-around best good." It was not the path of either of her contemporaries—H. D. or Mina Loy. But the fact is that the women's college of Moore's generation made possible a continuum of relationships and alternatives to marriage that helped support women scholars.

By 1913, M. Carey Thomas, as Barbara Cross has noted, "was ready to trust that the wave of history which had already carried women so far would eventually make possible the combination of marriage and a career" for women.[73] In a speech she gave at Mount Holyoke on the "Future of Woman's Higher Education," Thomas spoke of the "cruel handicap" that women scholars have had to face. "They may have spent half a lifetime in fitting themselves for their chosen work and then may be asked to choose between it and marriage. No one can estimate the number of women who remain unmarried in revolt before such a horrible alternative."[74] Thomas concluded her talk with a visionary statement about the future: "I have said that women's higher education was only part and parcel of the great social revolution which is now upon us. It is already clear that this transformation of society, of which universal woman suffrage is only a small part, will give equal opportunity to women in every field of human effort including teaching and scholarship."[75] Thomas went on to say that women will no longer be deprived "of a dearly loved profession because they wish to marry," a situation that "in the past" was the result of a misunderstanding, "because men do not yet understand that women, like themselves, find their greatest happiness in congenial work."[76]

Perhaps because women now perceived, like Thomas, that it was possible to combine marriage *and* a career, the percentage of Bryn Mawr women who married between 1910 and 1918 reversed itself. During this time, 65 percent of Bryn Mawr women married, while only 49 percent continued on with their education.[77] According to Smith-Rosenberg, "Wellesley and other women's colleges mirrored the Bryn Mawr trend."[78] A number of further factors may have been responsible for this shift. Smith-Rosenberg has suggested that as Victorian attitudes toward women's sexuality changed, warnings against lesbianism discouraged the kinds of close female relationships that had supported women of Moore's generation in their independence. Furthermore, once women gained the vote in 1920, they no longer had a central cause around which they built coalition and support, and so the promise of Thomas's vision began to disappear.[79] By the time Elizabeth Bishop, the subject of my next two chapters, entered Vassar in 1930, the idea of the women's college as an "Adamless Eden" had vanished, and women found themselves turning to different strategies of resistance to carve out space for themselves as writers and career women.

3
Elizabeth Bishop's "Queer Birds": Vassar, *Con Spirito,* and the Romance of Female Community

> Oscar Wilde once observed that alcohol, if taken in sufficient quantities, produces all the symptoms of intoxication. On the same principle, we have observed that education, if absorbed in sufficient doses, produces all the symptoms of intelligence in women.
> —*Con Spirito* "Editorial"[1]

IN 1933 DURING HER JUNIOR YEAR AT VASSAR COLLEGE, ELIZABETH Bishop and several of her friends decided to start their own "rebel" literary magazine, *Con Spirito,* as a rival publication to the college's established magazine, *The Vassar Review.* Or, as Bishop had put it somewhat more strongly in a letter to Donald Stanford, *Con Spirito*'s aim was "to startle the college and kill the traditional magazine."[2] Bishop's coconspirators were a brilliant group of women, including Mary McCarthy, Eleanor and Eunice Clark, Frani Blough, Margaret Miller, and probably Muriel Rukeyser.[3] Bishop had come up with the name *Con Spirito* for the magazine, according to McCarthy, as "a pun joining the musical notation meaning 'with zest' to the announcement of a conspiracy."[4] Betsy Erkkila has mentioned *Con Spirito* in passing as a "striking" example of a successful collaboration among women who are positioned in competition with other women in a "struggle" for literary territory.[5] Paying attention to struggles such as these, Erkkila argues, provides a richer reading of literary history, one that can account for the differences among women.[6] The editorial in the first issue of *Con Spirito*, however, also aligns these women in collaboration against a male-dominated literary tradition and particularly challenges the stereotypes of college-educated women put forward by the literary press.

Con Spirito was also a conspiracy, a clandestine and anonymous meeting of literary minds, in an attempt to create a space of freedom for the imagination within the boundaries of the women's college community and the larger literary world. Although it was short-lived (the magazine folded in November 1933 after only three issues), *Con Spirito* provided an important forum for the developing talents of its writers. Two of Bishop's *Con Spirito* pieces, "Then Came the Poor" and "Hymn to the Virgin," became her first professional publications when they appeared without significant changes in *The Magazine* in 1934. McCarthy took issues of *Con Spirito* to impress Malcolm Cowley at *The New Republic* when she was looking for review assignments.[7] T. S. Eliot praised the magazine when he came to the Vassar campus in May 1933.[8] Of the seven coconspirators, four went on to establish successful literary careers—Bishop, McCarthy, Eleanor Clark, and Rukeyser. But beyond its importance as a professional vehicle, *Con Spirito* provided a space of possibility for Bishop, who had not yet come to terms with her lesbian sexuality or her literary ambition. In a limited sense, *Con Spirito* allowed Bishop to "come out" as both a writer and (perhaps much more provisionally) a lesbian.

Moreover, the *Con Spirito* writers seemed to share a kind of fantasy of a productive female community, an idea of community that remained a powerful structuring fantasy in Bishop's work. Hence, the idea of literary community that I pursue through my reading of Bishop's experience at Vassar allows me to suggest new ways to see the enclosure fantasies that have long been noted by critics as an important feature of Bishop's work. These enclosure fantasies—among them the boarding house, the prison, and the island—serve as spaces of "possibility" in Bishop's work that provide a challenge to the fixed ideas of both gender and literary identity that she found constrained the artist in the 1930s.

But before moving to the inner spaces defined by Bishop's early writing in *Con Spirito* and beyond, I would like to examine the larger territory defined by the *Con Spirito* writers in their bid for literary power at the college. This bid, as I have suggested, involved a dual challenge to the boundaries of literary and sexual convention both inside and outside the Vassar community. In their first issue of *Con Spirito*, for example, the writers responded to an editorial that had appeared in the January 1933 issue of *The American Spectator*, a literary magazine that had recently been founded by Theodore Dreiser, Eugene O'Neill, James Branch Cabell, Ernest Boyd, and George Jean Nathan. *The Spectator* had criticized Smith and Vassar "girls" for wanting to be "carbon copies of men," called their professors "dessicated old maids," and lamented the loss of "femininity" in the educated woman.[9] *The Spectator* adopted the position put forward by theories of sexology that defined the independent college woman and all-female communities of the 1920s and 1930s as deviant.[10]

Although many college women graduated, married, and had children, this pervasive discourse labeled independent women "unnatural," because it was thought that their education would interfere with their becoming wives and mothers, roles assumed to be "natural" to their sex. In this sense, as Carroll Smith-Rosenberg has argued, their choices "violated normal gender categories."[11] *The Spectator* editorial had suggested that a woman's intellectual productivity would interfere with her reproductivity (hence the characterization of Vassar's female professors as "dessicated old maids"). Theories of sexology also attached masculine physical characteristics to independent women. The Viennese neurologist Richard von Krafft-Ebing, for example, had invented a new category in the nineteenth century for women who took on men's roles, the Mannish Lesbian.[12] The mannish lesbian symbolized social disorder and perversion not so much because of her sexual orientation, but because of her rejection of traditional feminine roles and her desire for "male privileges and power."[13] With this sexual classification, Krafft-Ebing connected women's independence "to cross-dressing, sexual perversion, and borderline hermaphroditism."[14] Krafft-Ebing's theories continued to have an enormous impact on early twentieth-century ideas about college women. George Jean Nathan's familiarity with such theories of sexology seems evident in his *Spectator* article on "The Theatre" where he complained that lesbians, or as he put it, women "who are of the sexual disposition of the Aeolian-Greek island colonizers," were ruining the theater with their "masculine hardness and chill undertone."[15] He concluded that, "you cannot cast Sappho as Cinderella, or as Juliet."[16] Finally, women's college communities were portrayed in terms of metaphors of disease and contagion and became in the words of one educator "'the great breeding ground' of lesbianism."[17] These attitudes toward women's colleges and independent women in general permeated a great deal of writing in the 1920s and 1930s.

Con Spirito writers responded to and challenged this discourse of biological determinism. After assuring *The Spectator* that their "femininity" was intact by claiming their right to both their degrees, via the Oscar Wilde notation I have included in my epigraph, and their "bottle of Chanel's and a Guerlain lipstick," they quoted *The Spectator*'s diatribe at length and proceeded to co-opt not only *The Spectator*'s layout but also its language in their effort to "refute" it.[18] The *Con Spirito* editors argued that, while they might seem "by the very launching of this publication to have become the prototype of dessicated womanhood," they felt confident that their "intellectual venture" would not interfere with their ability to have children, just as they presumed that "the literary dalliance" of *The Spectator* writers had not "interfered with their lawful begetting of infants."[19] At the end of their editorial, the *Con Spirito* editors further challenged the myth that aligned womanhood with motherhood by claiming the magazine as their child, a child they must keep nourished with "forward-looking" writing or it will die; they thus demonstrated they could produce children through the male channels of productivity and thereby distance themselves from reproduction. As they appropriated the productive power of men, the *Con Spirito* editors stepped confidently over the boundary *The Spectator* had established between feminine and masculine spheres. In other words, they make "gender trouble" in the ways that Judith Butler suggests by calling into question "those naturalized and reified notions of gender that support masculine hegemony and heterosexist power."[20]

They further challenge these fixed categories by appropriating certain aspects of masculine style, thereby calling attention to the performative aspects of masculinity. McCarthy describes, for example, how the idea for *Con Spirito* got started in the "smoking-room" of Cushing Hall at Vassar.[21] Bishop, McCarthy, and others sat around—"several sort of droll characters"—puffing and debating questions of art and making up bawdy rhymes, which were "mostly borrowed from men's colleges."[22] While *Con Spirito*'s response to *The Spectator* and adoption of masculine style challenged fixed ideas about gender categories, the battle between *Con Spirito* and *The Review* tended to reinforce the discourse of male writers engaged in what Nina Baym has called "melodramas of beset manhood."[23] According to Baym, masculine writers perceived themselves as being beset by "flagrantly bad best-sellers written by women" that threatened their "integrity and livelihood."[24] Their response to this perceived threat was the creation of a fiction about the woman author. In this melodrama, the woman author is excluded from the canon and becomes the creator of not art but "conventional works."[25] The *Con Spirito* writers used similar language in their criticism of *The Review*. *The Review* was "tame," according to McCarthy.[26] Bishop called it "dull and old-fashioned,"[27] and she makes the connections between gender and quality even clearer in her letter to Donald Stanford. In it she enclosed copies of *Con Spirito* with this note: "There are some very poor things in them —but for college writing, particularly women's college writing, I think they're pretty good" (*SL,* 13). Here Bishop repeats the logic of the melodrama. While proud of the writing in *Con Spirito,* Bishop aligns poor writing with women in particular rather than college literary magazines in general. *Con Spirito* writers seemed to want to put distance between themselves and what they saw as the more "feminine" *Vassar Review,* especially since this official college magazine had rejected their avant-garde work.[28]

Their various accounts of *Con Spirito*'s formation suggest that they imagined themselves to be part of a subversive underground. Eunice Clark called *Con Spirito* the "counter-establishment blast" and saw their efforts as "a tiny part of a worldwide literary revolution stretching, in variegated forms, from Walt Whitman to *Finnegans Wake.*"[29] Bishop's title for the magazine, which contained "an almost Joycean palimpsest of meaning" for Clark, emphasizes collective action *and* secrecy, the pleasure associated with music, something done "with spirit," and the danger associated with subversion and any close alliance among women.[30] To add to the conspiratorial atmosphere, the magazine was published anonymously. Even the *Con Spirito* editors didn't know who wrote what, except by guessing. "Manuscripts for submission were put, unsigned, on a wooden chair, to be read and argued over," McCarthy recalled.[31] In addition, the makeup of the editorial board was a secret to the campus. The coconspirators advertised the magazine "by posters we nailed up on trees in the dark of night."[32] They claimed they had "darkened [themselves] in anonymity" to avoid *The Review*'s "aristocratic" policies, *not,* as they put it, because they wanted to "wallow with impunity in 'communism and copulations.'"[33] But here the editors themselves brought together in their denial radical politics and illicit sexuality.

All this emphasis on secrecy plays on the danger associated with women's colleges at this time. Educators worried that "the invert" could lure other women into a life of perversion, because the woman-centered, secretive community of the women's college provided a perfect haven for such activity.[34] The language of sexology and popular psychology had linked such an alliance with sexuality, danger, and perversion. These Vassar "girls" had rejected their reproductive roles to be productive, according to the logic of *The Spectator*, and in so doing had cast off their femininity to adopt masculine style; they were therefore professional as well as sexual outcasts. McCarthy describes the college's reaction to *Con Spirito* in terms that maintain this alliance between literary "outsiderhood" and sexual "outsiderhood." When *Con Spirito* first came out in February 1933, it caused a tremendous stir on campus. It wasn't so much because of the writing in the magazine, it seems, although the magazine's focus on the experimental made it different in every way from *The Review*. The problem, according to McCarthy, was that it was "unsigned": "That was the outrage, the shameful crime, treated as such even by some of the faculty, who breathed the word 'anonymous' as though it were married to the word 'letter,' denoting something so scurrilous that it dared not sign its name."[35] McCarthy's allusion to Hawthorne, as well as "the love that dare not speak its name," suggests her solidarity with a group that has been cast out. While the tone registers outrage, it also indicates a romance of sorts, one that seemed to be shared by others in the group.

Read in the context of McCarthy's comment, Bishop's poem "A Word With You," published in the second issue of *Con Spirito*, becomes less the "panicky" fear of being identified with "outsiderhood" that Adrienne Rich sees in the poem than the controlled, satirized account of a women's college and the speaker's identification with a "select group" of outsiders:[36]

> Look out! there's that damned ape again
> sit silently until he goes,
> or else forgets the things he knows
> (whatever they are) about us, then
> we can begin to talk again. [37]

In this remarkably sophisticated poem, Bishop seems to connect the suspicion and scrutiny with which relationships were monitored in women's colleges in the 1930s with the production of words, for the production of "just one luscious adjective" creates a furor among the animals, much as *Con Spirito* had when it first appeared. Bishop's poem also suggests the contradictory positions of the women's college in the 1930s.[38] While providing a place for women to come together and form a sense of community, encouraging an atmosphere of free expression, women's colleges also harshly policed and censored that same expression. As Barbara Solomon has noted, a woman could be expelled from college not only "for staying out all night with a man" but also "for having too 'intense' a relationship with another woman."[39] The poem's ending reflects the kind of paranoia that such policies might produce:

> Quick! there's the cockatoo! he heard!
> (He can't bear any form of wit.)
> —Please watch out that you don't get bit;
> there's not a thing escapes that bird.
> Be silent,—now the ape has overheard.[40]

But Bishop's tone, and the zoo-like atmosphere, suggests that she turned panic and paranoia into a double-edged wit that sliced through the dullness she felt surrounded her.

While it could be argued that "A Word With You" recreates the limitations of the women's college in the 1930s, as well as *Con Spirito*'s resistance to them, Bishop's story "Seven-Days Monologue," also published in the second issue of *Con Spirito*, appears to provide a spatial metaphor for the working out of these conflicts. The setting for this story, related in a series of seven diary entries, is the female community of the boarding house, a space that by this time had become almost synonymous with lesbian community. This story perhaps most brings the theme of literary and sexual outsiderhood together and speaks to Bishop's desire to "gather her little society" together in one place.[41] The story is full of in-jokes and almost literally identifies the *Con Spirito* "birds" with the initial letters of each of their names. It is a witty and strange account fraught with the conflicts and pitfalls of such a community, which is dominated by the odd, watchful, and maternal presence of the landlady, at once menacing and fascinating.

"She is large, looming seriously now into my life, but unlabelled."[42] Her "unlabelled" status makes her hard to characterize and casts her as a source of suspicion. On "September 2nd" the narrator notes: "Now I am suspicious of the landlady. Every time I see her I see 'the house' floating over her head, like St. Paul with his church. I think she feels it there all the time: high and narrow and dark, its long stairways, black turns and lighted halls, fire-escapes and shut, white doors. We are all closed behind them, over her head, spidery legs and arms, little buttony heads."[43]

If those shut white doors lining dark, narrow passages remind one of a series of closets, the image of the landlady dressed in lavender provided earlier in the monologue seems a fairly obvious clue that Bishop's story has something to do with lesbian sexuality. As Lillian Faderman has argued, the color lavender was commonly used by lesbians in the 1930s as a code word for community.[44] The narrator, identified as a "female lodger" about midway through the story, is fascinated by the landlady who is described as the matriarch of this community: "There she sits on the sofa, like an ancient unculled pearl in a battered shell. She is constantly bedewed with perspiration and invariably wears a lavendar dress."[45]

Bishop twice uses the color "lavendar" as a description in her story, each time in a section of the story charged with eroticism. While this code word may not have been obvious to a straight person in 1933, it might have been to another lesbian. I am fully aware that Bishop was quite reticent about her sexuality, because of the consequences such a confession could have for her career and her life, but to those who understood and sympathized with her position, she seems to have been quite open. And "Seven-Days Monologue," even at this early date, seems a limited kind of "coming out" to me.

On "September 4th," the narrator describes how the landlady comes into her bedroom and sits down on the bed:

> Early this morning she came into the room like a thunder-cloud with a silver lining, her smiling face above all the rest of the *lavendarishness* and vastness, and a long white slit down the side where her dress had burst open.... I mustn't forget those feet: how her shoes have shaped themselves around them, how they bulged out and over and made themselves at home. There was something very compatible about her face and feet; you can look from one to the other without the slightest feeling of discrepancy.[46]

In this rather witty passage, the narrator mixes the grotesque with eroticism. The sexologists called the lesbian (and the educated woman) grotesque because she crossed acceptable gender boundaries. The idea that the women's college could be a "breeding ground" for lesbian sexuality indicates the concern over permeable boundaries, the idea that the women's college was a body that could be invaded by disease and thereby destroyed. The only hope for such a possible contagion was to police the borders and expel those who threatened them. In such a context this large and uncontainable landlady may represent the "excess" of same-sex desire—that is, what falls outside the boundaries of what can be narrated and thereby labeled within a story. It is also possible the landlady is a parody of the "aging Lady in Lavender," a persona for the independent woman that appeared in male literature of the 1920s, who "preyed upon the innocence of young girls, teaching them to fear men and their own sexual impulses."[47]

As if to quell any suspicion that might have arisen in the reader at this point about just what the relationship might be between the lodger and the landlady, Bishop introduces a heterosexual subplot, which clearly identifies the narrator as a "female lodger," who receives a male visitor one evening. But it seems simply a ruse for disguising what is really going on in the story, since the description of their relationship is so unappetizing as to suggest rejection: "It was hot as hell; we quarrelled slowly, back and forth, until I wanted to push him off the fire-escape and leave him to the mercies of the alleycats. The air was rigid; people's voices outside held to the same accent, on and on. The smell of their suppers was deathly, as if it would stick in their throats and choke them. I never thought the church steeple clock would have dared to strike the hour—or if it did it would declaim it like a death sentence and seal us all in leaden immobility."[48] While their quarrel mimics sexual intercourse, it could hardly be described as pleasurable. Heterosexuality is associated here with rigidity, death, argument, stale food, lack of motion, "leaden immobility." Heterosexualty is the death knell in this story and requires quite literally a shower to cleanse it. "Finally, thank God, it rained, a wonderful rain, almost like mercury, fluid and metallic."[49] While female sexuality is associated with the grotesque and the fluidity of boundaries in the figure of the landlady, it carries both "pleasure and danger," eroticism and power.[50] It is the landlady and the desire to know (about) her that drives both the narrator's desire and the reader's in this story.

In its adoption of the boarding house as an experimental space to test the boundaries and limits of both literary and sexual possibility, Bishop's story might be thought of in terms of the kinds of enclosure fantasies that have been noted in Bishop criticism.[51] Langdon Hammer has called Bishop's dream house in "The End of March" the most important of these enclosures and has pointed out not only its provisional nature but also its potential as a site of possibility. Hammer, using the object relations theory of D. W. Winnicott, has argued that the dream house, like Bishop's correspondence, creates a kind of "potential space" or "*third area*," which allows her to establish an "intimate relation" between poet and reader.[52] In this way, Hammer notes the "collaborative structure" not only of Bishop's correspondence but of her poetry as well.[53]

This "potential space" in Bishop's work also might be productively considered in terms of Mary Russo's discussion of such a space in her study of carnival theory and the female grotesque. Russo argues that female pilots, such as Amelia Earhart in the 1920s, created a kind of "provisional space" for taking risks through the "practice of stunting," which came to be defined as an "abnormal and increasingly liminal activity with regard to official flying."[54] In a theoretical sense, Russo argues, stunting is "a tactic for groups or individuals in a certain risky situation in which a strategy is not possible. . . . As a temporal category, the tactic, or in Earhart's terms, the practice of stunting, belongs to the improvisational, to the realm of what is possible in the moment."[55] The space created by such a practice is not, Russo is quick to point out, that boundless and "transcendent space associated with the Kantian sublime."[56] It is rather a space that "emerges within the very constrained spaces of normalization."[57] This practice of stunting strikes me as very much an aspect of the "improvisational" nature of *Con Spirito*'s formation, a practice as I have already suggested that emerged out of the normalizing discourse of the period that closely aligned literary ambition with sexual perversion. Such stunting can be heard in the language Bishop and McCarthy used to describe *Con Spirito*'s formation. For example, both of them tell of going to Signor Bruno's, a speakeasy in Poughkeepsie, to discuss the magazine. They drank "dreadful" red wine out of white coffee cups and got "slightly high."[58] Such descriptions underscore the improvisational as well as the risky behavior (drinking in a speakeasy; prohibition had only just ended that year) that marked so much of the discourse surrounding *Con Spirito*.

Bishop reproduced this improvisational space in her poetry. The boarding house, for instance, appears as an isolated space of community where a "grotesque" assortment of creatures assemble under the landlady's roof in "A Summer's Dream," a later poem that Bishop published in *A Cold Spring* (1955):

> To the sagging wharf
> few ships could come.
> The population numbered
> two giants, an idiot, a dwarf,
>
> a gentle storekeeper
> asleep behind his counter,
> and our kind landlady—
> the dwarf was her dressmaker.[59]

Bishop's assemblage of a community of grotesques not only suggests the discourse that labeled lesbians as outside and therefore perverse in relationship to "normal," heterosexual womanhood, but it also echoes the theme of difference and outsiderhood shared by the women of *Con Spirito*. At the end of "Seven-Days Monologue," the narrator identifies and brings together her community of outsiders. Describing herself in terms similar to the landlady in the passage about St. Paul, she aligns herself with that subject position: "Damn it all—I'm the Bird-Catcher, that's it. I must start going around balancing innumerable small silver-gilt bird-cages on my head and arms, to catch them in, and keep them all singing in the closet."[60] The image contains elements that would come to distinguish Bishop's poetry and prose throughout her career—that is, the collection of a "little society" within an enclosed space, a sense of the absurd, and what Jeredith Merrin has called Bishop's "obsession with transmogrification."[61] In Bishop's work, Merrin argues, "everything is always turning into something else."[62] This pleasure in changeability is inseparable from Bishop's "gayness," which Merrin defines as "her questioning of gender boundaries" in her work, "and the exploration (however oblique and shrouded) of the pleasures and anxieties of same-sex love."[63] The bird cage seems to stand in metonymically for the pleasure and danger of lesbian relationship in one of Bishop's unpublished poems written in Key West, which may have been about Marjorie Stevens, with whom Bishop was living in the early 1940s, or, as Alice Quinn has suggested, it may be earlier and refer to Bishop's college friend, Louise Crane.[64] The dating of the poem is unclear. The poem begins, "It is marvellous to wake up together / At the same minute; marvellous to hear / The rain begin suddenly all over the roof . . ." It continues with the onset of an electrical storm, which catches "the whole house . . . in a bird-cage of lightning," but the dreamy pair imagine that it is all "quite delightful rather than frightening."[65]

As the Bird-Catcher, the narrator takes on the role of the landlady, entrapping her prey, and so she lives the role assigned her by the sexologists, the role of a grotesque who can lure others into the closet with her. Like the color lavender, birds (or sometimes "queer birds") were code words for lesbians in the 1930s,[66] and its use here intensifies the sense that Bishop is identifying and establishing a community of society's deviants. At the end of the story, this sense of a possible lesbian community becomes closely associated with the idea of literary community. The Bird-Catcher not only attempts to lure others to her, but she distributes phallic symbols, among other objects, to all her friends, each of whom is identified by an initial letter that corresponds to the first letter of the names of the *Con Spirito* women: "One box of various articles to hand around, for conversational purposes only. The fans and tweezers and an occasional hat-pin for M. The anvil and hammer and the beautiful knives and forks for F. And a couple of genuine phallic symbols for E., nothing else. A new box of tricks."[67] The Bird-Catcher distributes the props and designates the players in this theater of the absurd in a parody of the way that Bishop might have, according to Eleanor Clark, "gather[ed] her little society" at Vassar.[68]

Bishop was not the only one to insert phallic symbols into her *Con Spirito* work. In Frani Blough's parodic play about D. H. Lawrence's "little society," Dionysius H. Lawrence enters carrying the "sweetly Phallic Symbol" aloft as a worshipful gaggle of female admirers and wannabes—Dorothy Brett, Catherine Carswell, Katherine Mansfield, Lady Cynthia Asquith, Eleanor Farjeon, Mabel Dodge Luhan, and Lady Ottoline Morrel—form a Greek chorus. "You are good. You are beautiful. You are tortured. We claim you as our own."[69] A bit later in the play, Aldington and Aldous (presumably Richard Aldington and Aldous Huxley) enter in drag. It seems there was no end to the desire of *Con Spirito* writers to call attention to the "performative" aspects of gender. Blough's play appears in the same issue of *Con Spirito* as Bishop's "Seven-Days Monologue" (the title is misprinted "Monolouge" in the issue), so they seem to consciously echo each other. Moreover, Blough may have included Huxley here, as well, to underscore McCarthy's dismissal of his work as outdated and pompous in a review she wrote for the previous issue of *Con Spirito*, a review that also mentions Lawrence and the "sentimental mysticism of his later work."[70] The responsive echoing of these writers throughout the three issues of the magazine not only makes for fascinating reading but also reinforces the collaborative structure of the enterprise.

Bishop's *Con Spirito* story "Then Came the Poor" also creates a kind of provisional space for community, but this time through a discourse of class politics, which would have been familiar to the *Con Spirito* writers. At the time, a number of the coconspirators, including Bishop, were interested in socialist politics. However, Bishop found their commitment to real change shallow, for as Blough recalled later, their theories "weren't grounded firmly enough in any action for them to last very long" and they would have been horrified at the idea of revolution, although that was "the bottom line."[71] "Then Came the Poor," according to Blough, was Bishop's response to this lack of commitment. But Bishop's story is more than just a send-up of what Blough had called a "childish" view of politics bandied about at Vassar. In the 1930s, when radical politics became the acceptable form of protest in intellectual circles, it served Bishop, at least in part, not as an answer for what was wrong with the world, but as a narrative "cover" for a different story, the story of same-sex love.

In "Then Came the Poor," the narrator's aristocratic family abandons its home after a communist takeover, while the narrator, who decides to stay behind, actually gets left behind by the family in the confusion. As the mob takes over and "ransacks" the house, they dress up in the clothing of the departed aristocrats, while the narrator dresses down in some old clothes he finds in the barn. Now dressed as a stable boy, the narrator successfully passes as one of the crowd and enters the house. In her article on Bishop and the left, Betsy Erkkila identifies the narrator in "Then Came the Poor" as female.[72] But there is very little in the story to indicate that this is the case, since the narrator is never named. There is no clear designation of gender in the story, until the narrator dresses up as a stable boy. At that point in the story, he is perceived as male by the other characters. It is this gender ambiguity and the ability to put on and take off gender identity that is important to Bishop and key to this story, which is consistent with Bishop's reluctance to align herself with fixed positions.[73]

Once inside the house, the narrator encounters a series of "scenes." Because of their erotic charge, their connection to parental objects and rooms, and the positioning of the narrator as voyeur in relationship to each of the scenes, they can be read as "primal" scenes that stage a reverse of what Freud has described as a family romance fantasy. The family romance, which is both a class fantasy and a sexual one, is a wish-fulfillment fantasy with two principal aims—erotic and ambitious.[74] In the typical romance fantasy, the child imagines that in getting rid of his own parents who are of low birth, he is free to replace them with those who occupy a higher social station. He does this by imagining a series of primal scenes to alter the conditions of his birth. In keeping with the socialist leanings of *Con Spirito*, Bishop's fantasy works in reverse.

In the first "scene" described in Bishop's story, the narrator sees two women in the hall, "fighting over the remains of a roasted chicken, both pulling."[75] On the "greasy and muddy" marble floor, the women are trampling red roses underfoot, the same red roses that the narrator had observed earlier in the story in association with objects belonging to the mother. The narrator explains that "people were coming and going in excited groups, pointing and grabbing and exclaiming, some of them dressed in fantastic costumes put together from the wardrobes of my departed family."[76] Here, a scene that seems meant to portray the workings of greed becomes erotically charged by the roses, a metaphor for the female body and sometimes for the female genitals themselves.[77] The representation here of women as petty, squabbling over the "remains" of some meager food, brings to mind the squabbling animals in Bishop's poem "A Word With You" and could perhaps be read in terms of Bishop's disdain for *The Review*.

The chicken scene (with its disturbing representations of women) can be connected to two later "scenes" viewed by the narrator as he makes his way through the house. In a later scene, an old woman sits on the drawing-room floor "in a ring of dirty petticoats . . . , carefully unhooking the cut glass pendants from the chandelier. . . . She was bedecked and a'dazzle from top to toe."[78] Finally, the narrator arrives at the mother's bedroom where he sees "In mother's French bed, canopied with lime-colored satin, someone had put two filthy babies to sleep."[79] Female sexuality in these scenes is associated with something not quite clean, something, in fact, sordid. The two women, fighting over the chicken on a "greasy and muddy" floor, trample the roses underfoot, while the old woman in her dirty petticoat greedily ransacks the chandelier. Two "filthy" babies fall asleep among the lime-colored drapery of mother's French bed.

A very different but related scene interrupts this wallowing femininity. Here is how the narrator describes it: "From father's large bathroom came loud laughter, splashings and slappings. I looked in and discovered two naked men jumping in and out of the shower and bath, throwing powder and bathsalts at each other, spitting shining spouts of water out the window into the sunlight and onto their amused friends below."[80] This is a decidedly campy scene that gains meaning only retroactively during the lottery at the end of the story, a scene that is unmistakably homoerotic. During the lottery, the men are drawing lots to see who will live in the narrator's house. As they do so, they call out the name of a man, Jacob Kaffir. Bishop's description of him at once labels him as other—he is dark, "the color of a well used penny"—and wears a fez. The narrator describes him as "an amazing little man," similar to the character in "A Flight of Fancy," a short story Bishop published in her high school literary magazine.[81]

Although Bishop's Vassar story "Then Came the Poor" itself dons the clothing of the highly politicized, social realism that was favored in literary circles of the 1930s, much of the story indicates that we are in another realm entirely. Jacob Kaffir himself belongs to that class of elflike creatures who show up in many of Bishop's early stories and poetry, signaling possible entrance into a kind of parallel universe, a fantasy world where some expression of same-sex desire becomes possible. Jacob acts as a similar bridge figure in "Then Came the Poor." He has no family, and so in order to get a room in the house, he must choose someone with whom to live. Like two men cruising each other in a bar, Jacob and the narrator exchange suggestive signals:

> I caught Jacob's eye and smiled as hard as I could, raising my forefinger like a man saying "One, next the wall," in a restaurant.
> "Him!" Jacob shouted. "He live with me. O.K. to you?"
> "You bet," I said. "Well it may be sort of fun for a while," I thought.
> Apparently Jacob had the same idea. "We'll have fun, huh?" he said, waving an empty bottle at me, and he gave me a wink I could almost hear. "Seems like home already, don't it."[82]

Although the narrator's attitude toward the situation is ironic, the "sexual undertones" in this passage, as James Longenbach has pointed out, are unmistakable, especially given the earlier bath scene.[83]

The scenes in this story that involve women, like the chicken scene, are charged with the same erotic, but they are much more fraught with dangers and difficulties, while in father's bathroom, the men are having good, clean fun and ejaculating out the window. The presence of the maternal hovering over the three scenes that involve women—or, in the cases of the chicken fight and the French bed, the absent mother—seems to disturb the representation in these scenes, so that it is only with two men and the space they occupy that Bishop can effectively distance herself from the taint of "femininity" and come briefly to some sort of space of "pure" pleasure, represented by their joyful "masculinity."

By June of Bishop's junior year, she was worried about the future of *Con Spirito*. Many of the magazine's formative writers had graduated—Eleanor and Eunice Clark, McCarthy, and Blough. She got out only one more issue in the fall of her senior year, but she didn't give up on the magazine. "I'd rather go on with it than anything else I can think of doing at college," Bishop said of the magazine in a September 1933 letter to Eleanor Clark (*SL*, 8). "What I should like would be to carry *Con Spirito* quite away from college next year & set it up in New England somewhere.... If you think there's anything to my idea of making it an *outside* magazine why let me know & I'll write to Frani and Mary" (*SL*, 8).

Letters between Blough and Bishop after Bishop's graduation share a mutual desire to maintain a sense of collaborative community, and the dialogue of improvisation continued even after Bishop graduated. In a 1935 letter to Bishop from Blough, with whom Bishop corresponded until her death, Blough discusses the possibilities of an opera that she and Bishop were planning to write together. Blough was in graduate school studying music in New York, and

Bishop was traveling in France. In this letter, Blough imagines an improvisational community of artists who might transform the world of opera with their innovative ideas:

> Opera needs to start all over again, it seems to me, and the best thing to do is to sweep away the Wagnerian debris and start as though the whole thing were quite a new idea, had by a few select people sitting around after dinner, then polished up.... I think satire could work very well in this sort of medium.... Something really funny and amusing and not heavy.... Also it would be a thing that a group of people could do with very little more preparation than an evening of quartet playing. Do come home and lend your able advice.[84]

Blough's description sounds very much like what *Con Spirito* had turned out to be—"quite a new idea, had by a few select people sitting around after dinner, then polished up."

The desire to carry her literary community with her outside of Vassar's walls was strong and continued to remain with Bishop throughout her life. Perhaps that longing and even a backward glance to Vassar is behind the prisoner's statement in her 1938 story "In Prison," when he says, "Many years ago I discovered that I could 'succeed' in one place, but not in all places, and never, never could I succeed 'at large.'"[85]

This fantasy of female community (expressed throughout her *Con Spirito* writing in terms of literary ambition, fear of a feminine taint, sexual perversion, and cross-dressing) continued to be part of her work throughout her career, attesting to the persistence of the discourse of perversion surrounding literary ambition and lesbian sexuality. "In Prison," for example, brings together ideas of gender ambiguity, literary influence, female community, and lesbian sexuality. Langdon Hammer has suggested that "In Prison" is a metaphor for life in the closet,[86] an idea that gains further reinforcement when one considers that the women the earliest sexologists defined as sexual inverts "were often a captive population in prisons and insane asylums, daughters of the poor."[87] The connection between inversion, captivity, and deviance resonates in Bishop's story. The prisoner, who is of ambiguous gender, begins the story in this way: "I can scarcely wait for the day of my imprisonment" (*CPr*, 181) and continues with a quotation from Hawthorne's 1844 story "The Intelligence Office": "I want my place, my own place, my true place in the world, my proper sphere, my thing which Nature intended me to perform . . . and which I have vainly sought all my life-time . . . ." (*CPr*, 181). Like Moore before her, Bishop, via Hawthorne, turns what has been defined as deviant, as unnatural, into what is "natural." As the prisoner claims, "I have known for many years in what direction lie my talents and my 'proper sphere,' and I have always eagerly desired to enter it. Once that day has arrived and the formalities are over, I shall know exactly how to set about those duties 'Nature intended me to perform'" (*CPr*, 181). Hawthorne's story is itself a fantasy about a government office in charge of fulfilling people's wants, whether it is a job or a lost object or a change of life. Some of the people that come to the office are successful. Some, like the man from whom the prisoner quotes, go away empty-handed. Hawthorne makes very clear in his story that this is a man "out of his right place." No matter where he is, he doesn't fit, a condition that resonates through Bishop's experience as orphan, lesbian, educated, childless woman, even literary outsider.

Bishop's prisoner wants the certainty of being "in" prison. To him (or her—gender is once again ambiguous), one is either in or out, and being "in," for the prisoner, "is the primary condition" (*CPr*, 182). Deciding that she/he cannot "'succeed'" on the outside (the goal of Bishop's dream for *Con Spirito*), the prisoner maps out a narrow sphere of influence. The prisoner's primary condition can be read not only as a metaphor for life in the closet, but as a metaphor for the literary influence that the female poet or the lesbian poet could hope to gain. Knowing that she/he cannot succeed in any big way outside the prison, the prisoner limits her/his sphere of influence and invites others inside. She/he decides to influence "style" on the inside by looking just a little different in her/his prison uniform. The prisoner notes wryly that she/he will attract "one intimate friend, whom I shall influence deeply" (*CPr*, 190). In this passage, Bishop links, with the words "intimate friend," the ideas of lesbian desire, literary style, and influence. For the prisoner's greatest influence within this horribly confined space comes from what she/he calls the "Writing on the Wall":

> I have formulated very definite ideas on this important aspect of prison life, and have already composed sentences and paragraphs (which I cannot give here) I hope to be able to inscribe on the walls of my cell . . . . I have thought of attempting a short, but immortal,

poem, but I am afraid that is beyond me.... They will be brief, suggestive, anguished, but full of the lights of revelation. And no small part of the joy these writings will give me will be to think of the person coming after me—the legacy of thoughts I shall leave him, like an old bundle tossed carelessly into a corner! (*CPr,* 188–89)

The question of influence is once again mixed up, as in the *Con Spirito* days, with secret, coded language. The prisoner's "joy" is not linked to the production of an "immortal" poem but to the reader who she/he imagines will occupy the cell after her/him and discover her/his "legacy of thoughts." Bishop's logic throughout these poems and stories of the 1930s turns on establishing provisional spaces, such as the prisoner's cell, where contact *is* possible.

Provisional spaces such as these can be found in Bishop's work throughout her career, but they are strikingly present in her well-known "Crusoe in England," published at the end of her career, although it is important to note that notebook entries from 1934 demonstrate that ideas for this poem are connected to the Vassar years and the discourse of the 1930s. Immediately following graduation from Vassar in 1934, Bishop stayed on Cuttyhunk Island in Massachusetts for several weeks. The landlord of her temporary home by the sea was Mr. Wuthenaur, a man who wanted to "simplify life" all the time, and his behavior led Bishop to consider writing a poem about "making things in a pinch—& how it looks sad when the emergency is over."[88] The idea was finally published in 1972 as "Crusoe in England." David Kalstone has written that the poems in *Geography III,* of which "Crusoe in England" is one, "revisit her earlier poems as Bishop herself once visited tropical and polar zones, and . . . they refigure her work in wonderful ways."[89] Bishop's "Crusoe in England" refigures the ideas of female community found in the *Con Spirito* work.

"Crusoe in England," like "In Prison," narrates the fantasy of a community both found and lost during the course of the poem. Alone on the island and oppressed by solitude, Crusoe has

> nightmares of other islands
> stretching away from mine, infinities
> of islands, islands spawning islands,
> like frogs' eggs turning into polliwogs
> of islands....
>
> (*CP,* 165)

3 / ELIZABETH BISHOP'S "QUEER BIRDS"

The images Bishop uses here are reminiscent of those I have already discussed that describe the lesbian who was supposed to be simultaneously sterile, the "dessicated old maid," and associated with a "breeding ground" for producing more of her kind.

This is an island that repeats in one sense the representations of lesbian community that Gabriele Griffith has argued were common to the early part of the twentieth century.[90] These representations create an image of lesbians "as the only one in their community, as isolated individuals . . . intended to arouse pity rather than condemnation."[91] This isolated figure is precisely the one we see as Crusoe sits dangling his legs over the edge of a volcano. "I often gave way to self-pity," he tells us:

> "Do I deserve this? I suppose I must.
> I wouldn't be here otherwise. Was there
> a moment when I actually chose this?
> (*CP*, 163)

If Crusoe is one of a kind, so is everything else on this island:

> The sun set in the sea; the same odd sun
> rose from the sea,
> and there was one of it and one of me.
> The island had one kind of everything:
> (*CP*, 163)

Crusoe's loneliness is alleviated temporarily, just as it is in Defoe's *Robinson Crusoe*, by the arrival of Friday. But while Crusoe in Defoe's colonial account is only able to construct Friday, the "savage," as a slave, even though he is clearly fond of him, Bishop's Crusoe calls Friday a "friend":

> Just when I thought I couldn't stand it
> another minute longer, Friday came.
> (Accounts of that have everything all wrong.)
> Friday was nice.
> Friday was nice, and we were friends.
> If only he had been a woman!
> I wanted to propagate my kind,
> and so did he, I think, poor boy.
> He'd pet the baby goats sometimes,

and race with them, or carry one around.
—Pretty to watch; he had a pretty body.
(*CP,* 165–66)

The narrator's elusiveness about the nature of his relationship with Friday and the cryptic phrase "(Accounts of that have everything all wrong)" suggest that the relationship between the two men was one of mutual desire. Bishop may be wondering at this late stage of her career what "accounts" will make of her personal relationships. Immediately following this cryptic parenthetical phrase, however, Crusoe utters what must be the most banal sentence in the world: "Friday was nice." He then repeats it in the next line and adds, "and we were friends," as if this would somehow explain the confusion.

Bishop wrote the poem long after she had read *Robinson Crusoe* and only reread the novel after she had written the poem, so she relies only on a hazy memory of the book to re-create her Crusoe. It was the idea of the desert island and making things do in an emergency that appealed to her. But it is clearly also the relationship between Friday and Crusoe that fascinated Bishop. In Defoe's account, Crusoe "civilizes" Friday and teaches him English. In Bishop's poem, Crusoe does not try to convert Friday. They are friends, on equal terms with each other. But immediately following these lines, Crusoe cries out,

> If only he had been a woman!
> I wanted to propagate my kind,
> and so did he, I think, poor boy.
> (*CP,* 165)

Bishop thereby adds a new factor to this story of Crusoe and Friday, a marriage plot that legitimizes Crusoe's feelings for Friday. However, as in "Seven-Days Monologue," Crusoe ultimately rejects the heterosexual narrative. Lorrie Goldensohn suggests in her reading of this passage that it is important to pay attention to "the pressure of [Bishop's] particular experience behind and within the poem," the suicide of her Brazilian lover Lota de Macedo Soares, and the desire she expressed in numerous letters to have children that she and Soares could raise together.[92] I would agree with this reading in part. But this stanza, with its qualifying and hedging, also suggests other ways of reading the phrase "I wanted to propagate my kind." What

Crusoe dwells on at the end of the stanza is Friday's body. Friday was, after all, "pretty to watch; he had a pretty body." Immediately following these lines, Crusoe and Friday are taken off the island and returned to England. In the last two stanzas of the poem, Crusoe—surrounded by his island possessions—is living on what he describes as "another island," England. There is no reason why he should not have found a woman in England, but the poem makes clear that he has stayed with Friday. The poem ends with the weight of loss: "And Friday, my dear Friday, died of measles / seventeen years ago come March" (*CP*, 166).

Loss is registered in the person of Friday. Crusoe took Friday "home" to England, and he died there. Certainly a tenuous connection can be made here, as Goldensohn does, between Friday's death and Lota's suicide, but leaving it there would ignore some of the complexity of the ideas of "home." Bishop's "home" in Brazil with Lota was perhaps the closest she ever got to a sense of real belonging, and yet, when she and Lota broke up, she found it more and more difficult to make a life there. Lota was her "home" in Brazil, not the country itself or the house she bought there, however much she tried to make it so. Much like Crusoe in Defoe's account, Crusoe in Bishop's finds a sense of purpose, of "home," when Friday arrives. The original title of the poem was "Crusoe at Home,"[93] which suggests that Bishop had initially thought of the poem in terms of an investigation of Crusoe's relationship to the idea of "home," or at least an ironic commentary on ideas of "home." In this sense, Crusoe finds a home with Friday much in the same way that the narrator in "Then Came the Poor" found a home with Jacob. Here again, as in that early story, an ambiguous but erotically charged relationship is represented through an investigation of the complex connections between two male personae. Joanne Feit Diehl has argued that "Crusoe in England" is "Bishop's most extreme poetic instance of gender-crossing fused with eroticism."[94] It is here within this space that the desire to "propagate my kind" is most strongly expressed.

Here, as in many of Bishop's stories and poems, we are presented with a circumscribed world in which a lonely individual or a societal misfit contacts another like himself and for a brief period finds a home. The circumscribed world of the island, like the prison, the boarding house, or the communal house in "Then Came the Poor," represents a landscape in which the poet, the woman, the orphan, or the lesbian can contact others like herself and form a community. It may represent that limited but also "capacious" space of the closet that Timothy Morris has suggested "resonates throughout her work."[95] Hence, Bishop's sense of community and influence cannot be thought apart from the desire to "propagate [her] kind," to create a language that would begin to speak of lesbian desire. Crusoe's phrase "I wanted to propagate my kind" cannot be interpreted simply as an expression of the biological urge of a childless poet to have children. Spoken by a character created by a lesbian poet wise to the homoeroticism of Defoe's original text, Crusoe's statement becomes a challenge to the biological determinism that hindered the careers of literary women of Bishop's generation. Crusoe's statement refers not simply to reproductive power but to productive power—the power to write, to influence future generations, and to build community.

Bishop's ideas of community and her own place in it might be productively considered in light of an essay she published at Vassar. Interested in the workings of time in the novel, Bishop offers us yet another spatial metaphor. Disturbed from her studies by a sound outside, she writes that she looked out her window and noticed the birds "going South."[96] They were "spread across a wide swath of sky, each rather alone" and yet connected by an "invisible thread." It was "within this fragile net-work," Bishop writes, that "they possessed the sky." Bishop built this fragile network at Vassar and maintained it in suggestive ways in the poetry and prose she published throughout her life. It is by establishing this connection that I have attempted to momentarily catch hold of the "invisible thread" that connected Bishop to a larger community of writers and artists who attempted, however briefly, to "possess[] the sky."

4
Con Spirito, Improvisation, and the Poetry of the 1930s

IN RECALLING HER VASSAR YEARS IN HER MEMOIR, MARY MCCARTHY notes that a defining moment came for her as a writer when she rejected Edna St. Vincent Millay, Vassar's most famous graduate. When did it happen, she wonders, as she considers the influence of one of her beloved teachers at Vassar. "Did Anna Kitchel 'kill' her for me with a jovial dart of satire? And James Branch Cabell? When did he go?"[1] Cabell was one of the editors of *The American Spectator,* the literary magazine that McCarthy and her coconspirators challenged in their own literary magazine, *Con Spirito.* Elizabeth Bishop, too, had found much to admire in Millay's poetry as a high school student, but by the time she got to Vassar, she and her fellow coconspirators were, as Frani Blough put it, "ready for something more modern."[2] The *Con Spirito* writers, it seems, defined who they were as writers, at least in part, in terms of what they were not. In this sense, they contributed to the growing New Critical marginalization of Millay that Cheryl Walker has outlined.[3] *The American Spectator* had just run a piece by Louis Untermeyer criticizing Millay. In "Daughters of Niobe," published in the November 1932 *Spectator,* Untermeyer outlines a "weeping" tradition in women's poetry classified by one commentator of the time and quoted by Untermeyer as the "O-God-the-pain-girls!"[4] As it turns out, such positioning was a crucial one for women writers of this period if they wanted to establish themselves in an increasingly masculinized literary marketplace. In reading the correspondence associated with their magazine, McCarthy's memoir, later interviews with Bishop and her coconspirators, and the magazine itself, it is clear that *Con Spirito* was viewed by its writers as a launching pad of sorts to literary careers, so exactly where they positioned themselves as writers became a concern for Bishop's group at Vassar.

So while they dismissed the misogyny of *The American Spectator* writers, who had labeled their Vassar professors in one editorial "dessicated old maids," they also rejected a narrow idea of what women's poetry should be like. Muriel Rukeyser, who was probably the author of at least one review in *Con Spirito*, registers this shift in her 1935 "Poem Out of Childhood" published in her first book of poetry *Theory of Flight*:

> We were ready to go the long descent with Virgil
> the bough's gold shade advancing forever with us,
> entering the populated cold of drawing-rooms;
> Sappho, with her drowned hair trailing along Greek waters,
> weed binding it, a fillet of kelp enclosing
> the temples' ardent fruit   :
>   Not Sappho, Sacco.
> Rebellion pioneered among our lives,
> viewing from far-off many-branching deltas,
> innumerable seas.[5]

Richard Flynn has remarked that Rukeyser is not rejecting Sappho, per se, but a particular model of women's poetry that embraces "victimization and suffering."[6] The anarchist Sacco, then, becomes a convenient and clever alliterative substitute for Sappho and her female community. Unlike Marianne Moore's generation at Bryn Mawr, feminist discourse had gone underground, and ambitious young poets of the 1930s worked hard to distance themselves from an overtly "female" tradition. While Rukeyser turned to the revolutionary as a suitable symbol for this shift, Bishop was more ambivalent about revolutionary promise. When Bishop toyed with putting her politics into action, she did not do so in Rukeyser's terms.[7] In a 1938 letter to Frani Blough dripping with sarcasm, Bishop writes that she had been reading Emma Goldman and had "just about decided to sign up with the Anarchists. . . . It's marvelous—all you have to do, apparently, is read Emerson's *Essays*, Whitman, and other equally dated and unpleasant works, and advocate 'free love'" (*SL*, 75). As a Vassar student, she was suspicious of any kind of "-ism," as Blough pointed out in a later interview, and tended to make fun of "the overly serious political theorizing of the day."[8]

Like Rukeyser, other *Con Spirito* writers were more overtly political about the impending threat of fascism in Europe. In her prose poem, "In Pace Requiescamus," which was published in the second issue of *Con Spirito* (April 1933), Mary McCarthy links fascism, anti-Semitism, and Catholicism. She writes that Mussolini "bellows out the command to be fertile to Italian womanhood. . . . The Pope . . . composes new encyclicals on birth-control," and Jews are "beaten with clubs . . . [and] kicked in the face."[9] While Bishop would never write this explicitly and politically in her own poetry, her interest in developing an art that was flexible enough to challenge absolutist thinking is evident in her college writing. During these years, Bishop was clearly casting around for a suitable tradition within which she could work, and so she turned to Eliot, Stevens, and finally Moore. However, as I will show later, she revised these writers, even using their own early work against their later work to advance her own theory of art in a series of essays, most of which were published in the *Vassar Journal of Undergraduate Studies*. Bishop's poems of the 1930s that became the basis of her first book of poems, *North & South* (1942), extend the "provisional" and "improvisational" emphasis she developed at Vassar and explore and challenge fixed ideas of both literary and gender identity. Bishop's early development of and interest in the "improvisational" would eventually lead to her investigation of the wider questions of race, gender, and identity taken up in the 1965 *Questions of Travel* and in her final volume, the 1976 *Geography III*.

CON SPIRITO AND MODERNISM:
LEARNING TO BE CRITICAL AT VASSAR

Not only did the name *Con Spirito* draw on musical terminology, but in emphasizing spontaneity, it also borrowed from music the concept of improvisation, playing a new tune on the modernist melodies already handed down to them. All three of *Con Spirito*'s issues emphasize "fresh," "experimental," "avant-garde" writing over both the staid, "genteel" tradition of the *Vassar Review*, the college's established literary magazine, and the social realism, as well as the misogyny, of the editors of *The American Spectator*. Many of the writers identified themselves with the political left, but challenged the notion that art, to be useful, must be polemical. Their manifesto, whether consciously or unconsciously, echoed another literary magazine of the period, *Hound and Horn*, which was concerned with maintaining high-quality writing in a literary marketplace that the editors felt was threatened by an emphasis on politics.[10] Compare *Hound and Horn's* 1929 statement ("We demand only that the given work should be well done")[11] to *Con Spirito*'s 1933 manifesto ("We demand nothing but fresh conception").[12] While the subtle change in the demand shows how *Con Spirito* wanted to shift the emphasis from the well made to the experimental and improvisational, these writers shared *Hound and Horn*'s desire to, as Richard Pells has noted, "maintain some literary standards in a period otherwise marked by shoddy thinking and cultural confusion."[13] Their manifesto continues, "Frankly we are more interested in experimental than in traditional writing. Anything—politics, science, art, music, philosophy—anything that is spontaneous, that is lively."[14]

Con Spirito, as I have suggested, was a kind of literary "stunt," and its highly educated writers were brilliant at staging raids on the monuments of modernism. Rukeyser wrote a parody of T. S. Eliot when he came to the Vassar campus. McCarthy trashed Aldous Huxley. Blough trashed D. H. Lawrence. And in a college essay, Bishop revised T. S. Eliot's literary monument "Tradition and the Individual Talent" to develop quite a different theory of poetry. A reading of the three issues of *Con Spirito* reveals not only high-quality writing, but also a critical edginess that places these women at the forefront of the literary and political debates of the 1930s. In her study of American women writers and college writing courses from 1880 to 1940, Katherine Adams argues that teachers, such as Anna Kitchel at Vassar, were very influential in encouraging students to critically evaluate contemporary writers. "Through assignments involving careful reading, analysis, and imitation, Kitchel invited McCarthy and her classmates to enter a community of writers and not simply to revere published models from afar."[15] Moreover, the experience of *Con Spirito* emphasizes just the kind of collaborative process that literary communities provide for the developing writer and the importance of such communities.

It is significant that both McCarthy and Bishop seemed to favor less charismatic and authoritarian teachers. As Mary McCarthy describes the Vassar of her college years in her memoir, the faculty were overwhelmingly socialist, given to converting the "dutiful Republican daughters" who made up the bulk of the student body "into Socialists [who would go] forth to spread the gospel."[16] Miss Helen Lockwood was in this camp, and, according to McCarthy, she encouraged a kind of discipleship among her students. "It was said that Miss Lockwood insisted that a girl completely break with her mother as the price of winning her favor."[17] The unpleasant Norine, a character in McCarthy's 1963 novel *The Group*, which is based on her years at Vassar in the 1930s, is an example of a Lockwood convert, a "disciple."[18] By all accounts, Bishop couldn't stand Lockwood, but her influence was powerful, and so, in her senior year, even Bishop "felt compelled" to take Lockwood's Contemporary Press class.[19] It was an "incredible mistake," according to Eleanor Clark, who said that Bishop was "quite authoritative in class without saying a word. Her presence was completely stymying and paralyzing to Lockwood."[20] Bishop, according to Clark, sounded "the death knell" to the class.[21] This incident suggests just how suspicious Bishop was of charismatic teachers who required a worshipful stance from their students. As McCarthy put it, Lockwood was "like a grotesque caricature of the Vassar teacher as shaker-up."[22] Bishop preferred the quiet Rose Peebles, for whom she wrote some of her best essays. McCarthy, like Bishop, also favored less charismatic more soft-spoken teachers, such as Bryn Mawr graduate Miss Sandison, whose tolerance extended to frank classroom discussions of homosexuality. McCarthy recalls how Sandison lectured on what she called the "Platonizing tendency—male homosexuality—of the Elizabethan period," and how it "woke [McCarthy] up to learn that the subject could be talked about so coolly in the classroom by a small pretty grey-haired full professor."[23]

These teachers, thought to be conservative by many on campus, also "shook up their girls," McCarthy said, but "more gently."[24] McCarthy suggests that it was in these classes that she learned to question and hone her critical skills, a critical stance that is certainly apparent in her *Con Spirito* writing. This particular aspect of their Vassar intellectual training—the skepticism and the dislike of the sentimental and of certitudes—is evident in the writing of Bishop's closest group of friends.

In the first issue, Margaret Miller, a painter, art historian, and Bishop's close friend, took on surrealism, calling it the "last Mohican of the primitives," a noble savage that found its roots in primitivism and would soon disappear.[25] There was Frani Blough's play about D. H.

Lawrence that I discussed in the last chapter. Rukeyser's clever parody of T. S. Eliot is more overtly political and revolutionary, but it contains many good poetic lines, and in its call to action, it anticipates Rukeyser's own experiments in bringing together aesthetics and politics. "Mr. Panfilo sits and grins / absorbed beyond hope in his own grinning— / collapsing in attempts to make an end / to his idea's beginning."[26] The audience is in thrall, "devoted lustfully to a conceit's expansion, / to an obscure line's scansion."[27] Meanwhile, the poem reminds us that "beyond these windows, China moans" and "nine dark boys" are beaten in Alabama.[28]

McCarthy's review of Aldous Huxley's *Brave New World* and Harold Nicolson's *Public Faces* ("Two Crystal-Gazing Novelists") is a prime example of how she and other *Con Spirito* writers sought to challenge the epic-scale claims to authority of certain strands of modernism. McCarthy praises Nicolson's humility over Huxley's arrogance. She concludes: "It has already been said that *Brave New World* is snobbish; it is also, in its retarded development, conceited. It feels superior about its Views; it mourns, Narcissus-like, over the hard fate of the Sensitive Man. Harold Nicholson is humble."[29] The technique that McCarthy values in Nicholson's work is remarkably similar to what Bishop outlined in her own work. Nicholson includes an appendix to his novel, which was supposedly written by a grandson in 1978. The novel is set in 1939. The appendix, McCarthy writes, "negates all that his hero's sacrifice for the twentieth century and for a woman has asserted."[30] The appendix, in short, forces the reader to adjust her thinking about all that has gone before, challenging notions of heroic art, an approach that Bishop would encapsulate in lines from her 1936 poem "The Gentleman of Shalott," who "loves / that sense of constant re-adjustment" (*CP*, 10).

Developing a Theory of Poetry: Bishop's College Essays

Bishop began to develop a theory of writing in college that anticipates the line from "The Gentleman of Shalott," particularly in her 1934 undergraduate essay "Dimensions for a Novel." Like the other poets of my study, Bishop's poetry as recognizably her own was slower to develop than her prose. All the writers in my study, including Bishop, wrote prose first that contained the seeds of what would become their best poetry. Bishop's college poetry, for the most part,[31] bore the mark of undigested Gerard Manley Hopkins, a hero of Bishop's at the time. "Hymn to the Virgin," for example, published first in *Con Spirito* and later in *The Magazine* includes such clotted, awful lines as: " . . . baby brood of / Strawberry-ice-cream-colored cherubim, tin- / winged, ascending, / Chub-toes a'dangle earthwards, fat-fists, pat-a- / cake for Thee, oh wooed of / Erstwhile eye-raised mortals!"[32] But her college essays—many of which were written for a favorite teacher, Rose Peebles, and published in *The Vassar Journal of Undergraduate Studies*—were luminous, full of descriptive passages that sound like Bishop's later poetry. Bishop's developing theory of poetry, contained in these essays, can be seen very much in the context of the overall project of *Con Spirito* and its improvisational nature.

In "Dimensions for a Novel," Bishop outlines a plan for the twentieth century novel that challenges traditional versions of canon formation, which would later be taken up by the New Criticism, equating that formation with monumentality. Bishop quotes the famous passage from Eliot's essay "Tradition and the Individual Talent" that, as she puts it, deals with "the individual artist's duty to the past."[33] When the new work of art arrives, Bishop quotes Eliot, "something . . . happens simultaneously to all the works of art which preceded it. The existing monuments form an ideal order among themselves, which is modified by the introduction of the new (the really new) work of art among them." Bishop points out that "Eliot is of course speaking of the placing of works of art in their place in the line of tradition," but Bishop suggests changing the subject of the paragraph from "monuments" to "moments" to disrupt linearity within the pages of a novel. What the passage also makes clear is that Bishop associates monumentality with canonicity. Moments—the idea of some sense of "experience-time," a mind in the process of thinking, disrupts the linearity of Eliot's monuments. As James Longenbach has argued, Bishop reads Eliot's essay against the grain "as a theory of hermeneutic indeterminacy."[34]

Bishop's revisionary reading of Eliot anticipates her later response to Wallace Stevens, but it also anticipates a revolutionary "moment" in poetry that James Breslin identifies with the late 1950s. Breslin rejects the monolithic terms modernism/postmodernism as a way of defining twentieth century poetry in favor of a more historically specific model.[35] Like Bishop's revision of Eliot's "monuments" to read "moments" in her college essay, Breslin emphasizes historical moments in poetry when something new emerges, which he describes using Thomas Kuhn's concept of the paradigm shift in science.[36] In this way, Bishop and her crowd at Vassar are already taking part in a redefinition of modern writing.

"Dimensions for a Novel" is one of a series of essays on prose and poetic style Bishop published at Vassar in which she asks how the writer can create and maintain fluid boundaries in writing; to this end, she analyzes how various writers, such as Joyce, Woolf, Stein, and Hopkins have used the concept of time in their work. Bishop's investment in breaking down the margins of poetry and prose and her exploration of the consequences of crossing boundaries are formal innovations that mirror her equally compelling interest in challenging fixed boundaries of gender and sexual orientation. In each of the three essays, Bishop emphasizes process and the fluidity of boundaries, and in each she illustrates her concept of this new kind of time with a visual metaphor.

In her essay on "Gerard Manley Hopkins," Bishop argues that some of Hopkins's techniques, such as sprung rhythm, enjambment, and slant rhyme, set the margins of the poetry free. Bishop, whose early college poetry was slavishly Hopkinesque, describes his work as "fluid," "hesitant," and "slurred." His verse "break[s] down the margins of poetry, blurr[s] the edges with a kind of vibration and keep[s] the atmosphere fresh and astir," causing his poetry to "[come] up from the pages like sudden storms."[37] In "Dimensions for a Novel," Bishop describes how the future novel may develop, not linearly, but like a "bramble bush." In "Time's Andromedas," Bishop studies the novels of Dorothy Richardson to elaborate more fully what she means by "experience-time." She emphasizes how in Richardson's books no one thing is valued more than another, a quality she also admired in Moore, a quality, she argues, that is "almost the secret of the whole thing."[38] The image of the bramble bush makes its appearance in a different form in a more elaborate visual representation of what Bishop means by time:

> Have you ever drawn lines with your fore-finger-nail on a windowpane just beginning to freeze over? The line remains clear on the opaque frostiness for just a minute . . . and then suddenly at angles away from it other lines spring out of their own accord and branch and grow under your eyes, with clean, crystalline edges.[39]

It strikes me that, in this image, Bishop emphasizes both boundaries, those "crystalline edges," as well as the multiplicity of possibilities, no one possibility valued over the other. Here fluidity and multiplicity are emphasized but so are precision and form, a quality that defines Bishop's best poetry perfectly; it is, to use her words, "almost the secret of the whole thing."

Bishop's Community Extended

When Bishop graduated from Vassar in 1934, Blough, Miller, and Louise Crane were already in New York, as was Marianne Moore. So Bishop, very much interested in remaining part of her adopted community, also headed to the city. In many ways, Bishop, who had lost both of her parents, really looked on her *Con Spirito* group, as well as other friends from Vassar, as her family. Bishop's connection with Blough went all the way back to high school. They both attended the Walnut Hill School together. As is well known, Bishop's father died when she was only eight months old, and her mother suffered a breakdown and was committed to an institution when Bishop was five, which was the last time Bishop saw her. She died in Bishop's senior year at Vassar. Bishop noted her death almost as an afterthought in a letter to Blough.[40] After her mother was committed, Bishop left her much-loved Great Village, Nova Scotia, family to live with her paternal grandparents in Worcester, Massachusetts, which proved to be a disastrous move for her both emotionally and physically. Realizing that Bishop was terribly unhappy, her grandparents eventually sent her to live in Boston with her Aunt Maud, who received a stipend from the family to take care of her. Although this turned out to be an arrangement that saved Bishop's life (Aunt Maud was generous and kind to her), she "always [felt] a sort of a guest," as she put it later.[41] It is not surprising that Bishop didn't feel quite like she belonged anywhere. Vassar, in many ways, fulfilled the sense of community and home that Bishop had lacked growing up. As Bishop moved to New York and then Key West, her "little society" that she had gathered at Vassar remained very much intact and an influence on Bishop's development through the shared experience of travel and through letter writing. I will focus here particularly on her wonderful correspondence with Blough from Key West.

Bishop's poems of the 1930s and her letters to Blough (later Frani Blough Muser) share that sense of the improvisational, uncertainty, and multiple possibility that her college essays explore. The half-man, half-looking-glass speaker of Bishop's 1936 "The Gentleman of Shalott," for instance, revels in multiple possibilities when it comes to questions of identity. He finds the "uncertainty" of his identity "exhilarating," and being "in doubt" is a necessary precondition for his very existence. Bishop's clever slant rhymes—"mirror," "error," "either"—contribute to the overall sense of uncertainty:

> But he's in doubt
> as to which side's in or out
> of the mirror.
> There's little margin for error,
> but there's no proof, either.
> And if half his head's reflected,
> thought, he thinks, might be affected.
> (*CP,* 9)

A letter she wrote to Blough the same year shares with this poem the same divided and carnivalesque representations. Bishop wrote that she was "quite recovered" from a recent "mastoid" operation, "except for a haircut that makes me look like the half-man-half-woman in the circus—clipped on one side, ordinary on the other."[42] She enclosed a decidedly campy picture of herself and her then lover, Louise Crane, heiress to the Crane Paper fortune and part of Bishop's group at Vassar. In the picture, Bishop had placed their heads on boxers' bodies, and Crane is giving Bishop a right hook to the side of the head. So, too, Bishop turns to the carnival for her representation of the gentleman, drawing on the transformative power of carnival mirrors.

Bishop's 1937 story "The Sea and Its Shore" created just such an improvisational character in Edwin Boomer, whose name is itself a kind of hybrid, a combination of Bishop's initials and her mother's maiden name. Moreover, Boomer, who occupies a provisional house, deals with the marginal occupation of ridding the beach of literary waste, because modern society turns out too much "paper covered with print" for the beach to "keep itself clean, as cats do" (*CPr,* 172). Boomer obsessively reads the scraps of paper he picks up on the beach before he burns them and tries to make meaning out of the fragments he collects. However, his activity and its impossibility not only draw on a discourse of inversion, they also question the validity of trying to fix meaning within a rigid categorical system.

Boomer's first group includes "everything that seemed to be about himself, his occupation in life, and any instructions or warnings that referred to it"; the second was about "the stories about other people that caught his fancy, whose careers he followed from day to day" (*CPr*, 175). Finally, Boomer's third category pertained to "items he could not understand at all, that bewildered him completely but at the same time interested him so much that he saved them to read. These he tried, almost frantically, to fit into first one, then the other, of the two categories" (*CPr*, 175). Boomer's system is flawed and creates anxiety precisely because he cannot fit the third category into the other two.

Boomer's relationship to print, like Bishop's, is fraught with pitfalls and "warnings": "The more papers he picked up and the more he read, the less he felt he understood. In a sense he depended on 'their imagination,' and was even its slave, but at the same time he thought of it as a kind of disease" (*CPr*, 177–78). Boomer expresses more than the mundane anxiety of authorship; he also resorts to the language of perversion to do so, a juxtaposition that had come together even more forcefully in Bishop's 1936 poem "The Man-Moth," which in itself is a poem based on an "error" in print, since the title comes from a newspaper misprint of the word mammoth. The language of perversion dominates the fifth stanza of the poem:

> Each night he must
> be carried through artificial tunnels and dream recurrent dreams.
> Just as the ties recur beneath his train, these underlie
> his rushing brain. He does not dare look out the window,
> for the third rail, the unbroken draught of poison,
> runs there beside him. He regards it as a disease
> he has inherited the susceptibility to. He has to keep
> his hands in his pockets, as others must wear mufflers.
>
> (*CP,* 15)

The *third* rail is that "unbroken draught of *poison,*" which the Man-Moth "regards . . . as a *disease* / he has *inherited* the *susceptibility to.*" And "he has to keep / his hands in his pockets," perhaps so that he does not contaminate others; we are back in the realm of the possible contamination, of which women's college students were warned with regard to the "invert." The Man-Moth can look but not touch. He carries the marks of his difference (his "abnormality") on his body, which "makes an *inverted* pin" (my emphasis; *CP,* 14). The Man-Moth's world is inverted in every sense. He "always seats himself facing the wrong way" on the subway trains he rides every night and "cannot tell the rate at which he travels backwards" (*CP,* 15). He is a solitary figure, although he is accompanied by his shadow:

> Up the façades,
> his shadow dragging like a photographer's cloth behind him,
> he climbs fearfully, thinking that this time he will manage
> to push his small head through that round clean opening
> and be forced through, as from a tube, in black scrolls on the light.
> (Man, standing below him, has no such illusions.)
> But what the Man-Moth fears most he must do, although
> he fails, of course, and falls back scared but quite unhurt.
>
> (*CP,* 14)

In the third stanza, the Man-Moth creates a kind of writing on the sky with his body, forced through the opening in the sky "in black scrolls on the light." Writing on the sky is a kind of public writing, like the writing on the wall in "In Prison." It is shared by others and becomes part of a community, and, like "In Prison," one gets the sense at the end of the poem that the solitary Man-Moth is attempting to contact others like himself:

> If you catch him,
> hold up a flashlight to his eye. It's all dark pupil,
> an entire night itself, whose haired horizon tightens
> as he stares back, and closes up the eye. Then from the lids
> one tear, his only possession, like the bee's sting, slips.
> Slyly he palms it, and if you're not paying attention
> he'll swallow it. However, if you watch, he'll hand it over,
> cool as from underground springs and pure enough to drink.
>
> (*CP,* 15)

The Man-Moth takes his hands out of his pockets for us, and the draught of poison becomes the Man-Moth's tear, "cool as from underground springs and pure enough to drink." The Man-Moth has let fall the tear that the hermit, in Bishop's 1936 poem "Chemin de

Fer"—another railroad tracks poem about a lonely, solitary individual trying to make contact—has been holding on to "year after year."[43] But this time, the Man-Moth finds a way to do it. For those readers who do not pay attention, or perhaps do not understand the Man-Moth's signals, the tear is lost as "[s]lyly he palms it." In this sense, "The Man-Moth" reverses the implied shunning of the hermit in "Chemin De Fer." That poem ends with the hermit crying out into the wilderness:

> "Love should be put into action!"
> screamed the old hermit.
> Across the pond an echo
> tried and tried to confirm it.
> (*CP,* 8)

As James Merrill points out in his afterword to David Kalstone's *Becoming a Poet,* an Elizabethan poet would have included the repeated syllable. But in "Chemin de Fer," "Bishop leaves it to the mind's ear: actions! . . . shun . . . shun . . . shun."[44] "The Man-Moth" turns this around, shunning those who would not understand him but making an intimate appeal to readers who might.

We can see in Bishop's development in her mid-1930s poetry an attempt to get "that sense of constant re-adjustment" into her work by engaging the reader at the end of "The Man-Moth," for instance, which, like "The Gentleman of Shalott," plays with the idea of changing perspectives. But it is really not until 1939 with "The Monument" that Bishop manages in poetry something approximating what she was trying to outline in her Vassar essays. Brett Millier has argued that "The Monument" is Bishop's "first mature manifestation of her undergraduate belief that poetry should portray the mind thinking."[45] "The Monument" is often read—when it is read at all—as a response to Stevens's 1936 *Owl's Clover.* There is no question that Bishop was responding to Stevens and studying his work intensively at the time, and her Key West poetry, as I will later show, gains further significance if we understand it at least in part as a dialogue with Stevens. But "The Monument" also emerges from the context of Bishop's attempts to define what art should be while she was still an undergraduate at Vassar and gains further significance in the context of the other writers at Vassar who shared in Bishop's project. As Bishop tried out her developing theory of art in her own poetry, Stevens became for her a crucial figure in helping her map her response to modernism, because in her reading of him she discovered both what she valued in art—the process of the mind thinking—and, occasionally, what she didn't value—some monumental and fixed idea of "ART," as she put it in all capitals in a letter to Marianne Moore (*SL*, 48).

Bishop read Stevens's work avidly as a college student and continued to follow his career closely after college. Lines from Stevens's *Harmonium* poem "Stars at Tallapoosa"—"The lines are straight and swift between the stars"—provide the epigraph for Bishop's 1934 "Dimensions for a Novel," which was one of her most important college statements about style and the modern novel. These lines are also yet another visualization of the "bramble bush" or the lines drawn on the frosty glass that represent for Bishop what writing at its best could be. But in a letter she wrote to Moore shortly after Moore had reviewed *Owl's Clover*, she complains of Stevens's tendency to create monuments: "I took [*Owl's Clover*] as a defense of his own position, and the statue—dear me—I felt, and still cannot help feeling, is ART—sometimes the particular creation, sometimes an historical synthesis, sometimes his own work—but always his own conception of such art" (*SL*, 48). Thus, the defense of a "monumental idea of 'ART'" that Bishop reads in Stevens, as John Lowney has pointed out, "is questionable, if not absurd, in her estimation."[46] Stevens himself wrote in a November 1935 letter to the mysterious Ronald Lane Latimer that the statue in "The Old Woman and the Statue" was a symbol for art, but he went on equivocally to explain art as "being a word that I have never used and never can use without some feeling of repugnance."[47] However, in "Mr. Burnshaw and the Statue," Stevens writes that the statue, "so far as I have defined it at all . . . is a symbol for things as they are."[48] Thus, in a sense, Stevens defines the shifting terrain of his own thinking about the statue that also characterizes the differing landscapes that Bishop herself read in his work. While Bishop upbraids Stevens for hitting a polemical note here, later in the letter to Moore, Bishop describes how he also, at times, hit exactly the right note. Although she qualifies this response a great deal, Bishop indicates that Stevens still comes through for her in the end: "What strikes me as so wonderful about the whole book—because I think there are a great many rough spots in it, don't you?—and I dislike the way he occasionally seems to make blank verse *moo*—is that it is such a display of ideas at work—making poetry, the poetry making them, etc. That, it seems to me, is the way a poet should think" (*SL*, 48). In the pages of *Con Spirito* and in her 1936 letter to Moore about *Owl's Clover*, Bishop was already initiating the shift—the second wave of modernism—that Stevens achieved in 1937 in *The Man with the Blue Guitar*, a sequence that Bishop praised in a 1938 letter to Moore as one in which Stevens achieves his vision of the statue as a "symbol for things as they are" (*SL*, 67).

Bishop's "Monument" shares its improvisational characteristics with many other poems of this period, including "The Man-Moth," "The Gentleman of Shalott," and even "Florida." Although it does not share their discourse of the grotesque and carnivalesque, "The Monument" is linked to these poems by the particular challenge it poses to fixed boundaries and its emphasis on the "provisional," which, as I have already noted, is inextricably linked to sexuality for Bishop.

Bishop's 1939 poem "The Monument" continues this trajectory of critique in its effort to put into practice what she praises in Stevens: to create "a display of ideas at work" and to represent the art of process. From the beginning we recognize the monument as antithetical to the idea of art as a well-wrought urn, an idea that can be traced back to *Con Spirito*'s manifesto. "Now can you see the monument?" the speaker asks in the first line. "It is of wood":

> built somewhat like a box. No. Built
> like several boxes in descending sizes
> one above the other.
>
> (*CP*, 23)

Not only is this structure decidedly not "beautiful" in any classical sense of that word, it is already undergoing revision almost before the initial description is fully underway. From the beginning, the monument is open to a voice of critique—actually several voices of critique. The poem's question at the beginning invites the reader in to participate in the construction and interpretation of the monument. The voice of the speaker is joined later in the poem by another, whiny sort of voice, which introduces the same Marxist critique of abstract art that Stevens was addressing in *Owl's Clover* in "Mr. Burnshaw and the Statue." This plurality of critique is itself a strike against epic-scale monumentalism.

The speaker's descriptions of the monument draw on a wide range of references to both Romantic and Modern poets, setting up a dizzying kaleidoscope of voices that pulls apart any sense that this monument is at all monumental.[49] The speaker's response to the observer's question—"'Where are we?'"—suggests the complexity of critical levels that are operating within the space of the poem. The speaker's description of the monument, for example, calls forth the artist-prince of Coleridge's *Kubla Khan*, itself a fragment poem. The speaker describes the scene in this way:

> An ancient promontory,
> an ancient principality whose artist-prince
> might have wanted to build a monument
> to mark a tomb or boundary, or make
> a melancholy or romantic scene of it . . .
>
> (*CP*, 24)

The observer's skepticism from within the poem seems intended to dismantle such grandiose claims to commemorative art:

> "But that queer sea looks made of wood,
> half-shining, like a driftwood sea.
> And the sky looks wooden, grained with cloud.
> It's like a stage-set; it is all so flat!
> Those clouds are full of glistening splinters!
> What is that?"
>
> (*CP*, 24)

The scene of the monument is staged, and yet the overwrought exclamations of this critique, and the amusing rhyming of "flat" and "that," leave the reader wondering where this critique is going. As if to calm us all, the unflappable tour-guide speaker enters once again, answering the observer's question with a matter-of-fact answer: "It is the monument." To which the observer responds with another tirade about the monument:

> "Why did you bring me here to see it?
> A temple of crates in cramped and crated scenery,
> what can it prove?
> I am tired of breathing this eroded air,
> this dryness in which the monument is cracking."
>
> (*CP*, 24)

The unsettling voices of this poem make it impossible for the reader to settle on any fixed idea of the monument or what it might represent. Unlike Yeats's 1938 poem "Lapis Lazuli," in which every "discoloration of the stone, / Every accidental crack or dent" is monumentalized into "avalanche" and "lofty slope,"[50] Bishop's "Monument" refuses to fill its cracks. Like the "Gentleman of Shalott," this poem also "loves / that sense of constant re-adjustment." The monument could be anything. It could harbor something, or not.

The final stanza of the poem, spoken by the practical, tour-guide speaker, moves definitively away from closure. Like the abandoned woodpile of Frost's poem or Stevens's jar in Tennessee, Bishop's monument changes the landscape in which it appears but nevertheless resists interpretation as Bishop leans heavily on possibility at the end in describing this monument:

> It may be solid, may be hollow.
> The bones of the artist-prince may be inside
> or far away on even drier soil.
> But roughly but adequately it can shelter
> what is within (which after all
> cannot have been intended to be seen).
> It is the beginning of a painting,
> a piece of sculpture, or poem, or monument,
> and all of wood. Watch it closely.
>   (*CP*, 25)

The open-ended appeal initiated by the adverb "closely" at the end of the poem invites the reader to become part of the process of making art. In so doing, the poet abandons all sense that the new resulting art would be anything other than collaborative and provisional.

Bishop's "Florida," written the same year as "The Monument," begins to bring together many of the overlapping issues that would become a major concern of her later work, suggesting the way that an emphasis on the provisional might be attractive in addressing the thorny questions and overlapping concerns of personal as well as national identity. "Florida," for instance, is an early attempt to understand how the poetic eye/I, the traveler, and the conqueror might share some of the same desires to order and tame, and, as Bishop puts it in "Arrival at Santos," enjoy "complete comprehension," a level of mastery that Bishop's developing theory of poetry resists. Insomuch as Bishop was investigating this desire, "Florida" also becomes a response to Wallace Stevens's Florida poems in both *Harmonium* and the 1936 *Ideas of Order*, volumes that Bishop studied closely.

Bishop's first visit to Florida was in the winter of 1937 when she and Louise Crane stayed at the Keewayden Club, a winter resort in Naples. Although Crane was not one of the writers in Bishop's *Con Spirito* group, she was a central figure among Bishop's coterie of friends at Vassar. That same year, Bishop saw the naturalist E. Ross Allen wrestle alligators and met Red and Charlotte Russell who would become lifelong friends. Much of the description of her poem "Florida" is taken from this initial encounter. As is well known, Bishop eventually bought a house with Crane in Key West, her first of "three loved houses," and traveled between New York and Florida for the next ten years or so. Florida became an extremely productive site for her poetic production of the 1930s and early 1940s, as would Brazil later. Her community there was very much an extension of the Vassar community she had formed from 1930 to 1934, particularly Louise Crane, Margaret Miller, and Frani Blough. Critics have focused primarily on Bishop's letters to Marianne Moore during this period, but Bishop's letters to Blough are far more candid about what Florida truly represented for Bishop—at least partly an escape from the sexual constraints of northern (specifically New England) culture. Key West was the "corrupt state," as Bishop calls it in "Florida," or as Stevens put it, land of "venereal soil."[51]

Bishop wrote at length in her letters about the natural world, and particularly the intervention of humans into that world. Hemingway, as one might expect, haunts this narrative. In one February 1940 letter, Bishop tells Marianne Moore that she is "sending you a real 'trifle,'" which turned out to be what would become her most anthologized poem, "The Fish" (*SL*, 87). "I'm afraid it is very bad," she writes, "and, if not like Robert Frost, perhaps like Ernest Hemingway!" In a 1948 letter to Robert Lowell, Bishop calls Florida "the land of big game fish and Hemingway" (*SL*, 153).

In one unpublished letter to Frani Blough, written during her first visit to Key West in January 1937, Bishop describes a fishing expedition with the "best captain," who she noted had been "Ernest Hemingway's [captain], my dear, for years and years."[52] In Bishop's description, we can certainly hear the beginnings of "The Fish." She writes, "It is so pretty when you have actually caught one of these monster fish and have him all the way up to the side—to see him all silver and iridescent colors in that blue water."[53] And in the swagger of the next lines, Bishop indulges in that moment of "victory" dramatized in "The Fish": "We had awfully good luck—we must have caught about twenty fish and all over twenty pounds. I caught (as I guess I couldn't resist telling you on the postcard) the biggest one—an Amberjack about 60 lbs. Of course our Ernest gets them, or something, up to 1,000 but we were pleased to learn he began by fishing off a pier, and besides, he's a 'Big, Powerful man.'"[54]

As in many of Bishop's letters to Blough—some of the funniest in Bishop's oeuvre—masculine braggadocio is heavily ironized, but still, Bishop was clearly attracted to certain aspects of masculinity—adventure, sportsmanship, the exhilaration of conquest. It is perhaps her understanding of what this exhilaration *feels like* that allows her to effectively criticize this position—the militarism rejected in "Roosters," for instance, and later her criticism of colonial conquest, while at the same time acknowledging how one can become complicit in this process. The astonishing shift at the end of "Florida" shows the extent to which Bishop was beginning to question the machismo she detailed in her letters with such fascination.

Still early in her first trip to Florida, Bishop wrote a letter to Moore (she was still calling her "Miss Moore" at this point) that describes the event that becomes the central focus at the end of "Florida." This was Bishop's trip to Fort Myers to see E. Ross Allen "wrestle with his alligator" (*SL*, 57). Bishop describes to Moore how Allen slipped silently into the water with the alligators and proceeded to imitate their calls, "his large solemn baby face apparently floating bodiless on the surface of the water" (*SL*, 58). Bishop's collagelike notebook from this period contains many clippings about Allen and the Florida Reptile Institute, for which he served as director. It is clear from these clippings, many of which were price lists, that the business of the institute was more capitalistic and exploitative than educational, for the institute sold everything from snake venom and alligator leather goods to what they called "preserved arthropodic specimens," such as black widow spiders. "All specimens," according to the brochure, "collected in Florida."[55] Keeping their "specimens" alive did not seem to be of particular concern for the institute. As with many of Bishop's newspaper clippings, scattered throughout her working notebooks, they are placed without comment, but they certainly point toward her penchant for the "strange," the exotic. And at the end of her letter to Moore, Bishop asks her mentor if she "can think of any object native to Florida that you might want—from alligators to grapefruit," and in so doing participates in the tourist trade in the exotic, a position Bishop would later question (*SL,* 59).

But Bishop's 1939 "Florida" begins to investigate the problems of this position, even as it explores the possibilities that Florida's "strangeness" opens up for the tourist as an escape from northern constraints. Women adventurers have long noted the freedom they experienced in travel where they are allowed to some extent to shed the cultural norms of home. Freedom in "exile," a concept that Bishop alternately embraced in these letters, can indeed be exhilarating as one explores the expanded boundaries that a confrontation with a different culture can provide. One of the subjects Bishop hints at in this perhaps more permissive environment (at least for Louise and her) is sexual freedom. Friends of Bishop described how she and Louise Crane used to hang out at the Square Roof, "an old whorehouse."[56] One friend described how "uncomfortable" it made her feel. "It was slumming—there were these black prostitutes sitting around, and there was somebody playing the piano."[57] But Bishop's letters suggest she enjoyed the freedom and anonymity of this kind of "slumming." In one letter to Blough, Bishop thanks her for a Hermès scarf. "I shall do the Rumba with it at Sloppy Joe's—with a tight white satin evening dress" (*SL,* 71). She then goes on to describe one of Joe's "girls," the Key West rumba champion, whose fleshy sensuality fascinates Bishop: "She is really wonderful, very very Latin, and fat, really more exactly like a Lachaise in the flesh than anyone I have ever seen, with very small feet and hands, and legs that taper in an almost isosceles triangle from the knees—five dimples in each, down. The last time I saw her she wore baby-pink satin, skin tight, no undergarments, and used a small raspberry-colored scarf" (*SL,* 71).

Bishop's description of the Key West rumba champion, one that would have been deemed too racy and campy for a letter to Moore, emphasizes the carnivalesque and grotesque. Like the body of the landlady in "Seven-Days Monologue," this body spills beyond its boundaries, thereby threatening bourgeois notions of the classical body. The Latin rumba itself, to Bishop's New England sensibility, with its strong, rhythmic movement and emphasis on sexuality, had the power to at least make one feel "uncomfortable."

Bishop's descriptions of Florida emphasize the state's grotesque characteristics with its "tanagers embarrassed by their flashiness," "hysterical birds," and "enormous turtles." Florida is the "careless, corrupt state," rotting at its core. It sits in "brackish water"; buzzards look for something dead they have "spotted in the swamp." Everything in this swamp leaves behind a ghost of itself. The mangrove roots "when dead strew white swamps with skeletons"; the turtles "die and leave their barnacled shells on the beaches, / and their large white skulls with round eye-sockets / twice the size of a man's" (*CP*, 32). What is most disturbing is that what is buried there does not remain buried. When "the tropical rain comes down / to freshen the tide-looped strings of fading shells," we glimpse a trace of Florida's violent history as "a gray rag of rotted calico, / the buried Indian Princess's skirt" is unearthed (*CP*, 32).

In *Harmonium*, particularly in the poem "O Florida, Venereal Soil," Stevens initiated a narrative about Florida and desire that Bishop seems to answer in her poem about Florida. At the end of the first stanza, Stevens imagines the state as a location for disclosure: "Florida, venereal soil, / Disclose to the lover," an occasion that brings about a sense of delicious torment:

> Swiftly in the nights,
> In the porches of Key West,
> Behind the bougainvilleas,
> After the guitar is asleep,
> Lasciviously as the wind,
> You come tormenting,
> Insatiable . . . [58]

This narrative of Florida and desire continues in Stevens's "Farewell to Florida," the first poem in *Ideas of Order*, and Bishop's tribute to Florida even echoes Stevens's contrasting images of north and south, as well as the skeletons in the swamp. But perhaps the most striking dialogue between the two poets takes place in the way that Bishop answers Stevens's appropriation of the Indian princess as a stand-in for Florida and desire. "O Florida, Venereal Soil" ends

> Donna, donna, dark,
> Stooping in indigo gown
> And cloudy constellations,
> Conceal yourself or disclose
> Fewest things to the lover—
> A hand that bears a thick-leaved fruit,
> A pungent bloom against your shade.[59]

I am reminded here of Bishop's "Brazil, January 1, 1502," and "those maddening little [Indian] women who kept calling, / calling to each other . . ." (*CP,* 92). But while that poem more obviously critiques the narrative of conquest, "Florida," in its response to Stevens's versions of Florida, also suggests a subtle critique, while acknowledging what Bishop learned from Stevens: that Florida was a location where disclosure *is* possible, a disclosure that Bishop could not investigate in either her letters to Moore, nor in any Moore-like imitation. She needed her Vassar coconspirators for this kind of disclosure.

Bishop's critique of Stevens's appropriation of the other, the Indian Princess, seems most pronounced at the end of "Florida" in its strange ventriloquism.

> The alligator, who has five distinct calls:
> friendliness, love, mating, war, and a warning—
> whimpers and speaks in the throat
> of the Indian Princess.
>
> (*CP,* 33)

In her letter to Moore, Bishop describes how Ross Allen appropriated the calls of the alligator. His "bodiless" head, "floating . . . on the surface of the water," as Bishop describes it, emitting "imitations of the alligator's calls: the 'bellow,' the love call, the warning, and the social call" (*SL,* 58). Allen's dinner table conversation later that day "consist[ed] of imitations of animals and birds," to which his guests would all respond mildly with a "murmur" and the word "Pretty." At the end of "Florida," the alligator gets his calls back only to be swallowed by the Indian Princess who had surfaced earlier in the poem. Not only that, but his "distinct calls" are reduced to what is no longer distinct, to what is neither a clear cry, nor silence, but something in between, something hybrid, broken, a "whimper." In "Florida," this strange displacement, the emotion that might have been attached to the unearthing of the Indian Princess (there is, in fact, no indication of emotion), becomes detached from its source and is perhaps contained in the alligator's whimper. Moreover, there is no appropriation or imitation of the alligator's call but rather a speaking through another, a kind of ventriloquism.

The poem's emotional weight is carried by the state's flora and fauna, not by its human subjects, since the poem's only human subject, the Indian Princess, is associated with an article of clothing, like the various lost articles of clothing—a glove, a stocking, a watch—that represent the lost mother in both unpublished and published Bishop poems. Instead, tanagers are "embarrassed"; pelicans take "delight"; turtles are "helpless and mild"; and mosquitos are "hunting to the tune of their ferocious obbligatos." And alligators call to their mates. The unearthing of a bit of Florida's buried past, its link to a history of violence and conquest—the same past, in fact, as Brazil—should elicit emotion but doesn't. Moreover, the fact that this object is a skirt, also links the princess to sexual repression as well. In the end, Florida and its past, and perhaps the poet's past as well, only reveal themselves in a whimper, a kind of third sound that we would be hard-pressed to fit into any particular category.

The cry—heard in Bishop's short story "In the Village" (1953) as a scream and as a cry of pain in "In the Waiting Room" (1976)—is difficult to place into any particular category; it is a hybrid, threatening the boundaries of the space it inhabits. When it emerges, it is closely linked to a sense of shame or embarrassment. When the child hears Aunt Consuelo's "*oh!* of pain," in the poem, for instance, as she sits in the dentist's waiting room—before she realizes it is "my voice, in my mouth"—she claims that she "might have been embarrassed, / but wasn't" (*CP,* 160).

In another displacement, the emotion that she should have felt in response to Aunt Consuelo's cry becomes attached to the images in the *National Geographic* she is reading, and specifically to the "horrifying" breasts of the naked natives represented in the magazine. Once again, we are confronted with the unassimilable, gendered, and native other, who is nevertheless somehow us. "Why should I be my aunt, / or me, or anyone?" the child, Elizabeth, asks in "In the Waiting Room":

> What similarities—
> boots, hands, the family voice
> I felt in my throat, or even
> the *National Geographic*
> and those awful hanging breasts—
> held us all together
> or made us all just one?
> How—I didn't know any
> word for it—how 'unlikely' . . .
>
> (*CP*, 161)

Again, as in "The Man-Moth," the question is one of inheritance. The "third rail," "those awful hanging breasts," and the "family voice"—representing in turn her sexual orientation, her gender, and her voice—all are characteristics the poet "has inherited the susceptibility to." Bishop recognizes, in her confrontation with gendered and racial otherness, that voice and vision are linked; that the poet's desire to order and tame through control of poetic voice and vision is never fully possible; that the traveler cannot enjoy "complete comprehension"; that such confrontations ultimately lead back to the very strangeness, the unlikeliness, of one's own self, and the inability, finally, of inserting a third category into the prescribed two, as Edwin Boomer finds in his activities on the beach. Alternately embracing, confronting, and noting the "strangeness" of alterity, Bishop, with her group at Vassar, developed a provisional, experimental community that embraced possibility and shunned fixity. It would take another fifty years for her critics to catch up with Bishop's early audience of coconspirators, to begin to answer the question of "The Monument's" inquisitor—"Why did you bring me here to see it?"

5
Sylvia Plath's Brave New World at Smith, 1950–1955

> I'm lost. Huxley would have laughed. What a conditioning center this is! Hundreds of faces, bending over books, fans whirring, beating time along the edge of thought. It is a nightmare... and I am torn in different directions, pulled thin...
>
> Sylvia Plath, *Unabridged Journals*[1]

SYLVIA PLATH'S *ARIEL* POEM, "LESBOS," BEGINS DRAMATICALLY WITH the line: "Viciousness in the kitchen!" In a flurry of sibilants—"The potatoes hiss"—the poem's speaker goes on to describe this kitchen as "windowless." Plath wrote the poem in October 1962, only a few days after her husband, Ted Hughes, had moved out of their home in Court Green, Devon, leaving Plath to fend for herself with two small children.[2] According to the dating of the poem given in *The Collected Poems*, "Lesbos" was written only two days after "Medusa," Plath's "most extreme poem of matricidal rage," as Susan Van Dyne has called it,[3] and "Lesbos" shares a considerable amount of that poem's ambivalence toward the stated object of its wrath—"you." Plath wrote "Medusa," "The Jailor,"[4] and "Lesbos" on October 16, 17, and 18, 1962 respectively, and if read in that order, which is how they are arranged in *The Collected Poems*, we are presented with a shocking triptych of failed motherhood, marriage, and female friendship at midcentury. In Plath's arranging of the *Ariel* manuscript (now restored in a new edition by Frieda Hughes), as well as in the 1965 *Ariel* arranged by Ted Hughes, these poems are spaced widely apart, so their concentrated bitterness is dissipated across the volume.

"The Jailor" did not appear in either the British or American editions of *Ariel*.

"Lesbos" is an important poem that has not received much critical attention, perhaps because its strange title and the poem itself really raise more questions than provide answers. The hissing that ends "Medusa"—"your wishes / Hiss at my sins—" is magnified in "Lesbos."[5] How did we wind up here in this "windowless" kitchen, hissing? If the women's college didn't exactly lead women here, it certainly did its share of contributing to the postwar period's push of women back into the home, even at the level of curriculum. No longer the "Adamless Eden" of Moore's 1905 Bryn Mawr, the women's college had become, as Plath suggests in her Smith College journals, both a place of opportunity for women *and* a Huxlean-style conditioning center.

In response, Plath developed a voice of consistent critique, honed to a fine edge in *Ariel*, but already evident in her Smith College writing, particularly in the prose. I would say that Plath, responding to the "violence without," to borrow from Wallace Stevens,[6] developed an art of counterviolence exemplified in her early 1956 poem, "The Goring" (*CP*, 47). In the violence of the bullring with its "ritual death," Plath writes, "The strongest will seemed a will toward ceremony," a critical phrase that could as easily be applied to the 1950s women's college where the tea ceremonies and rituals that had brought women together at Moore's Bryn Mawr served rather to prepare women to take their place as good wives and mothers. In the poem, the goring of the bull is described as merely "cumbrous routine, not artwork." The "instinct for art began" in the bull's act of turning on its oppressor, the bullfighter, and "lofting" his "lumped man-shape" into the mob (*CP*, 47). But Plath could turn her "instinct for art" as easily on women as on men. In fact, Plath's counterviolence was often directed towards how women failed each other and themselves. But the archival record also shows that Plath looked for and found women at Smith who would serve as friends and mentors who would not fail her and who did not hiss at her heels.

Although Plath's counterviolence dominates her poetry, another strand runs parallel to it, the possibility of "tenderness," best exemplified in a line filled with longing from her 1961 poem "The Moon and the Yew Tree": "How I would like to believe in tenderness," the speaker laments in that poem (*CP*, 173). The poem is about the possibility of artistic failure, as the poet tries to articulate her own vision: "I simply cannot see where there is to get to" (*CP,* 173). The poem links the poet's sense of artistic failure to a lack of tenderness, of nurturing in her life. If she could "believe" in tenderness, then perhaps she would be able to "see where there is to get to." The line, which appears in a number of Plath texts, including *The Bell Jar,* is implicitly and explicitly linked to women's failure to love each other. As Lillian Faderman has said of this period, it was "perhaps the worst time in history for women to love women."[7] While Faderman is talking specifically of lesbian relationships, a subject that Plath at times addresses in her work with ambivalence, Faderman's statement has wider implications for female friendships and mentoring relationships of all kinds within the context of the women's college.

The fear of women's colleges as "breeding grounds" for lesbianism that characterized Bishop's Vassar in the 1930s reached fever pitch by the 1950s in the wake of the McCarthy witch hunts,[8] further distancing women from a sense of community solidarity. Moreover, the importance placed on marriage in the 1950s women's college, as Barbara Solomon has noted, meant that, "the 'single' woman—whether unattached or involved in a heterosexual or lesbian relationship—was categorized as deviant in this time of social conformity."[9] Even contact with another lesbian, Faderman writes, like contact with a Communist, could open you up to suspicion.[10] Homosexuals, seen as part of a conspiracy by even the mainstream press, had to be "hunted down and purged."[11] It is in bringing the two strands of Plath's art together within this climate of fear—the search for "tenderness" in poems like the 1961 poem "The Babysitters" and the counter-violence of poems like "Lesbos"—that we can begin to understand how Plath's poetics can be read as one of the most significant and complex feminist statements of the post-war period. "Perfection is terrible," Plath wrote in the first line of the late 1963 poem, "The Munich Mannequins," "it cannot have children" (*CP,* 262). Women of Plath's generation labored under the terror of perfection—the perfect wife, the perfect mother, the perfect woman who brings forth the perfect children. Neither art nor children can be born under such conditions. The landscape is barren. "Instinct for art began," and ended, for Plath in "the goring" of these images of perfection in order to clear a space for something else.

The Smith Years

Sylvia Plath left behind a detailed record of her Smith College experience in the journals she kept, and in the hundreds of critical essays, poems and stories she wrote as an undergraduate. Her college years speak of an astonishingly prolific writer learning her craft. Plath was already a published writer when she came to Smith, and her promise was acknowledged and supported by the well-known, popular, and enormously successful writer Olive Higgins Prouty, whose novels *Stella Dallas* and *Now, Voyager* had both been made into Hollywood films. Plath used her college years to make herself into even more of a professional. Like her predecessors Moore and Bishop, but even more so, Plath used her college years as a way to launch her career. Smith provided opportunities, as Plath put it in a characteristic rush in one journal entry, for "Fulbright's, prizes, Europe, publication, males. . . . —going, seeing, doing, thinking, feeling, desiring" (*UJ,* 103).

Plath perceived Smith as crucially important to her "training" as a writer, a point she acknowledged again and again in her journals: "I am at Smith! Which two years ago was a doubtful dream—and that fortuitous change of dream to reality has led me to desire more, and to lash myself onward—onward" (*UJ,* 104). Plath's Smith experience also exemplifies what Langdon Hammer has called "a distinctly new situation for poetry" where "poetic expertise appeared as marketable technique like other specialized knowledges."[12] This increasing professionalization of the writer's craft is reflected in the curriculum at Smith where, as Hammer notes, "Plath took two prose writing courses in her second year . . . , a fiction writing course in her third, and another fiction writing course and a poetry writing tutorial in her fourth year."[13] Hence, according to Hammer, the college environment increasingly became "a scene of literary production," providing writers with "'networking' and mentorship" relationships that could lead to publication, and poets could make a living through "teaching, fellowships, and prizes."[14]

Hammer's is a crucial re-contextualizing of Plath's poetic production, but, as he himself acknowledges but cannot explore thoroughly, gender makes a difference to our understanding of how the conditions of poetic production are created. As Hammer points out, none of the male poets Plath wrote about while she was a guest editor at

Mademoiselle "advance his career by winning a guest-editorship at *Mademoiselle*."[15] The women's college, then, was fundamentally different from a male writer's experience of the liberal arts at mid-century. While Smith offered Plath, by her own account, enormous opportunities and a network of mentors who could help get her published, it was also a Huxlean-style conditioning center, a place that fed Plath's tremendous ambition and "led [her] to desire more" but also "conditioned" its students to "achieve" husbands and motherhood. This is the other fundamental shift of the women's college at midcentury. Just as women's colleges were training women writers to be marketable, they were also considering curriculum changes that would better prepare them to be wives and mothers.

Discussions in *Scan*, the college newspaper (later renamed *The Sophian*), centered during these years on whether Smith should offer vocational courses to better prepare students to be wives and mothers, joining a national debate on the subject. Mills College, for example, was offering courses in volunteerism as well as a "Marriage" major.[16] Even Millicent McIntosh, president of Barnard and niece of the radical feminist M. Carey Thomas who had been president of Bryn Mawr during Moore's years there, caved in to such challenges, joining other college presidents at Wellesley and Vassar to "caution" women that their "first duty is to their children," according to one *Times* headline.[17] Women's colleges seemed to be traveling backwards at an alarming rate. *Scan* reported on this debate, and although Smith College resisted such curriculum changes, Smith College President Benjamin Wright, in a baccalaureate speech he gave in 1952, told Smith women, "Women have an important role to play as housewives and mothers and are essential to the smooth operation of the reciprocal relationships which are the basis of our democracy."[18]

Plath's frustration at this "democratic" model of relationships is palpable throughout her Smith College journals. Understandably, Plath feared that marriage would destroy her professional ambition and sap her creative energies, which she might lose "in cooking scrambled eggs for a man" (*UJ*, 88). In the same month that Wright gave his baccalaureate speech, Plath wrote what could easily have been a critique of it in her journal in a long entry, dated May 15, 1952. Challenging the prevailing ideology of separate spheres suggested in Wright's speech, Plath imagines a partnership between men and women in marriage and describes herself and her partner as "two over-lapping circles, with a certain strong riveted center of common ground" (*UJ*, 105). Rather than being confined "solely to home, other womenfolk, and community service," Plath imagines that both of them would "arc" out into the world and then back again to share their experiences (*UJ*, 105). In short, Plath wants a productive union with a man that would allow her individual freedom. Plath emphasizes balance. "Not the continual subordination of one person[']s desires and interests to the continual advancement of another's! That would be too grossly unfair" (*UJ*, 106).

As a new student at Smith College in 1950, Sylvia Plath forged her identity as a writer and as a woman with the clear understanding that she was undergoing a long initiation into a community of women who would indeed pull her thin with their conflicted ideas of the purpose of higher education for women. Plath attended Smith at the height of the postwar backlash against women in the workplace, one that had a profound effect on the women's college. As Barbara Solomon has noted, debates surrounding the purpose of education for women used a pseudo-Freudian language in order to lend a "'scientific' rationale" to the argument that a woman's "natural" role in life was to be a wife and mother.[19] Examples of this discourse abound in Plath's experience at Smith. In her first year there, a Mrs. William Cole, who spoke at a marriage forum with her husband, warned Smith students, "The wife, who sets the whole atmosphere of the home, must achieve a willing sublimation of her desires to those of her husband and children. When this sublimation is not felt, often neurosis, frustration, and discontent result."[20] Mrs. Cole also told Smith students that, "among the higher educated women, greater sexual disorder is prevalent."[21]

In an August 1950 article published in the *Atlantic Monthly*, Agnes E. Meyer also uses pseudo-Freudian language to support a return to traditional gender roles for women. Plath took notes on this much-cited article in a notebook now housed in the Lilly Library.[22] The article, entitled "Women Aren't Men," warns that women must "sublimate" their sexual desires before marriage, if they are not to put themselves in danger of "warping [their] whole personality."[23] Meyer argues that women's freedom and greater autonomy, which they had gained during the war years, has sunk the nation into its lowest point of "sexual morality." Everywhere, women's organizations were lamenting this "moral lapse."[24] In 1950, as a response to the first Kinsey report on male sexuality, the National Council of Women adopted "an emergency resolution urging coordinated community effort to insure the security of the American home."[25] The second Kinsey report on women's sexuality came out in 1953 right in the middle of Plath's college career and generated even more vehement counterresponse.[26] The diversity and range of women's sexual appetites had suddenly been revealed, and America was clearly not ready for it.

Agnes Meyer had written that if a woman "guards her sex life," she will be more likely "to attract, to choose, and to hold the devotion of the right husband."[27] Meyers assumes that a "woman's sexuality" will be "destructive to her and to society," if she does not follow this advice.[28] Plath takes notes on this article without comment, but a number of journal entries reflect her resistance to this idea. In one she writes with exasperation, "I can only lean enviously against the boundary and hate, hate, hate the boys who can dispel sexual hunger freely, without misgiving, and be whole, while I drag out from date to date in soggy desire, always unfulfilled. The whole thing sickens me" (*UJ*, 20).

What is clear is that women, at least as much as men, if not more so, policed the borders of this community, adopting this discourse, leaving educated women, as one might imagine, unsure of their role in society. As Florence Kluckhohn wrote in the *New York Times* in 1950, "The American woman stands today confused by a culture that trains her to compete with men for a career, and then expects her to be content with being wife and mother."[29] In short, highly educated women were supposed to "guard their sex" before marriage, "sublimate" their ambitions to their husband's after marriage, and embrace motherhood as their highest achievement, a role that in reality was "so denigrated," as Eugenia Kaledin has argued, "that women who gave their serious energies to it for any period of time were considered unfit to do anything else."[30] In at least one popular study Plath read, Philip Wylie's *Generation of Vipers,* the mothers of consumer culture are turned into devouring monsters, she devils, harbingers of death, and "the black widow who is poisonous and eats her mate."[31] Plath included the book in her poem "The Babysitters," which I will discuss shortly.

Plath dramatizes these conflicts in a very early poem she wrote at Smith, "Metamorphoses of the Moon," which ends with these lines:

> Either way we choose, the angry witch
> will punish us for saying which is which;
>   in fatal equilibrium
> we poise on perilous poles that freeze us in
> a cross of contradiction, racked between
>   the fact of doubt, the faith of dream.
>
> (*CP*, 308)

The poem emphasizes the speaker's dilemma as one shared by others. "Either way *we* choose . . . / *we* poise on perilous poles that freeze us . . . ." Already, even at this early stage in Plath's career, she has the sense that what she has experienced as an individual has a wider significance, and she is beginning to try to convey that understanding in her poetry. The first stanza of "Metamorphoses of the Moon" dramatizes the speaker's ambition and her frustration that there is no one there to meet her challenge:

> Cold moons withdraw, refusing to come to terms
> with the pilot who dares all heaven's harms
>   to raid the zone where fate begins,
> flings silver gauntlet of his plane at space,
> demanding satisfaction; no duel takes place:
>   the mute air merely thins and thins.
>
> (*CP*, 307)

The cold moons, coded female in Plath's work, merely withdraw when faced with female ambition of such magnitude. There is no duel, and the speaker is left literally in "thin air." This poem dramatizes very well the problem of the women's college at midcentury and of relationships between women, which had become almost completely circumscribed by the relentless postwar ideology of domesticity.

However, there was clearly a line of resistance to this formulation. Many educators were concerned that conformity among students was killing democracy. Other articles in *Scan* track how conformity on college campuses had become a threat to democracy. In "Fear is Stifling College Liberals," Ann Rickenbaugh reports on an article published in the *New York Times* that warns, "New England's privately endowed colleges including Williams, Amherst, Smith and Wellesley are mentioned as seats of ebbing liberalism."[32] Rickenbaugh quotes from the *Times*, "Conformity of thought among students and the disappearance of radicalism from a number of college campuses including Smith constitute one of the present dangers to American democracy."[33] Since this debate applied equally to male and female communities, it is not in the least surprising that Plath would deal with these tensions almost exclusively in terms of female community, demonstrating that these struggles existed between and among women. When Plath audited a course with Alfred Kazin, who had a chair at Smith during the 1954–1955 school year, she wrote her mother that she was "appalled at the weak, mealy-mouthed apathy of the girls, who either were just too scared or just too stupid to have opinions."[34] Howard Mumford Jones, Harvard professor of English and president of the American Academy of Arts and Sciences, complained of the same thing in an article he wrote for the January 1952 issue of *Mademoiselle*, on which *Scan* reported. In that article he found college women "apathetic," "afraid to take a stand;" they have become women who have failed to "challenge" his " 'intellectual curiosity' . . . . Her simple aims are a temporary job and a husband. College girls want . . . jobs 'that are small, safe and secure,' jobs lacking in any mission, dedication or ambition."[35]

Plath's identity as a writer emerges from this context; she literally forges it by transforming "the general mumble" around her, as she put it in another early Smith poem, "Notes to a Neophyte" (*CP*, 306). She advises herself in this poem to "stiffen the ordinary / malleable mask / to the granite grin of bone" (*CP*, 306). And, to achieve "such a tempering task," she writes, "heat furnace of paradox / in an artifice of ice; / make love and logic mix . . . " (*CP*, 306). The poem, like many of Plath's Smith College poems, reflects the New Critical principles that Plath would have imbibed in heavy doses from her high school teachers and Smith College professors. Hammer notes that Plath owned and read Cleanth Brooks's *The Well Wrought Urn: Studies in the Structure of Poetry* (1947) and Brooks's and Robert Penn Warren's *Understanding Poetry* while she was in college.[36] Her "furnace of paradox" and "artifice of ice" come straight out of this educational background, but already we see in "the granite grin of bone" the shaping of that education into a poetry that would challenge such conformity.

Plath was also on the lookout, throughout her Smith College years, for female role models among established writers, among her teachers, and among peers. Prouty, her benefactor at Smith, was an important one for Plath, but probably too close to her mother's generation to be one that Plath could embrace without some degree of ambivalence. However, in the summer of 1952 between her sophomore and junior years of college, Plath met the writer Val Gendron in the Bookmobile. She cultivated the relationship and was rewarded for her efforts when Gendron invited Plath home to her "shack."

Plath's accounts of her initial visit with Gendron show just how much she treated her years at Smith as a writing apprenticeship. These notes range from descriptions of how she learned the disciplined practical aspects of a writer's life—"I start this fall. Four pages a day" (*UJ*, 124)—to stereotyped, if Joycean, descriptions of a woman alone: "She is small, skinny, sallow, with black hair done up in back in a bun and braids under a visor khaki cap. . . . Cats she has, in her shack, red-painted . . . and no phone. Signs of loneliness? Of living too long with Val Gendron? Who to talk to? Who?. . . . I will be no Val Gendron. But I will make a good part of Val Gendron part of me—someday" (*UJ*, 124–25).

One is reminded here of all the spinster stereotypes of Plath's early poetry, the "rat-shrewd," "root-pale," "bitter" spinster of the two 1956 poems "Two Sisters of Persephone" and "Spinster," or the pathetic "Ella Mason and Her Eleven Cats." But when Plath does make her "pilgrimage" to Gendron, she finds in her writer's life a Thoreau-inspired model of perfection. Her journal entry begins breathlessly: "Same time. After Val. God, the talk" (*UJ*, 131). She describes herself in the beginning as out of place in Val's environment. "I walk in, feeling big and new and too clean" (*UJ*, 131). There are dirty dishes on the floor, "[a]she-trays full of cigarettes," and cats. But the kitchen is also full of intoxicating smells—Val loves to cook—and Plath describes in loving detail the experience of smelling freshly ground coffee and spices. "She unscrews them and I smell each as she says, 'Thyme, Basil, Marjoram . . . ' and so on," and she speaks with admiration of Gendron's "preserving closet"—full of "jams, jellies, apple butter, beach plums. She picks and cans. Wild, sweet, tart, clear in glasses" (*UJ*, 131)—and her abundant garden. As Plath describes her, here is a woman who places her creative energies into living a domestic life for herself alone, not for a man, and whose life seems, at least to Plath, to seamlessly integrate the more creative aspects of that deeply domestic life—cooking, gardening, rug making, *and* writing—an integration that the speaker of Plath's bee poem "Winter-

ing" achieves herself, at least temporarily, when as "midwife" she extracts "six jars" of honey, "Six cat's eyes in the wine cellar" (*CP,* 217).
Plath describes Gendron's little house:

> It is all book shelves over the walls, Williamsburg blue-gray, and cream yellow. A rug she is braiding is on the floor, and balls of wool rag in a basket. A studio couch, a typewriter. Piles of manuscripts around, in boxes, on her desk. We sit cross legged on the floor, and start pouring ourselves cup after cup of coffee. I am a pig and have three hunks of cake. The four black kittens Prue is nursing come in and skitter around like black scritches of playful fluff. They are nosey, lean into my coffee cup, sneeze at the hot strong stuff and go skittering across the floor. One goes to sleep inside the edge of my skirt where it makes a comfortable fold on the floor. (*UJ,* 132)

Surrounded by a life, Plath is allowed to be "a pig," to indulge in a messy and productive life, to gorge herself on the meat and drink that she felt was so often denied her. As Gendron drives Plath home in her beat-up "jalop," as Plath calls it, Plath is "coffee-drunk. Exhilarated." Later, at home, she writes it all down and imagines the exchange between them in terms of a rejection of men and the achievement of perfection: "God," she writes, "she has been great to me. Tonight best yet. All the boys, all the longing, then this perfection. Perfect love, whole living" (*UJ,* 132).

Plath also seems to have found this perfection in her relationship with her college friend and roommate Marcia Brown. She devotes long, lyrical passages to Marcia in her journals, and even writes a poem about her. In everything she writes about Marcia, Plath expresses love and admiration, which is uncharacteristic of Plath's writing about other women. An unpublished poem, called simply "Marcia," among Plath's papers at the Lilly Library stages a domestic scene shared by two women that also seems to represent a kind of "perfect love, whole living" sensibility.[37] In this poem, Marcia and her poetic incarnation represent a kind of "authentic" sister, a counterbalance to the more dominant representation of female community and sisterhood in Plath. The two women sit across from each other and a breakfast of scrambled eggs, sharing a moment of independence where cooking scrambled eggs does not mean the dissipation of one's creative energies. This concept of "authentic" sisterhood is most notable in Plath's 1961 poem "The Babysitters." Brown serves as

Sylvia Plath and Marcia Brown (Stern), with dog, Castle Rock, Swampscott, MA, August 24, 1951. Mortimer Rare Book Room, Smith College, © Marcia Brown Stern.

the prototype for the sister of that poem, one of the few where Plath seems to embrace the possibility of a shared female solidarity.

Mother's Helpers

The poem is based on Plath's experience of working as a "mother's helper" in the summer of 1951, between her first and second years at college. Plath worked for the Mayo family in Swampscott, Massachusetts, while Marcia, then her college roommate, took a job with a neighboring family. The job was a typical one for Smith "girls" at the time, reflecting the general belief that a woman's primary role in life was to be a good wife and mother. These jobs, as Plath had written in one story she produced out of the experience and published during her Smith years in a conservative newspaper, helped her to feel "maternal." The second story she wrote was for a course at Smith. This one, a sophisticated social commentary, reflects Plath's education in class differences rather than in motherhood. Plath describes the workers here as a "federation," united against their oppressors.

Plath's use of this experience is significant because it reveals not only her method of working but also her complex understanding of sexual politics and class issues at midcentury, an understanding that would emerge finally in the poetry in 1961 in "The Babysitters." The poem, along with others Plath produced at the time, shares with her novel, *The Bell Jar*, also completed that year, Plath's acute observation of social conventions and of the powerful social and cultural forces that shaped relationships between women at midcentury.

The poem begins with a glance back to the summer of 1951 from the distance of ten years. The women of Plath's poem wear "black glasses," because they are so unhappy as babysitters they cry all the time—"little put-upon sisters." The first three stanzas of the poem describe the Gatsby lifestyle of the parents with "two huge, white, handsome houses in Swampscott," "eleven rooms and a yacht," and "a cabin boy who could decorate cakes in six-colored frosting." Plath's descriptions of this world in her journals occasionally idealize this realm of the rich in passages that sound straight out of Douglas Sirk's 1959 *Imitation of Life*, a film that itself suggested that women's happiness resided in choosing the roles of wife and mother. Plath describes Mrs. Mayo as "tall, slender and darkly beautiful in a flowing nylon gown of aqua," who rustled into the kitchen to make "cheese crackers to go with the cocktails" (*UJ*, 80).

At other times in her journals, Plath is highly critical, describing the upstairs/downstairs world that she inhabited. In one entry, she describes looking down at the party below from her perch above where she has been relegated to the nursery, like Jane Eyre who observes, unnoticed, Mr. Rochester's brilliant guests. Plath brings together these class issues in the poem. In one journal entry, Plath makes it clear what a "dictatorship" the Mayo household represents. She reports on an incident that took place when everyone, including the children, had gone out. Only Dr. Mayo remained, since he maintained an office in his home and was seeing patients at the time. Plath decides to play the piano, but before long, Dr. Mayo runs upstairs from his office to ask her in his "sharp thin annoyed voice" not to play the piano during office hours (*UJ*, 85). In response to the incident, Plath wonders "how human beings can suffer their individualities to be mercilessly crushed under a machine-like dictatorship— be it of industry, state or organization—all their lives long" (*UJ*, 85).

Plath makes it clear in a short story she wrote for her English 220 class her sophomore year, which was inspired by this experience, that the curtailing of liberty was not the job of men alone but was shared by the women of the household. The heroine of the story is a mother's helper whose employer, Mrs. Johnson, gives her no time to herself. The moment the heroine sits down with a book, Mrs. Johnson finds her, gives her a disapproving look, and suggests they bake something.[38] Plath casts Mrs. Johnson as a kind of dictator in the household, against which the household staff appears as "a cooperative federation of capable and magnanimous workers, united against would-be oppressors."[39] Plath brings together public and private spaces through the consideration of how people can "suffer their individualities to be mercilessly crushed under a machine-like dictatorship."

Such experiences were designed to teach the college woman how to be a good wife and mother, since Plath reminds us at the end of the story that she learned to hide her feelings and personal desires behind a cheerful and willing demeanor.[40] In another account she wrote for the conservative *Christian Science Monitor*, however, she adopts the expected persona, gushing that she felt "very benevolent" and "very maternal" when the children asked her for favors.[41] The sheer number of reworkings of this experience and its different presentations demonstrate Plath's method of working, of turning experience into marketable material on one level and art on another, all of which, of course, was marketable in different contexts.

The sisters' escape in "The Babysitters" shares with Plath's English 220 story a challenge to how women of Plath's generation were supposed to use this experience. The last two stanzas of "The Babysitters" narrate the afternoon of escape to the suggestively named Children's Island in a Wordsworthian echo that recalls the boat stealing incident of Book I of *The Prelude*.[42] The whole passage stages a series of returns to a finally impossible childhood innocence that nevertheless beckons toward a liberating possibility. Here, unlike many of Plath's poems, sisterhood is not a threat but a shared condition; they are "little put-upon sisters," but more than that, the apostrophe of the fourth stanza suggests both the presence and the loss of this sister and this day:

> O what has come over us, my sister!
> On that day-off the two of us cried so hard to get
> We lifted a sugared ham and a pineapple from the grownups' icebox
> And rented an old green boat. I rowed. You read
> Aloud, crosslegged on the stern seat, from the *Generation of Vipers*.
> (*CP*, 175)

In this stanza from "The Babysitters," sweetness—"a sugared ham and a pineapple"—is connected to illicit pleasure. Their reading aloud from Wylie's 1942 book *Generation of Vipers* suggests they are leaving behind the artificial, consumerist world of their employers in search of more "authentic" territory.[43] Plath had used Wylie's book in one journal entry to analyze her then current boyfriend's "mother complex," drawing specifically on Wylie's discussion of what he considers to be the archetypal American woman, which he splits between Cinderella and "Mom." Wylie's relentlessly misogynist text—he continually asserts the "natural" inferiority of women—rails against a consumer culture whose primary purpose is to produce things for Cinderella and "Mom" to consume, and the vapid emptiness that such a culture fosters. The equation of the American construction of "Mom" with consumption resonates strongly with Plath's construction of the devouring mother in her writing and explains in part how mothers become so closely aligned with conformity in Plath's work.

Wylie's criticism, although hard to stomach, is not without its merits; he argues, for instance, that a consumer culture where everything is designed around producing "the things the women consume" generates "a lazy female pattern."[44] It creates "the child wife, the infantile personality, the woman who cannot reason logically, the bridge fiend, the golf fiend, the mother of all the atrocities we call 'spoiled children. . . .'"[45]

The sisters of Plath's poem provide a counterfoil to the "vipers" of Wylie's book, who are the overbearing daughters and mothers that American consumer culture was producing, women who, according to Wylie, are "all tongue and teat and razzmatazz."[46] Finally, though, the epiphany that the poem promises with all its echoes of Wordsworthian Romanticism does not come. The image of the deserted island is "Stopped and awful as a photograph of somebody laughing, / But ten years dead." In the final lines of the poem, the speaker calls up the vision of the babysitters together: "I see us floating there yet, inseparable—two cork dolls." But while they remain inseparable, bobbing in the water in this image—"the thick salt" holding them buoyant so that they do not drown—the speaker wonders at the end:

> What keyhole have we slipped through, what door has shut?
> The shadows of the grasses inched round like hands of a clock,
> And from our opposite continents we wave and call.
> Everything has happened.
>
> (*CP*, 175)

By the time of the poem's composition, Marcia and Plath had both married, and Plath had moved to England. The last line of the poem suggests that "everything has happened" to keep these women apart. The escape from a tyrannous life of domestic service that the poem posits has been abandoned. In a 1957 journal entry, Plath laments the loss of the Marcia she had known at Smith. Marcia, now married to "weak Mike," is "set in her dogmatic complacency . . . jealous as a female fawn-colored bulldog, netted in by supermarkets, libraries and job-routine. . . . I wish she hadn't married Mike. Then she wouldn't have to shrink so small" (*UJ*, 316).

This elegy for Marcia is also an elegy for the lost possibilities for meaningful relationships between women, an idea that echoes throughout Plath's poems. Apart from "The Babysitters," women predominantly fail other women in Plath's poetry and prose. They are "cold moons withraw[ing]," "rivals," "honey-drudgers." In the strange 1961 poem "The Zookeeper's Wife," the speaker is digesting her sisters: "... my belly a silk stocking / Where the heads and tails of my sisters decompose" (*CP*, 154). In "Blackberrying," the speaker is disturbed by sisterly affection. The blackberries she picks literally stain her. They "squander" their juices on her fingers, and the speaker tells us that she "had not asked for such a blood sisterhood; they must love me" (*CP*, 168). But the blackberry bushes also have hooks, often associated with women's smiles in Plath's poetry. The speaker of "Insomniac" is kept awake as "Nightlong, in the granite yard, invisible cats / Have been howling like women, or damaged instruments" (*CP*, 163).

The poem "Heavy Women," from the same period, imagines a community of women that can exist together in harmony only because they have totally given into the stereotype (or the archetype). They sit content on the hillside, heavy with the weight of the history of Western art and its portrayal of women. They are "Irrefutable, beautifully smug / As Venus, pedestaled on a half-shell.... // Smiling to themselves, they meditate / Devoutly as the Dutch bulb.... // Pink-buttocked infants attend them. / Looping wool, doing nothing in particular, / They step among the archetypes" (*CP*, 158). They are knitting, a signifier for Plath of female conformity.[47] This is the portrait of terrible perfection that Plath treats with contemptuous irony here, for they are unaware that "far off, the axle of winter / Grinds round, bearing down with the straw, / The star, the wise gray men" (*CP*, 158).

All these poems were written in 1961 around the composition of *The Bell Jar* and share the emotional territory of the novel but with the critical distance and experience Plath had achieved by this stage in her career. During the spring and early summer of 1961, Plath wrote the first drafts of the novel and thereby returned to mine the raw emotions, desires, and events of her Smith College years that precipitated her breakdown and suicide attempt. These poems share much of the social critique that *The Bell Jar* offers about women's lives, demonstrate Plath's struggle to establish her poetic vision, and explore alternative lives and selves. Plath's self-explorations in all of these texts are often placed in the context of female relationships or use language that suggests such a context.

"The Babysitters," coming at the end of this series of poems, imagines a temporary "escape" from the tyranny of patriarchy and motherhood through an act of sisterly solidarity. But the women are gruesomely frozen, two "inseparable" "cork dolls." Dolls are neither sisters, nor women; they do not have that kind of agency. The outer reaches of the failure of sisterhood in Plath's time can be found in the wicked parody of Sappho's island of women, Plath's *Ariel* poem "Lesbos." This poetic statement of counterviolence that exists on the outer limits of such a possibility, exposes, I believe, not the limits of lesbian desire, but the abject limits of Sappho's ideal female community when that community becomes entirely aligned with reproductivity rather than productivity.

But before turning to "Lesbos," I want to consider the context that produced such a poem—midcentury attitudes toward the lesbian and Plath's response in her work.

Stalking the Lesbian

During Plath's years at Smith, as I have suggested, lesbian desire (or any suggestion of it) was what had to be violently purged to constitute normative heterosexuality. And heterosexual female desire had to be "guarded against" as well, at least until one was safely married. Smith created a culture in which its female students must maintain a "feminine masquerade" to belong to that community, a conditioning that Plath would critique in *The Bell Jar*. The creation of normative female subjectivity, through the purging of the "lesbian" and the channeling of female ambition and desire through the narrow conduit of marriage and children, represents an important and complicated nexus of competing desires in some of Plath's best work. Plath's treatment of the lesbian (and, by extension, relationships between women within the context of a female community) is significant, complicated, and important to her own efforts in positioning herself in relationship to other female writers and in creating the possibility for building a productive writer's life.

In her journals, poetry, and prose, Plath's response to the lesbian reflects her era's fascination and condemnation of that figure. As in previous decades, the lesbian was aligned both with deviance and with independence. These were women who had "got rid of the men," to borrow a line from Plath's bee poems. In her rather stereotyped but nevertheless interesting account of May Swenson at Yaddo, for instance, Plath admires Swenson as "independent, self-possessed," even "ageless" (*UJ*, 525). And she admits to her "old admiration for the strong, if Lesbian, woman" (*UJ*, 525). But the construction of heterosexuality at midcentury foreclosed on the possibilities of sharing this strength and independence without aligning oneself with deviance.

The women's college environment has been unique in that it has been subject to intense scrutiny over both the possibility and the threat of the lesbian, so it is one of the places where professional desire and lesbian desire seem to overlap. We can see these ideas coming together most notably in Plath's notes from 1959 when she was in Boston and undergoing psychoanalysis. Her notes from these sessions are now reprinted in Karen Kukil's edition of the *Unabridged Journals*. These are the famous, or infamous, sessions in which Plath's psychoanalyst gave her permission to "hate" her mother, and Plath proceeded to explore her relationship with not only her biological mother but surrogate mothers as well, some of whom had been her professors at Smith. In one session, Plath asks, "what does a woman see in another woman that she doesn't see in a man," to which her psychoanalyst responds, "tenderness" (*UJ*, 460). Plath lifts this dialogue from her journal almost intact in a discussion between Esther and *her* psychoanalyst, Dr. Nolan, in *The Bell Jar* in a section of the novel where the main character, Esther Greenwood, has been approached by Joan, a lesbian.[48] Dr. Nolan's comment about tenderness in the *Bell Jar* passage leaves Esther in silence. "That shut me up," she tells us (*BJ* 219).

The comment shows up in the journals, is recycled in the novel, and also appears in Plath's 1961 poem "The Moon and the Yew Tree," composed in late October just before "The Babysitters":

> The moon is my mother. She is not sweet like Mary.
> Her blue garments unloose small bats and owls.
> How I would like to believe in tenderness—
> The face of the effigy, gentled by candles,
> Bending, on me in particular, its mild eyes.
>   (*CP*, 173)

The line, "How I would like to believe in tenderness" read in the context of its repetitions in connection with lesbian desire, as well as its maternal references here, represents a kind of knot of difficulty in Plath's work, a complex longing. Both this poem and "Blackberrying" (written in September) are about the poet's creative struggle, a struggle that is bound up with, at least to some degree, the failure of relationships. In "Blackberrying," the speaker states, "I do not think the sea will appear at all" (*CP*, 168). In "The Moon and the Yew Tree," she tells us that "I simply cannot see where there is to get to" (*CP*, 173). Both poems speak to a failure of vision; both poems suggest that at least part of the problem might be that the ground on which the poet stands is a disablingly maternal and domestic landscape, "Slapping its phantom laundry in my face," in the case of "Blackberrying," or not providing the sought for "tenderness" in "The Moon and the Yew Tree" (*CP*, 169).

The novel rejects in no uncertain terms the possibility that a relationship with Joan might offer some tenderness that is not offered by the men in Esther's life. Esther responds with ambivalence to Joan. She says at one point, "In spite of the creepy feeling . . . Joan fascinated me" (*BJ*, 219). While Joan both repels and fascinates Esther, Esther rejects her, and her last comment to Joan is, "'You make me puke, if you want to know'" (*BJ*, 220). In his discussion of the novel's portrayal of the lesbian and the construction of femininity by women's magazines in the 1950s, Garry Leonard argues that "Plath presents a carefully constructed irony here" in her portrayal of heterosexual relationships versus lesbian ones: "The invariable physical and psychological abuse of Esther's heterosexual experience is viewed as 'normal,' while the idea of two women embracing makes her 'want to puke. . . .'"[49] When Joan tries to seduce her, Esther quickly recalls social attitudes towards the lesbian. "And as she stretched out on my bed with a silly smile, I remembered a minor scandal at our college dormitory when a fat, matronly-breasted senior . . . and a pious Religion major . . . started seeing too much of each other" (*BJ*, 219). A comparison with another novel that came out the same year is in order at this point, as it sheds some light on the treatment of lesbian desire at two different moments in the women's college experience.

Mary McCarthy's novel *The Group*, based on her Vassar class of 1933, was published in 1963, the same year Plath's novel *The Bell Jar* came out in London under the pseudonym Victoria Lucas. Not only do the characters of both novels emerge from women's colleges, both novels feature lesbian characters that in some way drive a major aspect of the plot. But there are some major differences, and I think these differences reflect the extreme homophobia that women experienced in women's colleges in the 1950s. McCarthy's lesbian character ends the novel; she gets to drive off into the horizon and the future, like John Wayne, leaving the insufferable white and homophobic male behind in the dust. The main heterosexual woman in the novel, Kay, who is married to the insufferable white male and quite dependent on him, either falls to her death from a window at the Vassar club twenty stories up or commits suicide. No one really knows. In *The Bell Jar*, the lesbian character, Joan, is a mental patient who tries unsuccessfully to seduce the narrator, Esther. The novel sacrifices the lesbian character in the end; she commits suicide, and, as Michael Davidson has argued, "In the larger sexual economy of the novel, heterosexuality must win out while lesbianism must be killed off."[50] While close attachments between women were viewed with suspicion and sometimes expulsion in the 1930s, by many accounts, the women's college environment still worked to protect these relationships on some level and to foster tolerance. When the women of McCarthy's novel find out that Lakey is a lesbian, some of them do respond with repugnance, but they don't reject her as a friend. McCarthy's narrative, though, treats her quite radically by turning her into the novel's romantic hero.

Plath did not deal overtly with the subject of lesbianism in her poetry, even though the title of her *Ariel* poem "Lesbos" suggests such a community. Plath's use of Sappho's island as the title is skillful and complicated. In contrast to Sappho's ideal community of women and Sappho herself, the great lyric poet, to which the title alludes, Plath's lyric speaks at every turn to the tyranny of domesticity in women's lives, women's inability to support other women, the lack of intellectual community, and the loss of lyric possibility—"I can't communicate." Given her own tendency to align lesbian poets, such as May Swenson, with independence, I'm tempted to read Plath's poem as an astute account of what it means for the female lyric poet to sever all ties to a community of women. Female friendships break down, and women can no longer talk to, or support, each other.

"Lesbos" hasn't received much critical attention. Susan Van Dyne rightly groups it with Plath's poems of "rage," but calls it one of her "incoherent, splenetic outbursts."[51] Steven Gould Axelrod lists it with

The Bell Jar as an example of work that "depicts lesbian feeling," but leaves it at that.[52] While I would agree with Van Dyne that this is a poem about rage, it is certainly not "incoherent," nor is it uncontrolled. It is rather a skillful, carefully constructed poem that turns inside out through a discourse of abjection a variety of signifiers surrounding the idea of female community. Jacqueline Rose argues that Plath "can be defined in Kristeva's terms as a writer of abjection, a writer for whom the limits of the body and of symbolisation are constantly worked over or put at risk."[53] The disgust that Esther expresses toward Joan in abject terms in *The Bell Jar*—"you make me want to puke"—dominates the imagery of the poem. But the poem has little to do with lesbian desire, despite its title. The horror at the center of this poem is, rather, a desire that becomes bound up with an idea of female community that is completely circumscribed and defined by a kind of tyranny of motherhood in the 1950s. The poem begins, after all, with the words,

> Viciousness in the kitchen!
> The potatoes hiss.
> It is all Hollywood, windowless,
> The fluorescent light wincing on and off like a terrible migraine,
> (*CP*, 227)

The "stink" at the center of this poem cannot be walled off; it permeates everything: "Their smell!" We seem to be back in the territory of Wylie's "all Hollywood" women here.

The poem centers on the circumscribed lives of two women; violence becomes commonplace and banal. The "you" of the poem suggests that the speaker "drown" both her daughter—because she is a useless girl—and her daughter's kittens, which the "you" of the poem has already locked up in a "cement well," "where they crap and puke and cry and she can't hear." The speaker wants to keep the other woman's "doggy husband" from leaving, not because he is of any interest but because he will absorb some of the shock waves from this other woman: "An old pole for the lightning, / The acid baths, the skyfuls off of you" (*CP*, 228). Only the poem's title and a couple of lines provide a hint of the unspoken desire that haunts the poem.

When Ted Hughes left Court Green, Plath's mother wrote to her daughter, suggesting that she return home to Massachusetts. On October 16, Plath responded, "Home is impossible. I can go nowhere with the children, and I am ill, and it would be psychologically the worst thing to see you now or to go home" (*LH,* 468). Plath told her mother that she must "make a new life.... I am a genius of a writer; I have it in me. I am writing the best poems of my life; they will make my name.... I feel only a lust to study, write, get my brain back and practice my craft" (*LH,* 468–69). Finally, Plath wrote: "After Ted left with all his clothes and things, I piled the children and two cats in the car and drove to stay with a ... couple I know in St. Ives, Cornwall.... Discovered Cornwall, exhausted but happy, my first independent act! I have no desire but to build a new life.... I must not go back to the womb or retreat. I must take steps out...." (*LH,* 469). Anne Stevenson has said that this trip and this American couple prompted the writing of "Lesbos."[54] But so much focus on a single incident as the catalyst for this poem obscures its much wider significance. The letter suggests that Plath associated returning home to her mother as a return to the protected but claustral closure of the womb, a metaphor that I will explore further in my final chapter. Suffice it to say here that this association was made as early as her college years, and Plath connected it very specifically with ideas of conformity, often figured as maternal. Whether Plath found another version of Wylie's "Mom" in Cornwall, she certainly represents the "you" of the poem as such a figure. This is not Sappho's ideal female community where women shared an intellectual life together. The problem with this community is that women have no intellectual life. Interestingly enough, Plath also wrote to her mother at this time that she would like to start a literary salon when she moved to London, so in taking "steps out," she hoped to form an intellectual community that might help ensure her own survival.

While these poems are clearly intensely personal and respond most pressingly to the breakup of her own marriage, that is only Plath's most immediate subject. Rather, these poems bring together one of the great subjects of Plath's work: the pathologies of a generation of women created by the horrifying postwar control and containment at the center of that society. The speaker does not escape self-criticism. She identifies herself early in the poem as a "pathological liar." The last line of "Lesbos" reads, "Even in your Zen heaven we shan't meet." The single-line stanza that ends this poem echoes "Medusa," which also ends with the single-line rejection, "There is nothing between us." Close to the end of "Lesbos," the speaker says:

> Now I am silent, hate
> Up to my neck,
> Thick, thick.
> I do not speak.
> I am packing the hard potatoes like good clothes,
> I am packing the babies,
> I am packing the sick cats.
> O vase of acid,
> It is love you are full of. . . .
>
> (*CP,* 229)

Like the German guttural sounds ("ich, ich") that choke the speaker of Plath's "Daddy," hate also chokes the speaker here and sets her packing in what seems a grotesque parody of Hughes's exodus, grotesque because the speaker is packing things that need to be cooked and taken care of. Packing is not an escape from domestic duties for her but a live burial in them. In "The Babysitters," the speaker cries, "O what has come over us, my sister!" And in the final stanza, the speaker wonders, "what keyhole have we slipped through, what door has shut?" The speaker's cry in "The Babysitters"—"O what has come over us, my sister"—is answered in the apostrophe of "Lesbos"—"O vase of acid, / It is love you are full of." It is a deadly love, filling the vase that stands at the center of Plath's poem, replacing the sister who has been lost to the domestic catastrophes of the midtwentieth century.

6
"Order[ing] a Box of Maniacs": Questions of Power in the Bee Poems

By all accounts, Sylvia Plath produced the five poems that make up her astonishing bee poem sequence in a tremendous burst of creative energy. She wrote them in six days between October 3 and October 9, 1962, even as Hughes was packing up and moving out of their house at Court Green in Devon. Plath's letters home and to friends during this period alternate between wondering how she is going to survive through another winter in Devon without central heating, without a husband, and with two small children, and a celebration of her own strength and self-sufficiency, her ability to manage in difficult times. As she wrote in one letter to her former Smith College roommate Marcia Brown, she felt "like a very efficient tool or weapon."[1] Certainly these events and concerns acted as an immediate biographical pressure on the production of the poems themselves.

But the seeds of these poems can be found much earlier in Plath's multiple and complex written meditations on power scattered throughout her college journals and essays, which were concentrated around questions of female community and authority, female sexuality, creative production, and reproduction. The bee community is the perfect metaphor, for the hive is valued for its productive capabilities, its ability to produce honey, but its production and survival depend on the manic reproductive capabilities of the queen bee.[2] This all-female community does not compete for men—"they have got rid of the men"—but rather with each other in a duel to become the queen bee. The desired duel of the early Smith poem "Metamorphoses of the Moon" can at last take place.

While the speaker of Plath's poem, the beekeeper, as critics have noted, provocatively takes over the father's role (Plath's father was an entomologist, kept honeybees himself, and wrote a book about bumblebees), this role of power and control is constantly called into question in the sequence, particularly when that power becomes one centered on the history of authoritarian conquest.[3] These five poems investigate the "web" of power relationships that, according to Michel Foucault, ensnare the individual within a mutually reinforcing system of power at the levels of family, community, state, and country. As Foucault suggests, sexuality is a particularly "dense transfer point for relations of power."[4]

Plath had tried this subject relatively unsuccessfully before in her effort to deal with the lost father. Her lack of knowledge about beekeeping, however, may have prevented her from treating the subject very convincingly or even from using the rich metaphorical possibilities that knowledge of beekeeping opened up to her. But Plath finally took up beekeeping seriously in June of 1962 when she reported triumphantly in a letter to her mother, "Today, guess what, we became *beekeepers*!" And she vowed to learn all she could about the subject (*LH*, 457). The year before in August 1961, she, Hughes, and their daughter, Frieda, then just a little over a year old, had moved from London into Court Green, a thatched cottage in North Devon, with three acres of land and orchards where Plath kept her hive of bees. Their son Nicholas was born there in January of 1962. What this newly acquired knowledge of beekeeping gave her was a way to bring together in complex and new ways issues that she had been dealing with since college.

One of those issues was what happens to the individual when he or she is initiated into a community. Plath had written an essay in May 1954 on Erich Fromm's 1941 groundbreaking psychoanalytic study of fascism, *Escape from Freedom*, for her history class. It is in Fromm's work where Plath found a link between individual psychodynamics and the actions of the individual within a larger human community. "Man" has two choices, argued Fromm, in a passage that Plath quotes in her essay. He can either "unite himself with the world in the spontaneity of love and productive work or else . . . seek a kind of security by such ties with the world as destroy his freedom and the integrity of his individual self."[5] This marks the fundamental struggle of much of Plath's work, from the portrait of Smith

College as a Huxlean-style "conditioning center" to the bee poems where the menace of a mechanistic community, the hive, reaches its apex. Along the way, we have the automaton bride and groom of "The Applicant," which might be said to pass into the machinery of war in "Daddy." As Fromm had argued and Plath quoted in her paper, "The appeal of authoritarianism, destructiveness, and automaton conformity has its roots in man's basic psychic need for a sense of community, significance, and security in all spheres of life."[6]

As early as her Smith College journals, Plath saw that this "appeal" could be witnessed in her own community at Smith, but also on the wider political landscape as well. Plath's response to this problem in her history paper and throughout her writing was to ask how one could claim "a spontaneous and creative individuality in the face of powerful, menacing, and even seductive monolithic forces."[7] This seduction is exemplified in one of Plath's most famous lines from "Daddy": "Every woman adores a fascist." Here Plath brings together the fields of sexual and governmental politics and exposes the mutually reinforcing and seductive forces of power that controlled both public and private spaces at midcentury.[8]

In her compelling essay on fascist fantasies in the work of Woolf, Plath, and Jong, Laura Frost treats Plath's often sophisticated appropriation of fascism for poetic purposes with the critical acuity it deserves but has not often received. Frost argues that Plath and Jong investigate fascist "fantasies of domination and submission" that have been "repudiated by progressive politics and particularly by feminism."[9] Plath's work, by understanding that fascism has a libidinally charged component, suggests that "even though institutions change and women gain ground in their struggle to separate from 'Daddy,' . . . he stubbornly persists as an object of sadomasochistic fantasy."[10] Frost argues that, "Fascism signifies a series of opposites for Plath: subjugation and oppression, control and freedom, sadism and masochism, and hate and love."[11] In both Plath and Jong, she argues, "The notion that 'Every woman adores a Fascist' is both a political fallacy and a persistent fantasy."[12] It is a concept that can be read in two ways and Frost argues, "Every woman fantasizes about submission, and every woman fantasizes about domination as an active agent."[13] A little later, I will discuss how Plath investigates this two-pronged fantasy in the bee poems.

Plath explored these issues during her college years in her deep and thoughtful reading of a wide range of writers from Dostoevsky and Joyce to Edith Sitwell. In her history paper, she brings together ideas from her reading in Fromm, Nietzsche, and W. H. Auden. Her interdisciplinary approach, as Al Strangeways has noted, reflects her liberal arts education where students were encouraged to seek "connections between the disciplines."[14] Moreover, Smith allowed Plath even more latitude than other students, allowing her to design her own program of courses and independent study. Her journal entries and college essays draw on her reading from a variety of disciplines to investigate social justice issues on many fronts. Entries on Stepford-like women overlap with those of bombs and war that use almost identical language. In an early entry written in the fall of 1950, Plath writes: "Woman is but an engine of ecstasy, a mimic of the earth from the ends of her curled hair to her red-lacquered nails. . . . Isn't it better to give in to the pleasant cycles of reproduction, the easy, comforting presence of a man around the house?" (*UJ*, 20) The "engine of ecstasy" gives way to the "cycles of reproduction" as the woman takes on her role as postwar baby-making machine. "Most American males," Plath wrote in one journal entry, "worship woman as a sex machine with rounded breasts and a convenient opening in the vagina, as a painted doll who shouldn't have a thought in her pretty head other than cooking a steak dinner and comforting him in bed after a hard 9–5 day at a routine business job" (*UJ*, 36). In her journals, this idea of a woman as a machine to fulfill man's desires, overlaps with mechanistic images of war, concern over the atomic bomb and the military machine of the Cold War. She writes of Nagasaki, Korea, Germany, Russia, and the "million, million microscopic men," the armies plotted on a map that appear in an unpublished poem, "Geography Lesson" (*UJ*, 59–62).[15]

In her analysis of freedom, Plath takes up the question that Fromm posits: How does one establish "a spontaneous and creative individuality" in a time of such stultifying (and seductive) conformity? It was the question that poets across the nation were asking as they responded not only to American society in the postwar period but also to a particular brand of conformity that marked poetry after modernism, as James Breslin has argued.[16] Many of these writers investigated questions of power and control specifically through writing that focused on mental illness and family dynamics. Plath's novel on the subject, *The Bell Jar* (1963), was published at about the same time as Ken Kesey's *One Flew Over the Cuckoo's Nest* (1962). Allen Ginsberg's *Kaddish*, about his own mother's terrifying mental breakdowns, shock treatments, and finally lobotomy, was published in 1959, the same year that the speaker of Lowell's "Skunk Hour" said, "My mind's not right." It is important to keep this context at the forefront of discussions of Plath's work to reestablish the historical moment that produced Plath and her contemporaries. But it is also important to keep in mind that Plath represented her struggle for poetic authority and individual autonomy in the context of all-female community, a battle represented most vividly in the bee poems when the queen bee, rising out of the all-female community of the hive, temporarily leaves behind the "honey drudgers" in her terrible flight.

In her history paper, Plath quotes Auden's poem "September 1939" in order to critique machine-like conformity. She cites the poem as a specific example of our willingness to accept authority without question.[17] In another essay she wrote on Part V of *Twelve Songs*, "Fish in the Unruffled Lakes," she suggests that Auden's concept of love might provide a way of establishing "a spontaneous and creative individuality."[18] She quotes Richard Hoggart as saying of Auden's idea of love that it finds its best expression in community. Loving in the sense that Auden meant it is synonymous with creative living.[19] Plath may be thinking of the final lines of Auden's song when she considers love's possibilities. In the last lines, the speaker praises his lover not only for his swanlike gifts—"Impulsive Nature," "majesty and pride"—but for the "voluntary love" that he bestows upon the speaker, his lover.[20]

Following Fromm's lead, Plath understands the process of creative and individual development in psychoanalytic terms. She compares the interaction between the individual and the world to that of the child and its mother. It is particularly telling that Plath's language is quite gendered in this passage; the child leaves behind the mother and the safety of the "womb."[21] Plath's language usage is similar in letters she wrote to her mother in October, 1962, "Home is impossible," she writes, apparently in response to her mother's suggestion that she return home to help her through the breakup of her marriage: "It would be psychologically the worst thing. I must not go back to the womb or retreat. I must take steps *out*. . . ." (*UJ*, 468–69). But as Plath's essay on Fromm suggests, the metaphor of retreating to the womb had much larger implications than simply returning home to her biological mother. It meant also a retreat to a conformist sense of community—most immediately what that meant for Plath as a woman was the loss of a productive self when she became a reproductive one. Earlier in the Fromm essay, Plath had written, "And [my mind] wants to climb still higher, out of the womblike security of complacent collective values into the realm of strong, individualistic winds."[22] Here, we find the rising metaphor that she uses so often in her writing and that would become important to the poetry as a figure for the emergence of an autonomous self, but it is also here that Plath takes "steps *out*," as she puts it in the letter, from family dynamics to join a larger community—she had begun writing to her mother about moving back to London and starting a literary "salon." It is this movement that is so central to an understanding of the bee poems' sequence, for the poems are all about initiation into a community and what that means for the individual.

Initiation

Most immediately the biographical impetus behind the bee poems is Plath's own initiation into a beekeeping community in a small village in England. The local midwife leads the initiation, thereby locating a female source of authority in the poem. Further, as Tracy Brain has argued, the bee poems investigate "the position of the foreigner in England and graft[] this tension between belonging and not belonging onto a battle concerning gender."[23] But these poems investigate questions of community that go back much farther than Plath's experience in England and have implications that range beyond Plath's immediate circumstances. "The Bee Meeting," the first poem of the sequence, is essentially an initiation ceremony that is ritualistic and frightening. The speaker of the poem is exposed. "I am nude as a chicken neck, does nobody love me?" Because everyone is veiled, except for the speaker initially, she cannot figure out who anyone is, and so the whole thing takes on the menace of a Klan meeting. "Which is the rector now, is it that man in black?" (*CP* 211).

The speaker is led and appears to have no control, as she is still excluded from the knowledge the others appear to possess. But as with all initiation ceremonies, she will soon become part of the group: "They are making me one of them" (CP, 211). Although the villagers are not all women, Plath's imagery throughout this poem suggests that the speaker is being initiated into a female community. As the speaker is led forward, she sees, "Feather dusters fanning their hands in a sea of bean flowers." The "shorn grove" where the villagers lead the speaker to the hives is itself reminiscent of the female body as it might be shaved and prepared for childbirth. Medical imagery throughout suggests some patient "etherized upon a table." The next stanza asks if they are conducting an "operation." All of this is reminiscent of the central sanitized birthing scene in *The Bell Jar*, when Esther Greenwood—because she is dating a medical student—gets to watch a child being born. Plath had just finished the novel when she wrote these poems, and, as Susan Van Dyne has pointed out, was composing the drafts of the bee poems on the back of pages of *The Bell Jar* manuscript. The bee poems were actually drafted on the back of this particular chapter. The images of both kinds of initiation are strikingly similar. In this scene, what Esther describes is anything but "natural" childbirth: "I was so struck by the sight of the table where they were lifting the woman I didn't say a word. It looked like some awful torture table, with these metal stirrups sticking up in mid-air at one end and all sorts of instruments and wires and tubes I couldn't make out properly at the other" (*BJ*, 65). The woman's "split, shaven place between her legs," as Esther describes it, is "lurid with disinfectant" out of which eventually a "fuzzy thing" emerges (*BJ*, 66). Women clearly have no control over this oddly sterile process. The doctors are dressed in "lime-green coats and skull caps" in *The Bell Jar* chapter; in "The Bee Meeting," the villagers stand around waiting for "the surgeon" who arrives as "this apparition in a green helmet." In the same chapter of *The Bell Jar*, Esther is initiated into another kind of strangely sterile scene when Buddy Willard suggests that they get naked together but don't actually have sex since as Esther makes clear, she is supposed to remain a virgin until marriage. When he takes off his clothes and stands before her, she only stares at him: "The only thing I could think of was turkey neck and turkey gizzards and I felt very depressed" (*BJ*, 69). The scene makes Buddy vulnerable, a vulnerability shared by the speaker in the bee poems whose exposure is compared to a chicken neck.

WOMAN AS ENGINE, REPRODUCTIVE MACHINE

Long before writing the bee poem sequence, Plath had used machine and insect metaphors to describe female sexuality in journal entries she wrote at Smith. As I suggested earlier, in one 1950 journal entry woman as "engine of ecstasy" gives way to the "cycles of reproduction" as the woman takes on her role as postwar baby-making machine. In either case, she exists to provide her services to a man. As the speaker of Plath's "The Applicant," written just two days after the last of the bee poems, puts it, this automaton woman is "willing / To bring teacups and roll away headaches / And do whatever you tell it" (*CP*, 221). In a Kafkaesque journal entry, dated May 5, 1953, Plath imagines what it would be like to marry a rather pathetic and unsuitable man she has recently dated: "All your life long feeling big and swollen, lying like mother earth on your back and being raped by a humming entranced insect and begetting thousands of little white eggs in a gravel pit" (*UJ*, 181).

She invokes the insect metaphor again in a paper she wrote for a Russian class she took at Smith—this time to designate the negative effects of community, which could produce a "collective mass of weaklings in the Grand Inquisitor's prosperous ant-heap."[24] In these journal entries and in Plath's Smith college writing, we have the beginnings of the overlapping concerns that would culminate in the bee poems—questions of productive and reproductive control; the costs of "automaton conformity," as Fromm had called it;[25] the menace and possibility of an all-female community; and, as Plath had noted in her history paper on Fromm, Auden, and Nietzsche, "the affirmation of a spontaneous and creative individuality in the face of powerful, menacing, and even seductive monolithic forces."[26]

Questions of control for women over their sexuality and reproduction were, and remain absolutely central to their lives in a way that they have never been for men. While Plath was in college, not only are we looking at a period before *Roe v. Wade,* but it was illegal in Massachusetts for anyone to provide even birth control information, let alone contraception to unmarried women. Plath addresses this problem in a central passage in *The Bell Jar* where Esther equates birth control with freedom not to become a slave or machine.[27] Though it is illegal, she has been able to get an appointment for birth control through her female psychoanalyst who knows the doctor. After a long wait in the examining room when she reads an issue of *Baby Talk* and thinks she is "so unmaternal and apart" for not wanting one, Esther finally goes into the examination room for her fitting: "I climbed up on the examination table, thinking: 'I am climbing to freedom, freedom from fear, freedom from marrying the wrong person . . . just because of sex'" (*BJ*, 223).

The way that the bee poems treat fertility is complex and informed by Plath's written investigations of it throughout her life, as well as her personal experiences of childbirth and how that experience contrasted with a typical American birth at the time. The birth of Nicholas in England was very different from the American birth she describes in *The Bell Jar*. She had the baby at home with very little intervention, as she describes it in a letter to her mother (*LH*, 442–43). The midwife "sat at one side of the bed and Ted on the other, gossiping pleasantly together," while Plath sucked in gas from the cylinder the midwife had brought to ease her pain during contractions (*LH*, 443). Finally, all participated completely in the messiness of birth, as Plath describes it, as "this great bluish, glistening boy shot out onto the bed in a tidal wave of water that drenched all four of us to the skin, howling lustily" (*LH*, 443). The doctor didn't even make it in time. This is clearly a scene in which Plath, at least as she relates it, had a lot more control over the birthing process; and it was far less medicalized and sanitized than the typical American birth of the early 1960s.

The bee poems suggest a sterile environment, as well, perhaps providing the only environment where the beekeeper, as a kind of surgeon, can take control over the means of production. In the initial poem, "The white hive is snug as a virgin, / Sealing off her brood cells, her honey, and quietly humming" (*CP,* 212). At the end of the second poem, "The Arrival of the Bee Box," the speaker recognizes the power she has as a newly initiated beekeeper. "Tomorrow I will be sweet God, I will set them free" (*CP,* 213). In the third poem of the series, "Stings," the speaker has developed enough confidence in her abilities to work "bare-handed." But from the beginning, the images are both highly sexualized and paradoxically chaste, as the beekeeper and her instructor, a "man in white," work together: "He and

I // Have a thousand clean cells between us" (*CP,* 214). The imagery here suggests the sterility of the hospital, the man in white a kind of doctor, but it also seems like a wedding ceremony of sorts. Hughes has suggested in *Birthday Letters,* his 1998 poetic response to Plath's *Ariel* poems, that this was a staged wedding between Plath and the mythic father, which closed Hughes out of the picture: "I never guessed a wedding," the speaker tells us in "The Bee God"; "But you bowed over your bees / As you bowed over your Daddy."[28] Plath's own early bee poem, "The Beekeeper's Daughter" (1959), suggests this reading in its last line, "The queen bee marries the winter of your year" (*CP,* 118).

This reading is plausible, if a bit reductive, saying more, perhaps, about Hughes's attachment to the myth than Plath's. Or perhaps Plath is merely taunting Hughes here with a parodic primal scene. Plath had a rather wicked sense of humor, as she demonstrated in *The Bell Jar.* The instructor and the newly initiated beekeeper are passing clean cells between them in a mock bridal night, a parody of the "bride flight" mentioned in the first poem where the queen copulates with as many males as she can. The scene also shares imagery with Plath's 1961 poem "The Surgeon at 2 a.m." In that poem, the speaker ventriloquizes the voice of the surgeon himself, who moves confidently through the hospital. "I am the sun, in my white coat, / Gray faces, shuttered by drugs, follow me like flowers" (*CP,* 171). The death in life image of the gray faces is repeated in the grayness of the brood cells, which "terrify" the speaker, "they seem so old."

The speaker identifies a "third person" who watches, who is superfluous, and "has nothing to do with the bee-seller or with me." Plath ties this figure to Hughes in a letter she writes to her mother. The voyeur that he is literally runs away and is gone, "in eight great bounds, a great scapegoat," in an image that casts him more as a big, silly dog than a man. He loses clothing as he goes, further shedding any claim to power, first one "slipper," then another, then the "square of white linen / He wore instead of a hat" (*CP,* 215). Although he watches, he literally has no control of vision in the scene. Plath had been eviscerating Hughes's creative power throughout the poems of these years—most notably in a poem not chosen for *Ariel,* "Burning the Letters," where Hughes's emblematic animal, the fox, is gutted in the last lines (*CP,* 205). In "The Detective," another Hughes animal, the crow, shadows the scene of a crime, which the reader learns is the "vaporization" of a woman through the gradual silencing of her voice in marriage (*CP,* 209). Moreover, in this poem from the bee sequence, he plays the scapegoat, a word that wickedly anticipates the role he would actually play for some of Plath's supporters after her death, further intensifying the delicious dismissiveness of this passage; but it doesn't last. Rather, the speaker remembers her own longing as she looks after him, disappearing: "He was sweet, // The sweat of his efforts a rain / Tugging the world to fruit," a reprise of the longing and loss the speaker expresses in the lines from "The Moon and the Yew Tree, "how I would like to believe in tenderness" (*CP,* 215). The lines echo the sexual imagery that precedes these lines where we find the hive "Opening in spring, like an industrious virgin / To scour the creaming crests / As the moon, for its ivory powders, scours the sea" (*CP,* 215).

Both the movement of the hive "opening" in spring, as well as the implied opening of the speaker to her lover, is without violence or coersion but freely given in both cases, and in each instance the opening yields sweetness—honey and fruit. There is no rape scene; rather, within this space, there is some suggestion of the creative possibilities of both production and reproduction, except that Plath identifies the hive as an "industrious virgin," suggesting a machinery that is at odds with the natural imagery of spring and rebirth that follows. Moreover, sweetness, as Plath so often has shown in her poetry, can hide deception, as indeed it does in this case, and "the bees found him out" and turn on him, "Molding onto his lips like lies, / Complicating his features" (*CP,* 215). It is almost as if with the recognition of longing, the speaker must double the punishment to protect herself.

This primal scene, as it were, is interrupted though with a moment when the speaker identifies intensely with the bees. Despite the seeming mastery of the situation, feelings of terror and shame mingle in the speaker's mind, further suggesting the feelings associated with a primal scene. The queen is "old." She is "poor and bare and unqueenly and even shameful" (*CP,* 214). The speaker imagines herself then as one of the queen's attendants:

> I stand in a column
>
> Of winged, unmiraculous women,
> Honey-drudgers.

> I am no drudge
> Though for years I have eaten dust
> And dried plates with my dense hair.
>
> And seen my strangeness evaporate,
> Blue dew from dangerous skin.
> Will they hate me,
> These women who only scurry,
> Whose news is the open cherry, the open clover?
> <div align="right">(<i>CP</i>, 214)</div>

Here the identification with the all-female worker bee community signifies powerlessness; she is reduced to domestic drudgery, her productivity destroyed; and her "strangeness" evaporates into the glow produced by electroshock therapy, the ultimate 1950s medical answer to wayward and deviant personalities. Yet the speaker worries about being accepted and liked by this community. The question, as the bee poems make clear, is one of power. How different can one be?

Plath explored this question quite exhaustively in her journals and in various college stories about initiation, always investigated in terms of female community. Shortly after moving to Smith, Plath was awakened by a fire drill, and she and the other women in her house filed outside. Plath wrote in her journal, "So this is what we have to learn to be part of a community: to respond blindly, unconsciously to electric sirens shrilling in the middle of night. I hate it. But someday I have to learn—someday—" (*UJ*, 23). Again, we are reminded of Alfred Kazin's class at Smith where Plath is "appalled at the weak, mealy-mouthed apathy of the girls" (*LH*, 147). This is just one example among many of how Plath portrayed herself as standing apart from the "honey-drudgers," which no doubt she did, since any reading of her work at Smith clearly shows how much she did, in fact, distinguish herself in comparison with other undergraduates. At the end of the poem, the stupidity of the honey drudgers is exemplified in their suicidal stinging of the intruder. "They thought death was worth it," the speaker claims. The speaker, identified briefly with the queen bee, but now reclaiming the power of the beekeeper and the queen, rises above this deathlike conformity:

> ... but I
> Have a self to recover, a queen.
> Is she dead, is she sleeping?

> Where has she been,
> With her lion-red body, her wings of glass?
>
> Now she is flying
> More terrible than she ever was, red
> Scar in the sky, red comet
> Over the engine that killed her—
> The mausoleum, the wax house.
>   (*CP*, 215)

The queen's obvious poetic analogs are Lady Lazarus who "eats men like air" and "God's lioness" in "Ariel," as Tim Kendall has pointed out.[29] In this case the queen rises out of the ashes of a dead marriage, even a dead female community, represented by the way that the worker bees conform to the male lips. It is, after all, a mausoleum that is associated quite distinctly with adversarial sisterhood in the 1961 poem "The Rival" where the speaker points out that the Medusa-like rival's "first gift is making stone out of everything," and the speaker "wake[s] to a mausoleum" (*CP* 166).

Napolean

The queen's flight out of the hive initiates the swarm of the next poem in the sequence, which begins with the most violent and extreme solution to swarming behavior—that is, shooting the bees down. "The Swarm," the fourth poem of the sequence, calls attention to the power dynamics already set up in the previous poems and aligns them with the history of power in the figure of Napoleon. Because of the power issues already raised in the second of the sequence, "The Arrival of the Bee Box," these two poems work as a pair that aligns the beekeeper's declaration "Tomorrow I will be sweet God" with the egomania of Napoleon's dictatorship (*CP*, 213). Plath may have adopted Napoleon as her central figure due to the immediate fact that she had been commissioned by the *New Statesman* to write a review of Hubert Cole's *Josephine*, a biography of Napolean's wife.[30] The fact that the poem was left out of the British edition indicates how difficult readers have found it to fit this poem into the sequence. Plath herself seems to have been unsure about the "fit" of this poem as she included it on the contents page of the *Ariel* manuscript with parentheses around it, but did not include it in the manuscript itself.[31] The poem dramatizes another aspect of beekeeping, something you want to avoid if you have a hive, and that is the possibility of the bees swarming and deserting the hive. Plath metaphorically links this crisis to Napoleon's army deserting.

"The Swarm," an essential but sometimes puzzling poem in the bee sequence, seems to make a political statement about ambition and its costs that can be linked to questions about the poet's ambition. In a journal entry she wrote in October 1959, Plath suggests this connection when she writes, "Ideas are tyrants to me: the ideas of my jealous, queen-bitch super-ego: what I should, what I ought" (*UJ*, 520). Plath seems to have realized well enough the dangers of personal ambition, and yet in claiming ambition as the prerogative of her own super-ego, she rejects the social norm. A woman's superego at this time should police her own ambition, not spur it on.

Moreover, Plath's complex overlapping of personal tyrant (one's own superego) with local tyrant (the beekeeper but also the villagers) with historical tyrant (Napoleon), really cannot be understood without recourse to Plath's extensive reading in psychological theory. Unlike the women who came to speak at Smith or wrote about the need for women to "sublimate" their desires, adopting a pseudo-Freudian discourse, Plath really read Freud and knew his work well, as well as those writers who used Freud's theories in sophisticated ways to understand human history, such as Erich Fromm.

To make this connection, I need to return for a moment to "The Arrival of the Bee Box," a poem that might be said to be the more localized representation of the global power relations of "The Swarm." When her box of bees arrives in "The Arrival of the Bee Box," the second poem in the sequence, the newly initiated beekeeper tells us in the fifth stanza that "I have simply ordered a box of maniacs" (*CP*, 213). The adverb is telling. On the one hand, she has "simply ordered" the box of bees, which she can send back if she wants. She doesn't have to do this; it is in her power and under her control to refuse or reject what she cannot master. "They can be sent back. / They can die, I need feed them nothing, I am the owner" (*CP*, 213). So on that level, the problem is simple. But the word "maniacs" makes it not so simple. Plath is most certainly drawing on the Greek origin of the word *maniac,* meaning divine madness or passion, as well as on the later clinical meaning of the word. The narrative of the bee poems, as the drafts suggest, is at least in part about the poet her-

6 / "ORDER[ING] A BOX OF MANIACS"

self trying to bring her own "madness" under control, as well as her creative power.

On another level, the poet/beekeeper is trying to make sense out of, make order out of, what at this point seems like a Roman mob. And, since she describes this problem specifically in terms of ordering language—"the unintelligible syllables," "The Arrival of the Bee Box" asks how the poet is to order language. How does the poet control language and become "the owner"? The poet's difficulty finding or ordering or speaking language fluently is dramatized in "Daddy," where the father's German and its links to a totalitarian past get stuck in the speaker's throat. Here, in the bee poems, metaphorical language seems elusive, the "unintelligible syllables," the "Roman mob," or even "furious Latin" that needs to be brought under control. And finally, it is a "box of maniacs" that has been ordered and defies ordering. The simultaneous link to madness and desire of the plural *maniacs* provides an opportunity to contextualize Plath's ambition, as well as her search for a language to convey it, for the word "maniac" also speaks to the poet's ambition.

The speaker's power, though, is also linked to larger historical issues of power, specifically slavery:

> I put my eye to the grid.
> It is dark, dark,
> With the swarmy feeling of African hands
> Minute and shrunk for export,
> Black on black, angrily clambering.
> (*CP,* 213)

A similar word usage links this passage on slavery to the slavery of femininity suggested in Plath's psychoanalytic sessions when she expresses the need to escape the "smarmy matriarchy of togetherness" fostered by her mother (*UJ,* 429). These hands pose a threat, just as the bees do, because they can swarm, they can refuse to be controlled, or, in the case of Napoleon's army, they can desert. I don't believe Plath is co-opting historical catastrophes to represent extreme psychological states, but rather she is using these events to link the dangers of extreme psychological states to political issues. After all, Plath had extensive experience with how the medical profession treated those who did not conform, and, as Foucault has shown, the medical profession is just one level of the web of power. Plath's imagery here plays in sophisticated ways on the commodification of African slaves, as well; their hands are "shrunk for export." Besides, Plath implicates herself in the web of power in one of the most disturbing but revealing statements of her poetry, "Every woman adores a fascist," the speaker proclaims in "Daddy" (*CP*, 223).

An inability to make this connection between the personal and the political in Plath has led some scholars to abandon feminism in reading "The Swarm." Lynda Bundtzen, for example, tells us that she is going to move her reading of Plath's "The Swarm" in a "less overtly feminist direction in terms of how Plath unites the personal and the political."[32] Why? Is Plath's complex investigation of power relationships less feminist here than it is elsewhere? The imagery that describes Napoleon's defeat at Waterloo also echoes the imagery at the end of the first bee poem, "The Bee Meeting." In the last stanza the speaker compares herself to "the magician's girl who does not flinch." In "The Swarm," the speaker tells Napoleon, "It is you the knives are out for / At Waterloo, Waterloo . . . " (*CP*, 216). The shift in subject positions is complex here; first, Napoleon is seen as a victim of his own army's desertion, yet in the next stanza, the speaker addresses Napolean as the victimizer, "These are chess people you play with. . . . / The mud squirms with throats, / Stepping stones for French bootsoles," which in turn is an echo of the "swarmy" African hands (*CP*, 216). But although the poem continually refers to Napoleon's defeat and the desertion of his armies, in the end the bees are eventually brought under control:

> The dumb, banded bodies
> Walking the plank draped with Mother France's upholstery
> Into a new mausoleum,
> An ivory palace, a crotch pine.
>
> (*CP*, 217)

The honeybee was an important emblem for France during Napoleon's reign, and everything was embroidered with this insignia. But the reference to "Mother France" makes it a specifically gendered reference as well, reminding us again of those women stitching the story of woman's entrapment into their samplers in an early Plath poem "Virgin in a Tree." In the end, the bees simply do as they are told, returning once again to the "mausoleum," with their "black intractable mind" (*CP*, 217). The poem emphasizes the collective conformity of this "black ball," "A flying hedgehog, all prickles" (*CP,* 216). In the end, order is restored and Napoleon (as beekeeper) revels in conquest, suggesting in complex ways the speaker's own complicity in these power relationships:

> Napolean is pleased, he is pleased with everything.
> O Europe! O ton of honey!
>
> (*CP,* 217)

The final poem, "Wintering," shifts uneasily, adopting a variety of stances towards power. Initially, the beekeeper establishes control:

> This is the easy time, there is nothing doing.
> I have whirled the midwife's extractor,
> I have my honey,
> Six jars of it,
> Six cat's eyes in the wine cellar . . .
>
> (*CP,* 217)

But the basement room where the honey is stored in jars (a terrible echo of the scene of Plath's first suicide attempt in 1953) takes on a menacing quality:

> This is the room I have never been in.
> This is the room I could never breathe in.
> The black bunched in there like a bat,
> No light . . .
>
> (*CP,* 218)

Midway through the fourth stanza, the beekeeper loses control:

> . . .
> Possession.
> It is they who own me.
> Neither cruel nor indifferent,
>
> Only ignorant.
>
> (*CP,* 218)

In a reprise of Napoleon's army, the bees file "like soldiers / To the syrup tin // To make up for the honey I've taken" (*CP,* 218). Who is in control here? The whole world is frozen in a porcelain smile, "a mile-long body of Meissen," this poem seems to suggest, the "Black /

Mind" of the bees in a ball against all that white. Unlike the moment when the queen bee rises in "Stings," I am not convinced of the hopefulness of this female community. Although the men are clumsy bumblers, the female community of the hive does not fare much better. In the final lines, a lone woman sits by a cradle, knitting. She is cold and "too dumb to think."

While the final stanza offers the consolation of survival, for the bees fly out of the hive in the spring, I agree with Van Dyne's reading that the hope is tentative, not transcendent, as some critics have claimed.[33] Plath's investigations of power are simply too complex to argue for transcendence. Plath's knowledge and investigation of the power relations that circumscribed her life came too early for her to find a way out; her whole experience (combined with her temperament and very real struggle with mental illness) was too much of a Huxlean-style conditioning. Rather, Plath made *steps out* only through the effect her work and life had on the next wave of feminists, who read her work with shock and recognition.

"Could the world really be like this. . . ?"

Sandra Gilbert's now classic feminist essay on the Plath myth initiates that first wave. Gilbert begins with Plath's college writing, which she discovered while still a high school student. She read Plath's college story "Den of Lions," which was published in 1951 in *Seventeen*. Gilbert recalls that, although the plot of "Den of Lions" "was fairly conventional," the story affected her in "inexplicable, almost 'mythic' ways."[34] She writes, "Could the world really be like this, I wondered. Was it like this? How had selves of blood and meat been admitted into the glossily sanitized pages of *Seventeen*? How could anyone so close to my own age have imagined such selves?"[35]

Gilbert herself followed Plath's path as guest editor of *Mademoiselle*, just four years later, and they shared the same editor, fictionalized as Jay Cee in *The Bell Jar*. Years later, after the feminist movement brought to consciousness the domestic slavery of a generation of women, Gilbert realized, "What I had unconsciously responded to in 'Den of Lions,' what had made me uneasy about it, was probably that it was a story of female initiation, an account of how one girl learns to see herself as intelligent meat—victim and manipulator of men, costumes, drinks, cigarettes—flesh and artifice together."[36] Gilbert writes that the *Mademoiselle* experience itself "was a kind of initiation ritual, a dramatic induction into that glittery Women's House of fashion and domesticity. . . . We had entered the house of female work."³⁷ As female workers, they were given "tokens of what we were and where we were" by the editors and staff, "tokens quite unlike those we had become accustomed to at school. Instead of tests or books or grades, for instance, they gave us *clothes*."³⁸

On February 11, 1963, Plath committed suicide, but left on her desk the completed manuscript of *Ariel*. The British edition of *Ariel* with Hughes's additions and deletions was published in 1965, and the American edition came out in 1966. But Plath's completed manuscript belongs to 1963, along with Adrienne Rich's *Snapshots of a Daughter-in-Law* and Betty Friedan's *The Feminine Mystique*. Each of these books has been described by one woman or another as "eye-openers," books that were instrumental in initiating them into the second wave of feminism, a wave that transformed the women's college once again into a place of activism and a catalyst for change. In *Ariel*, Plath had successfully created herself as a virago not only of the new poetry but of the feminist movement itself. Her years at Smith College, it turns out, overlap with those of Gloria Steinem. And although all of it came too late for Plath, her influence as part of this wave should not be underestimated.

Early in her career at Smith, Plath wrote an entry on the bombing of Nagasaki: "They're really going to mash the world up this time, the damn fools," she wrote after reading a description of the Japanese victims. "God save us from doing that again. For the United States did that. Our guilt. My country" (*UJ*, 46). Here, as in her meditation on Napoleon, she claims both national and personal guilt. As part of a nation that murders, she, too, might be implicated as a murderer. Her entry ranges freely from Nagasaki to the atomic bomb tests in Nevada to the Germans to the Russians. "What could we do with the Russian nation if we bombed it to bits? How could we 'rule' such a mass of foreign people. . . . How could we control them under our 'democratic system,' we who even now are losing that precious commodity, freedom of speech?" (*UJ*, 46). Plath notes that her own beloved high school teacher, Mr. Crockett, "was questioned by the town board" as a possible subversive. "All he is is a pacifist," she writes. "That, it seems, is a crime" (*UJ*, 46). Plath's writing here is as passionate as any of her writing that addresses the curtailment of her own personal liberties, and in the bee poems, she fashioned a poetry that was able to do what her Smith College journals could do—that is, move flexibly between the registers of the personal and the historical, the personal and the political. I think it is Plath's ability here and elsewhere in her work to establish what Fromm had called "a spontaneous and creative individuality" in a time when Auden's "evolving conception of love" no longer seemed possible that continues to make Plath relevant to her best readers, readers who can respond to the life, not the death. "How I would like to believe in tenderness," Plath had written in her 1961 poem "The Moon and the Yew Tree." But what she also wrote about was ". . . hate / Up to my neck, / Thick, thick." Her *Ariel* volume, as she arranged the manuscript, true to the New Critical principles she learned in college, began with the word "love," she noted, and ended with the word "spring." Even as Plath recorded and absorbed the hate that dominated this period, she wanted to believe in something else, and she wanted us to believe it, too.

Coda

IN HER 1989 POETRY COLLECTION, *NURTURE*, MAXINE KUMIN INCLUDES a poem called "Marianne, My Mother, and Me." The poem is an act of reclaiming mothers—both biological and literary ones. Kumin writes of her own mother, as well as Marianne Moore, claiming her as a poetic foremother. I discovered this poem in the early stages of this project, and it has remained uncannily relevant to the literary history of women poets and the women's college experience, since Kumin's own women's college experience provides the significant institutional and historical context for her individual exploration.

The poem begins with Marianne Moore arriving for an iconic modernist "*dejeuner sur l'erbe*" at Alfred Kreymborg's house in the country before the Great War, and, as the speaker tells us, ". . . everyone / sits on the ground in attitudes of such grace / that tears come into my eyes for what is gone, // for the intensity of it."[1] Kumin notes that Moore is the same age as her mother and then contrasts Moore's cool elegance with her own mother's lack of control, as "housebound," she becomes "crazed with her first born," so much so that she "opens the lid of the Steinway with an axe" (41).

As a student herself, Kumin tries on Moore's words "like a negligee," but she notes the lack of other female role models during her years as an undergraduate at Radcliffe. "But not once in my four years as a Cliffie, / humble in Harvard Yard, do I find that phantom / I long for, a woman professor, trailed by her covey" (42). Later at Wellesley in the 1950s, Kumin, then a "freshman English instructor" and a "freshman poet," hears Moore read her poetry, "but the black tricorn bending low deflects / that flat small voice from reaching anyone" (43). What Kumin sees is "an eccentric spinster / whom I can't emulate, however much / I admire her words that 'cluster like chromosomes'" (43–44). Throughout the poem, Kumin reports on the doings of both her mother and Moore in parallel lines, and in the end: ". . . I claim them both as mine / . . . both shapers of my alphabet" (45–46).

Kumin's poem speaks to the profound human longing for recognition, support, and approval from a woman whom we can admire, who has done something with her life—that female professor with her "covey" of female students, for poetic models, for a new kind of woman. Adrienne Rich's similar search for female role models in poetry caused her to reject Moore and initially Bishop and search for Emily Dickinson at home in Amherst.[2] Rich, who graduated from Radcliffe in 1951, has been at the forefront of debates over the future of the women's college. In 1984 she addressed the students at Scripps College in her lecture "The Soul of a Women's College" in which she asked questions that have been central to the debates about women's colleges since Emily Dickinson's time. "Is a women's college a place for women to be protected or a place for women's empowerment? . . . . What is a women's college for? . . . . What does it mean to educate women?"[3] Rich did not ask, as Freud had done, "What do women want?" She asked rather, "What do women need?" in order to thrive. The answer seems to be that women need other women, or perhaps I should say that women need intellectually powerful women.

One of the best recent statements of what women need again emerges from the women's college. Jill Ker Conway's elegant memoir of her decade as president of Smith College from 1975 to 1985 speaks to those heady days when the women's college was again able to advance an agenda to transform women's lives through its engagement with the second wave of feminism, the feminist wave, I might add, that made it possible for Kumin to reclaim both her mother and Marianne Moore.

Conway's penultimate chapter, "The Politics of Women's Education," returns us to many of the questions that M. Carey Thomas herself faced at the beginning of the century as president of Bryn Mawr. As president of Smith, Conway wanted to focus on women's minds, but found that she could not avoid addressing their sexuality. Conway notes that one of her challenges as a college president was to address perceived notions of women as not interested in the life of the mind. Why, her questioners often asked, do you want to run a women's school? Why would women want to be educated separately?

She realized that the "subtext" of these questions was that "if women chose to be educated separately from men, their reasons couldn't be intellectual—they must be sexual and involve sexual rejection of males."[4] Conway realized that such homophobia, which she had assumed to be a "redneck reaction of the undereducated," was something that she would have to face "daily from highly educated professionals, male and female, and from all places in the political spectrum."[5] When Conway told questioners that "Smith educated ... people's minds, and their sexuality was no business of our administration, ... that answer didn't satisfy."[6] When Conway asked whether the questioner thought the administration should be policing the sex lives of male students and faculty at Harvard, Yale, and Dartmouth, the questioner would reply that that was different. "What young men did was their own business, but society still had ownership in women's sexuality and should control it."[7] Conway speaks to how "illuminating" these conversations were; and she found they were instrumental in "convert[ing] my standard liberal commitment to tolerance to a passionate defense of gay rights, because I came to see those rights as fundamental feminist issues. They were part of the fight for women to own every aspect of themselves and not to be a form of property."[8]

Conway's thoughts about these issues suggest that female sexuality and reproduction continue to circumscribe the lives of women in higher education in ways that they simply do not for men. On every level, the debates over women in higher education have had to contend with definitions of female sexuality that mitigate the life of the mind. All the poets I have considered in this study have dealt with that split in some way.

Like M. Carey Thomas before her, Conway wanted to focus on "the work," the intellectual life, but found that there were other issues that had to be confronted as well. Thomas had said, "Women, like men, find their greatest happiness in congenial work." And, like Thomas, Conway recognizes that what she had experienced of women's lives was not well represented in writing: "Watching generations of young women grow intellectually, discover intellectual vocations, and begin to take charge of their lives had been a powerful experience. I couldn't find that women's story written about much.... We clearly needed more writers who could make the serious woman intellectual's life experience come alive for both women and men."[9]

Conway warns that "the sentimental view of the female—which emphasize[s] maternal bonding, blurred or permeable boundaries to the female personality, and intuitive versus rational knowledge" has reemerged among "young women eager to mute or call a truce in the gender wars."[10] Such a view, Conway argues, ignores "the rationale and institutional framework for women's intellectual life, something still quite problematic in many areas of scholarly inquiry, and something of critical importance for the future."[11] In discussing the work of Moore, Bishop, and Plath, I have tried to recreate that institutional framework.

As an undergraduate myself of a women's college in the years from 1976 to 1980, I loved the independence and the focus on the life of the mind, so different from my experience of high school. Unlike the colleges I study here, my women's college was not elite, but it nevertheless helped to form, in ways that I am only beginning to realize now, the scholar in me. And despite its limitations, the women's college has held tremendous potential throughout its history for women's growth and transformation. That transformative potential has been at the heart of this study, always tempered by the knowledge that such potential is only ever provisional and contingent. As a professor at a liberal arts college, I still believe in that potential, and occasionally I work with a student who, like the scholar hero of Marianne Moore's poem, might possibly make the journey in those four years from undergraduate to student.

Notes

Introduction

1. I prefer Moore's more complex 1932 version of this poem published in *Poetry* magazine as part of the sequence "Part of a Novel, Part of a Poem, Part of a Play." However, I have quoted from the revised *Complete Poems* version here, because the lines more succinctly convey the essence of the poem's message. See Marianne Moore, *The Complete Poems of Marianne Moore* (New York: Penguin, 1981), 101. Subsequent quotations from this work are cited parenthetically in the text.

2. More work has been done on women's colleges and narrative practice than on poetic practice. One of the best is Susan Leonardi's study of women's colleges and the narrative practice of British writers Dorothy Sayers and Vera Brittain. I am particularly interested in Leonardi's study because she looks at the attempts of these writers to find representation for the educated New Woman and her college experience. See Susan J. Leonardi, *Dangerous by Degrees: Women at Oxford and the Somerville College Novelists* (New Brunswick, NJ: Rutgers University Press, 1989). See also Shirley Marchalonis, *College Girls: A Century in Fiction* (New Brunswick, NJ: Rutgers University Press, 1995). Marchalonis looks at the representation of college women in popular fiction, as well as in the small press fiction produced by the alumnae of the women's colleges themselves.

3. Gail McDonald, *Learning to Be Modern: Pound, Eliot, and the American University* (Oxford: Clarendon Press, 1993), vi.

4. Lynn D. Gordon, *Gender and Higher Education in the Progressive Era* (New Haven, CT: Yale University Press, 1990), 10.

5. Ibid., 3.

6. Helen Lefkowitz Horowitz, *The Power and Passion of M. Carey Thomas* (New York: Alfred A. Knopf, 1994), 407.

7. Ibid.

8. Ibid., 321.

9. In a fascinating article on Marianne Moore and portraiture, Stacy Carson Hubbard argues that Moore drew on the Mannerist style to represent herself in photographs and paintings made of her throughout her life. Hubbard argues, "In her portraits, Moore visually 'quotes' a body of Renaissance art and literature which makes of the ungloved hand and the artful arrangement of double-jointed digits an intricate vocabulary of desire and power." Perhaps it was the Thomas portrait that originally inspired her to present herself in this way. See Stacy Carson Hub-

bard, "Mannerist Moore: Poetry, Painting, Photography," in *Critics and Poets on Marianne Moore: "A Right Good Salvo of Barks,"* ed. Robin G. Schulze (Lewisburg, PA: Bucknell University Press, 2005), 118.

10. Gordon, *Gender and Higher Education*, 38.

11. Barbara Miller Solomon, *In the Company of Educated Women: A History of Women and Higher Education in America* (New Haven, CT: Yale University Press, 1985), 162.

12. Gordon, *Gender and Higher Education*, 39.

13. Michel Foucault, *The History of Sexuality, Vol. I: An Introduction*, trans. Robert Hurley (New York: Vintage Books, 1980), 101.

14. "Editorial," *Con Spirito* 1, no. 1 (February 1933): 1.

15. Solomon, *In the Company of Educated Women*, 191.

16. Ibid., 194.

17. Ibid.

18. "Most of Smith Single: Only 112 Sport Rings," *Scan*, May 15, 1951, 1. Solomon reports, "In 1957 the average woman in the United States married at age twenty; the typical college woman, if she graduated, married somewhat later, at the age of twenty-two or twenty-three" (Solomon, 195).

19. Ibid, 194.

20. Eugenia Kaledin, *Mothers and More: American Women in the 1950s* (Boston: Twayne Publishers, 1984), 51.

21. Lillian Faderman, *Odd Girls and Twilight Lovers: A History of Lesbian Life in Twentieth-Century America* (New York: Penguin, 1991), 150 and 57.

22. Solomon, *In the Company of Educated Women*, 97.

23. Katherine H. Adams, *A Group of Their Own: College Writing Courses and American Women Writers, 1880–1940* (Albany: State University of New York Press, 2001), 67 and 60.

24. Betsy Erkkila, *The Wicked Sisters: Women Poets, Literary History & Discord* (New York: Oxford University Press, 1992), 4.

25. Ibid., 3.

26. Elizabeth Bishop, "As We Like It: Miss Moore and Edgar Allan Poe," *Quarterly Review of Literature* 4, no. 2 (1948): 135.

27. See Patricia Ann Palmieri, *In Adamless Eden: The Community of Women Faculty at Wellesley* (New Haven, CT: Yale University Press, 1995), xx.

28. Roland Barthes, *The Pleasure of the Text*, trans. Richard Miller (New York: The Noonday Press, 1975), 4.

29. Ibid.

30. See Susan Rubin Suleiman, *Subversive Intent: Gender, Politics, and the Avant Garde* (Cambridge, MA: Harvard University Press, 1990).

31. Joan Wallach Scott, *Gender and the Politics of History* (New York: Columbia University Press, 1988), 8.

1. To Work "Lovingly"

1. Letter to Bryher dated August 31, 1921. In Marianne Moore, *The Selected Letters of Marianne Moore*, ed. Bonnie Costello, Celeste Goodridge, and Cristanne

Miller (New York: Alfred A. Knopf, 1997), 178. Subsequent quotations from this work are cited parenthetically in the text.

2. Bryher was the name used by the novelist Winifred Ellerman, who was also H. D.'s lover and literary patron.

3. According to Solomon, women of the second generation attended college between 1890 and 1910. Solomon, *In the Company of Educated Women*, 95.

4. Gordon, *Gender and Higher Education*, 1.

5. Carroll Smith-Rosenberg, "The Female World of Love and Ritual: Relations between Women in Nineteenth-Century America," in *Disorderly Conduct: Visions of Gender in Victorian America* (New York: Oxford University Press, 1985), 53–76.

6. Gordon, *Gender and Higher Education*, 1.

7. Ibid., 36.

8. Ibid., 39.

9. McDonald's book is entitled *Learning to Be Modern*.

10. I am indebted to Robin Schulze's indispensable volume, Marianne Moore, *Becoming Marianne Moore: The Early Poems, 1907–1924*, ed. Robin G. Schulze (Berkeley: University of California Press, 2002). It reprints the 1924 *Observations* in its entirety and provides commentary and facsimile pages of Moore's early publications of these poems in little magazines, allowing us to trace her development as a poet in a way that has never been available to scholars before. All quotations from the early poems are from this volume and are cited parenthetically in the text. "Black Earth" was first published in *The Egoist* in 1918. John Slatin dates the composition of "Peter" as 1919 or 1920. See John Slatin, "The Town's Assertiveness: Marianne Moore and New York City," in *Marianne Moore: Woman and Poet*, ed. Patricia C. Willis (Orono, ME: National Poetry Foundation, 1990), 66.

11. Patricia C. Willis, "The Owl and the Lantern: Marianne Moore at Bryn Mawr," *Poesis* 6, no. 3–4 (1985): 96.

12. Marilyn Brownstein's article, for example, relies on a rather uncritical reading of Julia Kristeva to discuss this relationship in semiotic terms, removing it entirely from the cultural sphere. See Marilyn Brownstein, "The Archaic Mother and Mother and Mother: The Postmodern Poetry of Marianne Moore," *Contemporary Literature* 30, no. 1 (1989): 13–32. She repeats this argument in her preface to the otherwise useful publication of a small selection of the family correspondence in "Marianne Moore (1887–1972)" in an anthology edited by Bonnie Kime Scott, *The Gender of Modernism: A Critical Anthology* (Bloomington: Indiana University Press, 1990), 323–34. For other discussions that briefly refer to the importance of Moore's relationship with her mother, see Jeredith Merrin, "Marianne Moore and Elizabeth Bishop," in *Columbia History of American Poetry*, ed. Brett C. Millier and Jay Parini (New York: Columbia University Press, 1993). In this essay, Merrin argues that Moore's and Bishop's positioning as poets was the result of the "creatrix" behind the scenes (343–69). For an earlier study, see Laurence Stapleton, *Marianne Moore: The Poet's Advance* (Princeton: Princeton University Press, 1978). Stapleton says of Mrs. Moore's death in 1947, "It was the end of an extraordinary relationship for which I can think of no comparison" (148).

13. Palmieri, *Adamless Eden*, 61.

14. Charles Molesworth, *Marianne Moore: A Literary Life* (Boston: Northeastern University Press, 1991), 9.

15. Marianne Moore, *The Complete Prose of Marianne Moore*, ed. Patricia C. Willis (New York: Penguin, 1987), 572. Subsequent quotations from this work are cited parenthetically in the text.

16. See Patricia C. Willis, "Comment," *Marianne Moore Newsletter* 5, no. 1 (Spring 1981): 2–4. Willis provides a good summary of Bryn Mawr's academic requirements during this period.

17. "Fangs" refers to the name of a dog in Sir Walter Scott's *Ivanhoe* (*SL*, 4). It is one of many names that Moore was given by her family, which as she explained in a letter to Bryher included also "a weasel, a coach-dog, a water-rat [from *Wind and the Willows*], a basilisk and an alligator" (*SL*, 137). Only those who were closest to the family received nicknames. Mary Norcross, probably the closest, was sometimes called "Rustles" and "Beaver." These pet names signified community, and, outside the family, were only used with other women. The use of noms de plume was typical of the letters between intimates in Victorian society, according to Carroll Smith-Rosenberg, "The Female World of Love and Ritual, in *Disorderly Conduct*, 55. Often one woman would take the name of a man and the other the name of a woman. The use of pet names in Moore's family similarly crosses gender boundaries fairly fluidly, at least in one direction. Moore was often referred to by her mother and brother with the male pronoun.

18. Mary Warner Moore to Marianne Moore, October 4, 1905, RML.

19. M. Carey Thomas, "Marriage and the Woman Scholar," in *The Educated Woman in America: Selected Writings of Catharine Beecher, Margaret Fuller, and M. Carey Thomas*, ed. Barbara M. Cross, Classics in Education (New York: Teachers College Press, 1965), 174.

20. Mary Warner Moore to Marianne Moore, April 17, 1907, RML.

21. Ibid.

22. Marianne Moore to Family, April 22, 1907, RML.

23. Mary Warner Moore to Marianne Moore, April 23, 1907, RML.

24. This was the opinion of Dr. Edward Clark, whose popular book *Sex in Education*, published in 1873, still held sway in the medical community when Moore was at Bryn Mawr. He is quoted in Solomon, *In the Company of Educated Women*, 56.

25. Marianne Moore to Family, January 19, 1908, RML.

26. Marianne Moore to Family, December 17, 1905, RML.

27. Marianne Moore to Family, November 5, 1905, RML.

28. Carroll Smith-Rosenberg, "The New Woman as Androgyne," in *Disorderly Conduct*, 258.

29. Ibid.

30. Marianne Moore to Family, April 22, 1907, RML.

31. Solomon, *In the Company of Educated Women*, 98–101.

32. Smith-Rosenberg, "The New Woman as Androgyne," 254.

33. Palmieri, *Adamless Eden*, xx.

34. Marianne Moore to Family, February 11, 1906, RML.

35. Marianne Moore to Family, April 16, 1907, RML.

36. Marianne Moore to Family, February 20, 1908, RML.

37. Willis, "Owl and Lantern," 88.

38. Marianne Moore to Family, April 7, 1907, RML.

39. Linda Leavell, "Marianne Moore, the James Family, and the Politics of Celibacy," *Twentieth-Century Literature* 49, no. 2 (Summer 2003): 221.

40. Ibid.: 226.

41. "Pym" is reprinted in *Complete Prose*, 12–16.

42. Marianne Moore to Family, dated Rosenbach, Spring 1908, RML.

43. Willis, "Comment."

44. The professor was Miss Fullerton in Moore's letter to her family dated March 20, 1907; quoted in Willis, "Owl and Lantern," 91.

45. Marianne Moore to Family, October 14, 1907, RML.

46. Quoted in Patricia C. Willis, "MM on the Literary Life," *Marianne Moore Newsletter* 5, no. 1 (Spring 1981): 6.

47. Ibid.

48. Ibid.: 7–8.

49. Marianne Moore to Family, October 30, 1907, RML.

50. Marianne Moore to Family, October 27, 1907, RML.

51. Leavell, "Marianne Moore, James Family," 227.

52. Mary Warner Moore to Marianne Moore, 12 February 1907.

53. Peggy James to Marianne Moore, 16 June 1907, RML.

54. Ralph Waldo Emerson, "Friendship," in *Emerson's Essays* (Apollo Editions, 1961), 142.

55. Ibid., 139.

56. Ibid.

57. As Schulze explains, another, syllabic version of "When I Buy Pictures" came out just after *The Dial* version. Somehow H. D. and Bryher obtained a copy of the earlier version and published it without Moore's "immediate knowledge or consent" in the 1921 Poems (*BMM*, 256).

58. Mary Warner Moore to Marianne Moore, January 11, 1908, RML.

59. Marianne Moore, "A Jelly-Fish," *The Lantern* 17 (Spring 1909): 110.

60. Patricia C. Willis, *Marianne Moore: Vision into Verse* (Philadelphia: The Rosenbach Museum and Library, 1987), 35.

61. One of Moore's earliest readers attributed Moore's carefully observed poems to "a novel intelligence, a strange sensibility, and a unique scholarship." See Glenway Westcott, "Concerning Miss Moore's *Observations*," *The Dial* 78 (January 1925): 2.

62. Such revisionary chopping was not unusual for Moore. Moore's epigraph to her *Complete Poems* (1967), "Omissions are not accidents," tempts one to read these revisions or "omissions" as instructive, perhaps even revealing. The most extreme example of Moore's revisionary chopping was her poem "Poetry," which was 38 lines long when it was published in *Observations* in 1924. Moore cut it to three lines when it was reprinted in her far-from-complete *Complete Poems*.

63. Willis, *Vision into Verse*, 6.

64. Marianne Moore, Lecture Notebook for Georgina Goddard King's Imitative Writing Class, Bryn Mawr, Spring 1909, Folder VII:05:07, RML.

65. Willis notes, "While T. S. Eliot is credited with rediscovering the seventeenth century for the modernist generation, his 'Metaphysical Poets' did not appear until 1921 when he reviewed Grierson's anthology for the *Times Literary*

Supplement." She goes on to say, "His essays on seventeenth-century prose writers were published still later. Moore's study of seventeenth-century prose in 1909 took her to the writers those poets themselves were reading, from Bacon's humanistic essays to the sermons of Protestant divines. The rhythms of the King James Bible, the devices of classical rhetoric, and the careful splicing of eclectic subject matter characteristic of that prose were to influence not only her prose, but also the *materia poetica* she was to choose for her verse, so evident in the famous bibliographical notes she appended to her poems." Willis, *Vision into Verse*, 6.

66. Willis speculates that King "might well have reported on the December 1908 review of Pound's *A Lume Spento* in the New York *American Journal Examiner.* . . . Marianne might have seen any of the seven articles Pound had published by that time in *Book News Monthly*, a Philadelphia periodical, although his translations of late medieval Latin verse were his only poetry to appear there." Ibid.

67. This entry is undated, but the date several pages before it is "Summer 1909," and immediately after it is the date October 1909, so it was probably written during the summer of 1909. From Marianne Moore, "Reading Notebook," dated 1882–1915, Folder VII: 01:01, RML.

68. Marianne Moore to Family, February 1909, RML.

69. Angelique Richardson and Chris Willis, eds., *The New Woman in Fiction and in Fact: Fin-De-Siecle Feminisms* (London: Palgrave Macmillan, 2002), 1.

70. Ibid., xi, 12.

71. Smith-Rosenberg, "The New Woman as Androgyne," 247.

72. Cristanne Miller, *Marianne Moore: Questions of Authority* (Cambridge, MA: Harvard University Press, 1995), 32. Miller's book played a significant role in initiating the shift in Moore studies to seeing Moore as a poet of authority rather than as one of humility that had dominated Moore criticism. Miller focuses on the early poetry and relies for her readings on the earlier versions of the poems, as I do, rather than on the later ones that Moore sometimes radically revised for her 1967 *Complete Poems* and in so doing destroyed some of their power. Although Miller does not focus specifically on Bryn Mawr, she does quote in her first chapter a number of the Bryn Mawr letters to show Moore's engagement in social activism and suffrage while she was a student. In Chapter 4, "Your Thorns are the Best Part of You: Gender Politics in the Nongendered Poem," Miller provides an excellent discussion of gender and the development of Moore's authority.

73. Marianne Moore to John Warner Moore, January 17, 1908, RML.

74. Linda Leavell, *Marianne Moore and the Visual Arts: Prismatic Color* (Baton Rouge: Louisiana State University Press, 1995), 42.

75. Ibid.

76. "Black Earth" had also appeared in *Poems* (1921), Moore's first volume of poetry, which was published by H. D. and Bryher without Moore's knowledge. As with "Radical," I quote from *Observations* here. "Black Earth," one of her most powerful and seductive poems, which reappeared as "Melanchthon" in 1951, was not included in the *Complete Poems*.

77. Willis, *Vision into Verse*, 6.

78. Marianne Moore, unpublished poem, Folder I:03:12, RML.

79. Ibid.

80. Pound's "Sestina: Altaforte" was published in the 1909 edition of *Exultations* published by Elkin Mathews in London and purchased by Moore in his bookshop in 1911. I quote from Ezra Pound, *Collected Early Poems of Ezra Pound* (New York: New Directions, 1976), 108.

81. Kirstin Hotelling, "'The I of Each Is to the I of Each, a Kind of Fretful Speech Which Sets a Limit on Itself': Marianne Moore's Strategic Selfhood," *Modernism/Modernity* 5, no. 1 (1996): 76, 77. This argument is presented in revised form in Kirstin Hotelling Zona, *Marianne Moore, Elizabeth Bishop, and May Swenson: The Feminist Poetics of Self-Restraint* (Ann Arbor: The University of Michigan Press, 2002).

82. *The Little Review* published Eliot's "The Hippopotamus" in June 1917. See John Slatin, *The Savage's Romance: The Poetry of Marianne Moore* (University Park: The Pennsylvania State University Press, 1986), 79.

83. Ibid., 7.

84. In his review, "Marianne Moore and Mina Loy," Ezra Pound wrote that "these girls have written a distinctly national product" (46). This review, which originally appeared in *The Little Review* in March 1918 was reprinted in Charles Tomlinson, ed., *Marianne Moore: A Collection of Critical Essays* (New York: Prentice Hall, 1969), 46–47.

85. Letter to Marianne Moore from London, December 16, 1918, in Ezra Pound, *The Selected Letters of Ezra Pound, 1907–1941*, ed. D. D. Paige (New York: New Directions, 1971), 143.

86. Cristanne Miller, "Marianne Moore's Black Maternal Hero: A Study in Categorization," *American Literary History* 1, no. 4 (Winter 1989): 787.

87. Ibid, 807–8.

88. Leavell, *Marianne Moore*, 155.

89. Marianne Moore to John Warner Moore, October 18, 1915, RML.

90. "The Love Song of J. Alfred Prufrock," in T. S. Eliot, *The Complete Poems and Plays, 1909–1950* (San Diego: Harcourt Brace Jovanovich, 1952), 5.

91. Rachel Blau Du Plessis has argued that Moore's experiments in syllabic form were a crucial aspect of her "feminist poetics." See Du Plessis, "No Moore of the Same: The Feminist Poetics of Marianne Moore," *William Carlos Williams Review* 14, no. 1 (Spring 1988): 8.

92. Pondrom argues that after repeated unsuccessful attempts to get her work published in a volume, "Moore withdrew into a posture that publication for her work would be premature" (376). See Cyrena N. Pondrom, "Marianne Moore and H. D.: Female Community and Poetic Achievement," in *Marianne Moore: Woman and Poet*, 371–402. Pondrom's essay looks at Moore's poetry in the context of female community.

93. Mary Warner Moore to Marianne Moore, October 20, 1905, RML.

2. Serpents in Paradise

1. Horowitz, *Power and Passion*, 318.

2. M. Carey Thomas, "The 'Bryn Mawr Woman.'" Reprinted in abridged form in Cross, *Educated Woman in America*, 140.

3. Ibid., 141.

4. *A Book of Bryn Mawr Stories*, ed. Margaretta Morris and Louise Buffum Congdon (Philadelphia: George W. Jacobs, 1901).

5. Smith-Rosenberg, "The New Woman as Androgyne," 281.

6. Rachel Blau DuPlessis, "'Corpses of Poesy': Some Modern Poets and Some Gender Ideologies of Lyric," in *Feminist Measures: Soundings in Poetry and Theory*, ed. Cristanne Miller, *Women and Culture* (Ann Arbor: University of Michigan Press, 1994), 77.

7. Harriet Jean Crawford, "Catherine's Career," in *A Book of Bryn Mawr Stories*, 235. Crawford was Bryn Mawr class of 1902.

8. Georgina Goddard King, "Free among the Dead," in *A Book of Bryn Mawr Stories*, 153–54.

9. Ibid., 159.

10. M. Carey Thomas, "Present Tendencies in Women's College and University Education." Reprinted in abridged form as "Motives and Future of the Educated Woman" in Cross, *Educated Woman in America*, 167.

11. Ibid.

12. Gordon, *Gender and Higher Education*, 32.

13. Ibid.

14. Marian MacIntosh, "Her Masterpiece," in *A Book of Bryn Mawr Stories*, 13, 18.

15. Ibid., 64.

16. Charles Berger, "Who Writes the History Book?: Moore's Revisionary Poetics," *Western Humanities Review* 53, no. 3 (Fall 1999): 279.

17. Ibid.

18. Ibid.

19. Ibid.

20. Marianne Moore, "Reading Notebook," Folder VII:01:04, pp. 29–30, RML.

21. Lynn Keller, "'For Inferior Who Is Free?': Liberating the Woman Writer in Marianne Moore's 'Marriage'," in *Influence and Intertextuality in Literary History*, ed. Jay Clayton and Eric Rothstein (Madison: University of Wisconsin Press, 1991), 227. Keller notes that Moore misquotes this passage. Bacon's original read "rovers" for the word "errors" and "auricular" traditions rather than "circular" (n. 11). The misquotations are slightly different, though, because Moore quotes "rovers" in her reading notebook but changes it to "errors" in the poem, but she transcribes "auricular" as "circular" in her notebook, perhaps suggesting all kinds of interesting possibilities about how the process of composition works at both the conscious and unconscious levels.

22. Margaret Holley, *The Poetry of Marianne Moore: A Study in Voice and Value* (Cambridge: Cambridge University Press, 1987), 71.

23. The reader must be quite wary in using the Schulman edition as there are many errata in the text that must be checked against the original manuscripts at the Rosenbach.

24. Marianne Moore, *The Poems of Marianne Moore*, ed. Grace Schulman (New York: Viking, 2003), 40. See also manuscript version of " 'And Shall Life Pass an Old Maid By?,'" Folder I:01:04, RML. Subsequent quotations from this work are cited parenthetically in the text.

25. Schulze outlines the effect of Bryher's marriage on Moore in her publication biography of the Manikin edition of "Marriage" (BMM, 455–65).

26. Shaw was a suffragist, minister, doctor of medicine, and author, who spoke often on college campuses during this time for suffrage in an attempt to get college-educated women interested in working for the cause.

27. Susan Kingsley Kent, *Sex and Suffrage in Britain, 1860–1914* (Princeton, NJ: Princeton University Press, 1987), 85.

28. Ibid., 86.

29. See particularly Pamela Hadas, "Treading Chasms," in *Modern Critical Views: Marianne Moore*, ed. Harold Bloom (New York: Chelsea House, 1987), 25–41. See also Sabine Sielke, "Snapshots of Marriage, Snares of Mimicry, Snarls of Motherhood: Marianne Moore and Adrienne Rich," *Sagetrieb* 6, no. 3 (Winter 1987), 79–97. Both argue that Moore's poem describes matrimony as a modern *Paradise Lost* and is a feminist rereading of Milton. Moore's poem "Marriage" has a long history of being read as a feminist poem, reaching as far back as its inclusion in the 1973 feminist anthology of poetry *No More Masks!* In their introduction, the anthology's editors called it a poem that sprang from "revolutionary spirit." See Florence Howe and Ellen Bass, eds., *No More Masks! An Anthology of Poems by Women* (New York: Anchor, 1973), xxix.

30. Berger, "Who Writes the History Book?," 279.

31. Ibid., 280.

32. Miller, *Questions of Authority*, 118.

33. Book IX, Line 433. Quoted here from John Milton, *The Complete Poetry of John Milton*, ed. John T. Shawcross, rev. ed. (New York: Anchor Books, 1971), 431.

34. Molesworth, *Marianne Moore: A Literary Life*, 106.

35. This earlier line appeared in the notebook Moore was using to work on poems of the 1920s, including "Marriage," "An Octopus" and "Sea Unicorns and Land Unicorns," Folder VII:04:04, RML.

36. Moore goes on to say, "Until recently, I took [chastity] for granted—like avoiding 'any drugs'" (*CPr*, 503). The essay, "If I Were Sixteen Today," was originally published in *World Week* 33 (7 November 1958), 16–17.

37. Elizabeth W. Joyce, *Cultural Critique and Abstraction: Marianne Moore and the Avant-Garde* (Lewisburg, PA: Bucknell University Press, 1998), 73.

38. Ibid.

39. My emphasis here. Marianne Moore, unpublished notebook, Folder 1250/2, RML.

40. Cross, *Educated Woman in America*, 160.

41. Ibid.

42. Leavell, "Marianne Moore, James Family," 235.

43. Ibid.

44. Ibid., 223.

45. Quoted in Leavell from an unpublished letter from Mary Warner Moore to John Warner Moore, February 17, 1914.

46. Moore's attitude toward Freud's theories has often been thought to be dismissive, largely because of the comment she seems to have made to Elizabeth Bishop about psychoanalysis, which Bishop quotes in her memoir of Moore "Ef-

forts of Affection" (in *Elizabeth Bishop: Collected Prose*, 155), but as Moore writes in a letter to Bryher, "The pterodactyl has an open mind with regard to Freud and child and parent protective measures" (*SL*, 142). And her discussion of the concept of sublimation certainly suggests she was reading Freud with some attention. Freud even advised in the case of Thayer's mental instability, which was causing Moore a great deal of trouble when she was editor of *The Dial*, and Moore approved of his advice (*SL*, 212, 222, 224).

47. Molesworth, *Marianne Moore: A Literary Life*, 190.

48. From an undated letter, perhaps February 1929, from Mary Warner Moore, quoted in Miller, *Questions of Authority*, 264n19.

49. Alyse Gregory, "The Dilemma of Marriage," *The New Republic* 4 (July 1923): 151.

50. Ibid.

51. Ibid.

52. Ibid.: 152.

53. Hilda Doolittle, "Circe," in *H. D.: Collected Poems, 1912–1944*, ed. Louis L. Martz (New York: New Directions, 1983), 119.

54. Ibid., 120.

55. Du Plessis, "'Corpses of Poesy,'" 88.

56. Ibid., 77.

57. Ibid., 78.

58. Ibid., 77.

59. Ibid.

60. Gregory, "The Dilemma of Marriage," 151.

61. Ibid.

62. Heather Cass White, "Morals, Manners, and 'Marriage': Marianne Moore's Art of Conversation," *Twentieth Century Literature* 45, no. 4 (Winter 1999): 503.

63. Moore only remembered this one line from Nearing's parody, according to a note in the *Selected Letters, 142*. The manuscript has been lost.

64. M. Carey Thomas, address given at Mount Holyoke College, 1913, "The Future of Woman's Higher Education." Reprinted as "Marriage and the Woman Scholar" in Cross, *Educated Woman in America*, 172–73.

65. Marianne Moore to family, April 15, 1909, RML. See also Moore's comments on Thomas's struggles as Bryn Mawr's "impassioned emancipator" in her 1948 review of Edith Finch's biography of Thomas (*CPr*, 416–19).

66. Mary Wollstonecraft, *Vindication of the Rights of Woman*, ed. Carol H. Poston, 2nd ed., *Norton Critical Edition* (New York: Norton, 1988), 30. The reference is from Chapter II, "The Prevailing Opinion of a Sexual Character Discussed" where Wollstonecraft responds to Dr. John Gregory's *A Father's Legacy to His Daughters*, first published in 1774, a text that was popular during the eighteenth century. Wollstonecraft spends much of this chapter pointing out the disservice Gregory is doing to women and how his beliefs encourage them to be weak and feeble wives.

67. Kent, *Sex and Suffrage*, 16.

68. Ibid., 86.

69. Gregory, "The Dilemma of Marriage," 151.

70. William Carlos Williams, "Marianne Moore," in *Selected Essays* (New York: New Directions, 1954), 128.
71. Smith-Rosenberg, "The New Woman as Androgyne," 252–53.
72. See Palmieri, *Adamless Eden*, xx.
73. See head note in Cross, *Educated Woman in America*, 170.
74. Ibid., 172.
75. Ibid., 173.
76. Ibid., 174.
77. Smith-Rosenberg, "The New Woman as Androgyne," 281.
78. Ibid.
79. Ibid.

3. Elizabeth Bishop's "Queer Birds"

1. This editorial appeared on page 1 of the first issue of *Con Spirito*, which came out in February 1933.
2. Elizabeth Bishop, *One Art: Elizabeth Bishop Letters*, ed. Robert Giroux (New York: Farrar, Straus and Giroux, 1994), 13. Subsequent quotations from this work are cited parenthetically in the text. Bishop began corresponding with Donald Stanford, a first-year graduate student at Harvard, in the fall of 1933. Yvor Winters, then regional editor of *Hound & Horn*, encouraged Stanford to write to Bishop. See Gary Fountain and Peter Brazeau, *Remembering Elizabeth Bishop: An Oral Biography* (Amherst: University of Massachusetts Press, 1994), 56.
3. Rukeyser's participation in the group is uncertain. McCarthy writes in her memoir that she thought Rukeyser was part of the group but was unable to identify anything she wrote for the magazine, except perhaps for a verse account of T. S. Eliot's visit to campus in the fall of 1933 entitled "Lecture by Mr. Eliot," which I discuss in chapter 4.
4. Mary McCarthy, *How I Grew* (New York: Harcourt Brace Jovanovich, 1987), 226.
5. Erkkila, *Wicked Sisters*, 100.
6. Ibid., 4.
7. McCarthy, *How I Grew*, 262.
8. Fountain and Brazeau, *Remembering*, 51.
9. "Editorial," *The American Spectator* 1, no. 3 (January 1933): 1.
10. Smith-Rosenberg, "The New Woman as Androgyne," 265.
11. Ibid.
12. Ibid., 272.
13. Ibid., 271.
14. Ibid., 272.
15. George Jean Nathan, "The Theatre," *The American Spectator* 1, no. 1 (November 1932): 2.
16. Ibid. *The Spectator* printed an article by the leading sexologist in British and American circles, Havelock Ellis, on the front page of the same issue. See Ellis, "The Physician and Sex," *The American Spectator* 1, no. 1 (November 1932): 1. Although Ellis's article was not specifically about "inversion," its presence here

would seem not only to confirm the popularity of Ellis within the literary community but also to authenticate *The Spectator's* views on educated women. Nathan's familiarity with the theories of the sexologists is also evident in a play he wrote in 1933 that parodied Noel Coward's *Design for Living*. Called *Design for Loving*, Nathan's play featured a hermaphrodite, an onanist, a flagellant, a transvestite, a male homosexual, a lesbian, and another woman with "tribade tendencies" among its cast of characters. See Faderman, *Odd Girls*, 104.

17. Faderman, *Odd Girls*, 49. Smith-Rosenberg also notes that "articles complaining of lesbianism in women's colleges, clubs, prisons, and reformatories—wherever women gathered—became common" after World War I as Progressive women reformers gained more power. Smith-Rosenberg, "The New Woman as Androgyne," 280.

18. "Editorial," 1.

19. Ibid.

20. Judith Butler, *Gender Trouble: Feminism and the Subversion of Identity* (New York: Routledge, 1990), 33–34.

21. McCarthy, *How I Grew*, 226.

22. Fountain and Brazeau, *Remembering*, 43.

23. Nina Baym, "Melodramas of Beset Manhood: How Theories of American Fiction Exclude Women Authors," in *The New Feminist Criticism: Essays on Women, Literature & Theory*, ed. Elaine Showalter (New York: Pantheon Books, 1985), 63–80. See also Andreas Huyssen, "Mass Culture as Woman," in *After the Great Divide: Modernism, Mass Culture, Postmodernism* (Bloomington: Indiana University Press, 1986), 44–62. Huyssen argues that in modernist discourse "mass culture is somehow associated with woman while real, authentic culture remains the prerogative of men" (47). See also Sandra Gilbert and Susan Gubar's massive study of male modernist rage against women writers in *No Man's Land*, vol. 1.

24. Baym, "Melodramas of Beset Manhood," 70.

25. Ibid., 77.

26. McCarthy, *How I Grew*, 257.

27. Ashley Brown's interview with Elizabeth Bishop in Lloyd Schwartz and Sybil P. Estess, eds., *Elizabeth Bishop and Her Art* (Ann Arbor: University of Michigan Press, 1983), 293.

28. Eunice Clark Jessup, "Memoirs of Literatae and Socialists 1929–1933," *Vassar Quarterly* 55 (1979): 17.

29. Ibid.

30. Ibid.

31. McCarthy, *How I Grew*, 258.

32. Ibid.

33. "Editorial," 1.

34. Smith-Rosenberg, "The New Woman as Androgyne," 280.

35. McCarthy, *How I Grew*, 258.

36. Adrienne Rich, "The Eye of the Outsider: Elizabeth Bishop's Complete Poems, 1927–1979," in *Blood, Bread, and Poetry: Selected Prose 1979–1985* (New York: Norton, 1986), 128. Rich reads this poem as one that illustrates Bishop's divided sense of self. The poem, she argues, is "a tense, panicky, one-sided conversation during which a whole menagerie gets out of control."

37. I quote here from the *Con Spirito* version of "A Word With You," which was reprinted in *The Complete Poems* (218–19). Elizabeth Bishop, "A Word with You," *Con Spirito* 1, no. 2 (April 1933): 2.

38. Ibid.

39. Solomon, *In the Company of Educated Women*, 162. Novels of the 1920s reflected the fear that intimacy between women could carry severe consequences. In Wanda Fraiken Neff's 1928 roman à clef *We Sing Diana*, the protagonist says of women's colleges, "Intimacies between two girls were watched with keen, distrustful eyes. Among one's classmates, one looked for the bisexual type, the masculine girl searching for a feminine counterpart, and one ridiculed their devotions" (199).

40. Bishop, "A Word With You," 2.

41. Eleanor Clark uses this phrase to describe Bishop's group at Vassar in Fountain and Brazeau, *Remembering*, 37.

42. Elizabeth Bishop, "Seven-Days Monologue," *Con Spirito* 1, no. 2 (April 1933): 3.

43. Ibid.: 4.

44. Faderman, *Odd Girls*, 106.

45. Bishop, "Seven-Days Monologue," 4.

46. My emphasis. Ibid.

47. Smith-Rosenberg, "The New Woman as Androgyne," 282.

48. Bishop, "Seven-Days Monologue," 4.

49. Ibid.

50. As Carole Vance argues, "Sexuality is simultaneously a domain of restriction, repression, and danger as well as a domain of exploration, pleasure, and agency." Carole Vance, "Pleasure and Danger: Toward a Politics of Sexuality," in *Pleasure and Danger: Exploring Female Sexuality*, ed. Carole Vance (Boston: Routledge and Kegan Paul, 1984), 1.

51. Thomas Travisano was one of the first to label this aspect of Bishop's work. He refers to these spaces as "fables of enclosure" in chapter 2 of his book on the phases of Bishop's development. See Travisano, *Elizabeth Bishop: Her Artistic Development* (Charlottesville: University Press of Virginia, 1988), 17–51.

52. Langdon Hammer, "Useless Concentration: Life and Work in Elizabeth Bishop's Letters and Poems," *American Literary History* 9 (1997): 173.

53. Ibid. David Bromwich also notes the conversational nature of Bishop's work and the risks she is willing to take to communicate with the "readers she cares for." In David Bromwich, "Elizabeth Bishop's Dream-Houses," in *Modern Critical Views: Elizabeth Bishop*, ed. Harold Bloom (New York: Chelsea House, 1985), 160.

54. Mary Russo, *The Female Grotesque: Risk, Excess and Modernity* (New York: Routledge, 1994), 19.

55. Ibid., 22.

56. Ibid., 11.

57. Ibid.

58. McCarthy, *How I Grew*, 258. Schwartz and Estess, *Elizabeth Bishop and Her Art*, 293.

59. Elizabeth Bishop, *Elizabeth Bishop: The Complete Poems* (New York: Farrar, Straus and Giroux, 1991), 62. Subsequent quotations from this work are cited parenthetically in the text.

60. Bishop, "Seven-Days Monologue," 4.

61. Jeredith Merrin, "Elizabeth Bishop: Gaiety, Gayness, and Change," in *Elizabeth Bishop: The Geography of Gender*, ed. Marilyn May Lombardi (Charlottesville: University Press of Virginia, 1993), 154.

62. Ibid., 153.

63. Ibid., 154.

64. From Alice Quinn's excellent notes in Elizabeth Bishop, *Edgar Allan Poe & the Juke-Box: Uncollected Poems, Drafts, and Fragments*, ed. Alice Quinn (New York: Farrar, Straus and Giroux, 2006), 267–68.

65. Ibid., 44.

66. Faderman, *Odd Girls*, 106.

67. Bishop, "Seven-Days Monologue," 4.

68. Fountain and Brazeau, *Remembering*, 37.

69. Frani Blough, "The Bacchae, or Revelling Women," *Con Spirito* 1, no. 2 (April 1933): 2.

70. Mary McCarthy, "Two Crystal-Gazing Novelists," *Con Spirito* 1, no. 1 (February 1933): 1.

71. Fountain and Brazeau, *Remembering*, 50.

72. Betsy Erkkila, "Elizabeth Bishop, Modernism, and the Left," *American Literary History* 8 (1996): 286.

73. For another reading of this story in relationship to Bishop and the politics of the left, see John Palatella, "'That Sense of Constant Re-Adjustment': The Great Depression and the Provisional Politics of Elizabeth Bishop's *North & South*," *Contemporary Literature* 34, no. 1 (Spring 1993): 18–43.

74. Sigmund Freud, "Family Romances," in *The Freud Reader*, ed. Peter Gay (New York: Norton, 1989), 299.

75. Elizabeth Bishop, "Then Came the Poor," *Con Spirito* 1, no. 1 (February 1933): 4.

76. Ibid.

77. For excellent discussions of the rose metaphor in Bishop, see Bonnie Costello, "Attractive Mortality," in *Elizabeth Bishop: The Geography of Gender*, 126–52. See also Lorrie Goldensohn, "The Body's Roses: Race, Sex, and Gender in Elizabeth Bishop's Representations of Self," in *Elizabeth Bishop: The Geography of Gender*, 70–90.

78. Bishop, "Then Came the Poor," 4.

79. Ibid.

80. Ibid.

81. In this story, Bishop's narrator mocks the intense female friendships that marked Moore's Bryn Mawr experience. During a conversation about George Meredith's *Diana of the Crossways*, the narrator balks at his companion's interest in Meredith who admits that such stories of "a passionate female friendship" have become "a little quaint" (25). Since such intense friendships had become a "little quaint" (or downright dangerous), Bishop had to cast around for another way to convey such passion. Elizabeth Bishop, "A Flight of Fancy," *The Blue Pencil* (December 1929).

82. Bishop, "Then Came the Poor," 4.

83. James Longenbach, "Elizabeth Bishop's Social Conscience," *English Literary History* 62 (1995): 470.

84. Frani Blough Muser to Elizabeth Bishop, October 7, 1935, VC.

85. Elizabeth Bishop, *Elizabeth Bishop: The Collected Prose*, ed. Robert Giroux (New York: Farrar, Straus and Giroux, 1984), 190. Subsequent quotations from this work are cited parenthetically in the text.

86. Langdon Hammer, "The New Elizabeth Bishop," *Yale Review* 82, no. 1 (1994): 144.

87. Faderman, *Odd Girls*, 41.

88. Entry dated July 1934, Notebooks: 1934–37, Folder 72A.3, VC.

89. David Kalstone, *Becoming a Poet: Elizabeth Bishop with Marianne Moore and Robert Lowell*, ed. Robert Hemenway (New York: Farrar, Straus and Giroux, 1989), 252.

90. Gabriele Griffith, *Heavenly Love? Lesbian Images in Twentieth Century Women's Writing* (Manchester, England: Manchester University Press, 1993), 11.

91. Ibid.

92. Lorrie Goldensohn, *Elizabeth Bishop: The Biography of a Poetry* (New York: Columbia University Press, 1992), 68.

93. Brett C. Millier, *Elizabeth Bishop: Life and the Memory of It* (Berkeley: University of California Press, 1993), 366.

94. Joanne Feit Diehl, "Bishop's Sexual Poetics," in *Elizabeth Bishop: The Geography of Gender*, 20.

95. Timothy Morris, *Becoming Canonical in American Poetry* (Urbana: University of Illinois Press, 1995), 125.

96. Elizabeth Bishop, "Time's Andromedas," *Vassar Journal of Undergraduate Studies* 7 (May 1933): 102.

4. CON SPIRITO

1. McCarthy, *How I Grew*, 209.

2. Fountain and Brazeau, *Remembering*, 26.

3. See Cheryl Walker, "Antimodern, Modern, and Postmodern Millay: Contexts of Revaluation," in *Gendered Modernisms: American Women Poets and Their Readers*, ed. Margaret Dickie and Thomas Travisano (Philadelphia: University of Pennsylvania Press, 1996), 170–88.

4. Louis Untermeyer, "Daughters of Niobe," *The American Spectator* 1, no. 1 (November 1932): 4.

5. Muriel Rukeyser, *Theory of Flight*, (New Haven, CT: Yale University Press, 1935), 11.

6. Richard Flynn, "'The Buried Life and the Body of Waking': Muriel Rukeyser and the Politics of Literary History," in *Gendered Modernisms*, 266.

7. In an unpublished letter to Bishop dated August 9, 1935, Frani Blough reports that Rukeyser had been awarded a prize by Stephen Benét "with remarks by him that Muriel is a revolutionary who speaks with the conviction of a revolutionary but the feeling of a poet," VC.

8. Fountain and Brazeau, *Remembering*, 50.
9. Mary McCarthy, "In Pace Requiescamus," *Con Spirito* 1, no. 2 (April 1933): 1.
10. Richard H. Pells, *Radical Visions and American Dreams: Culture and Social Thought in the Depression Years* (Middletown, CT: Wesleyan University Press, 1973), 34.
11. Quoted in Pells, 34.
12. "Editorial," 1.
13. Pells, *Radical Visions*, 34.
14. "Editorial," 1.
15. Adams, *Group of Their Own*, 67.
16. McCarthy, *How I Grew*, 205.
17. Ibid.
18. Ibid., 206.
19. Fountain and Brazeau, *Remembering*, 54.
20. Ibid.
21. Ibid.
22. McCarthy, *How I Grew*, 206.
23. Ibid., 204.
24. Ibid., 206.
25. Margaret Miller, "Sur-Realism, the Last Mohican of the Primitives," *Con Spirito* 1, no. 1 (February 1933): 3.
26. Muriel Rukeyser, "Lecture by Mr. Eliot," *Con Spirito* 2, no. 1 (November 1933): 2.
27. Meyer, 35.
28. Ibid.
29. McCarthy, "Two Crystal-Gazing Novelists," 2.
30. Ibid.
31. "A Word with You," which I discussed in the last chapter, is a notable exception in its freshness and clear description. Bishop also wrote a delightful ballad when she was 16, "The Ballad of the Subway Train," that offers a glimpse into the surprises of her later work. See Thomas Travisano, "Heavenly Dragons: A Newly Discovered Poem by Elizabeth Bishop," *Western Humanities Review* 45, no. 1 (Spring 1991): 28–33.
32. Elizabeth Bishop, "Hymn to the Virgin," *Con Spirito* 1, no. 2 (April 1933): 3. This poem was reprinted in the back section of *The Complete Poems* entitled "Poems Written in Youth," 221–22.
33. Elizabeth Bishop, "Dimensions for a Novel," *Vassar Journal of Undergraduate Studies* 8 (May 1934): 96.
34. James Longenbach, *Modern Poetry after Modernism* (New York: Oxford University Press, 1997), 24. Longenbach's work has been instrumental in helping me see the way that Bishop was using these college essays to work out her poetic theory and how that translated into the later poetry. My work places those investigations more within the context of Bishop's specific experience of the women's college and particularly in conversation with her group of very close friends.
35. James E. B. Breslin, *From Modern to Contemporary: American Poetry, 1945–1965* (Chicago: University of Chicago Press, 1984), 51–53.
36. Ibid., 51.

37. Elizabeth Bishop, "Gerard Manley Hopkins: Notes on Timing in His Poetry," *The Vassar Review* 23 (February 1934): 7. Bishop continued to work on her Hopkins paper after college, presumably with an eye toward publishing it. In a 1935 letter to Moore, she writes that Hopkins's "own ideas of composition seem almost to forecast some of Schönberg" (*SL*, 32).

38. Bishop, "Time's Andromedas," 113.

39. Ibid., 109.

40. See Millier, *Life*, 60.

41. Ibid., 29.

42. Elizabeth Bishop to Frani Blough, February 14, 1936, VC.

43. In her use of the railroad tracks, Bishop also brings to mind a familiar icon of 1930s America—the hobo. According to Lillian Faderman, statistics gathered in 1933 estimated that there were about 150,000 women hobos in the United States and that working class lesbian couples were not uncommon among this group. See Faderman, *Odd Girls*, 94–95. It is not hard to imagine the fantasy of sexual freedom that Bishop might have found in this trope.

44. Kalstone, *Becoming*, 253.

45. Millier, *Life*, 77.

46. John Lowney, "'Littered with Old Correspondences': Elizabeth Bishop, Wallace Stevens, and the 1930s," *Arizona Quarterly* 55, no. 2 (Summer 1999): 89.

47. *Letters of Wallace Stevens*, ed. Holly Stevens (Berkeley: University of California Press, 1996), 290.

48. Ibid.

49. In his reading, Guy Rotella usefully uncovers many more of the poem's possible sources to emphasize its intertextuality and, hence, "less than monumental" qualities. See his *Castings: Movements and Monumentality in Poems by Elizabeth Bishop, Robert Lowell, James Merrill, Derek Walcott, and Seamus Heaney* (Nashville, TN: Vanderbilt Univerity Press, 2004), 32.

50. In W. B. Yeats, *The Poems*, ed. Richard J. Finneran, vol. 1, *The Collected Works of W. B. Yeats* (New York: Scribner, 1997), 300.

51. In "O Florida, Venereal Soil," *The Collected Poems of Wallace Stevens* (New York: Vintage, 1982), 47.

52. Elizabeth Bishop to Frani Blough, January 4, 1937, VC.

53. Ibid.

54. Ibid.

55. Bishop Notebooks: 1934–37, Folder 72A.3, VC.

56. Fountain and Brazeau, *Remembering*, 78.

57. Ibid.

58. Stevens, *Collected Poems*, 47–48.

59. Ibid, 48.

5. Sylvia Plath's Brave New World

1. Sylvia Plath, *The Unabridged Journals of Sylvia Plath, 1950–1962*, ed. Karen V. Kukil (New York: Anchor Books, 2000), 26–27. Subsequent quotations from this work are cited parenthetically in the text.

2. Hughes left the family in late August, but he returned to Court Green "during the second week of October" to pack his things. See Diane Middlebrook, *Her Husband: Hughes and Plath—a Marriage* (New York: Viking, 2003), 183.

3. Susan R. Van Dyne, *Revising Life: Sylvia Plath's Ariel Poems*, ed. Linda K. Kerber and Nell Irvin Painter, *Gender and American Culture* (Chapel Hill: The University of North Carolina Press, 1993), 93.

4. The American edition of *The Collected Poems* uses the American spelling of jailer. I use the British spelling that Plath preferred in the original *Ariel* manuscript now available in Sylvia Plath, *Ariel: The Restored Edition*, ed. Frieda Hughes (New York: HarperCollins, 2004), 23.

5. Sylvia Plath, *The Collected Poems of Sylvia Plath*, ed. Ted Hughes (New York: HarperPerennial, 1981), 226. Subsequent quotations from this work are cited parenthetically in the text.

6. In his 1942 essay "The Noble Rider and the Sound of Words," Stevens outlined the ability of the poetic imagination to respond to violence. The full quotation is as follows: "It is a violence from within that protects us from a violence without. It is the imagination pressing back against the pressure of reality. It seems, in the last analysis, to have something to do with our self-preservation; and that, no doubt, is why the expression of it, the sound of its words, helps us to live our lives." Wallace Stevens, "The Noble Rider and the Sound of Words," in *The Necessary Angel* (New York: Vintage, 1951), 36.

7. Faderman, *Odd Girls*, 157.

8. Senator Joseph McCarthy spoke on the Smith College campus in the spring of 1952 while Plath was there.

9. Solomon, *In the Company of Educated Women*, 195.

10. See Faderman's chapter on this period, "The Love that Dares Not Speak Its Name: McCarthyism and Its Legacy," 139–58.

11. Faderman, *Odd Girls*, 146.

12. Langdon Hammer, "Plath's Lives: Poetry, Professionalism, and the Culture of the School," *Representations* 75 (2001): 61–62.

13. Ibid., 76.

14. Ibid., 61.

15. Ibid., 64.

16. Kaledin, *Mothers and More*, 53.

17. Ibid., 51.

18. Mary Curley, "President Notes Role of Women," *Sophian*, June 9, 1952, 6. Adlai Stevenson, who spoke at Plath's graduation, gave Smith women the same message.

19. Solomon, *In the Company of Educated Women*, 194.

20. Nancy McChesney, "Coles Discuss Components of True Marriage," *Scan*, April 13 1951, 1.

21. Ibid.

22. Smith College Memorabilia, Box 12, Folder 10, LL.

23. Agnes E. Meyer, "Women Aren't Men," *Atlantic Monthly* 186.2 (August 1950): 35.

24. Ibid.

25. "Moral Lapse Laid to Kinsey Report," *The New York Times* October 21, 1950, 14.

26. The Kinsey report on female sexuality turned up the volume on the hysteria of the McCarthy era. According to a review essay in the *American Quarterly*, Congress acted swiftly to try to block the report. New York Representative Louis B. Heller requested that the Postmaster General "bar the Female Report from the mails until it could be investigated" and "charged Kinsey with 'hurling the insult of the century against our mothers, wives, daughters and sisters.'" See Regina Markell Morantz, "The Scientist as Sex Crusader: Alfred C. Kinsey and American Culture," *American Quarterly* 29, no. 5 (Winter, 1977): 575.

27. Meyer, 35.

28. Ibid.

29. Quoted in Kaledin, *Mothers and More*, 51.

30. Ibid., 48.

31. Philip Wylie, *Generation of Vipers* (New York: Rinehart, 1946), 203.

32. Ann Rickenbaugh, "Fear Is Stifling College Liberals," *Scan*, May 11, 1951, 1.

33. Ibid.

34. Sylvia Plath, *Letters Home: Correspondence 1950–1963*, ed. Aurelia Schober Plath (New York: Harper, 1975), 147. Subsequent quotations from this work are cited parenthetically in the text.

35. Marcia Damon, "College Women Evince Negativistic Attitutude," *Scan* January 15, 1952, 2.

36. Hammer, "Plath's Lives."

37. Sylvia Plath, Unpublished Poetry, Box 7A, Folder 13, LL.

38. Plath, "Somebody and We," College Essay, November 15, 1951, Plath Mss. II, Box 10, Folder 8, p. 4, LL.

39. Ibid., 7.

40. Ibid., 8.

41. Plath, "As a Baby-Sitter Sees It," newspaper article for *Christian Science Monitor*, Family Features, Youth Section, n.p., November 6, 1951, Box 9, Folder 1, LL.

42. Lines 357–400 in William Wordsworth, "The Prelude, Book I," in *William Wordsworth: Selected Poems*, ed. John O. Hayden (New York: Penguin, 1994).

43. Jacqueline Rose has noted the connection between *Generation of Vipers* and "The Babysitters" in order to show how "Plath situates herself . . . within the framework of popular culture" (165). However, apart from its mention in the context of Wylie's book, Rose gains no insight on the poetry based on this juxtaposition. Jacqueline Rose, *The Haunting of Sylvia Plath, Convergences: Inventories of the Present*, ed. Edward W. Said, (Cambridge, MA: Harvard University Press, 1991), 165.

44. Wylie, *Generation of Vipers*, 48.

45. Ibid., 50.

46. Ibid., 186.

47. Knitting was a popular pastime for college women in the 1950s; *Scan* was full of knitting ads during Plath's years there, but Plath refused to take it up.

48. Sylvia Plath, *The Bell Jar* (New York: Perennial, 1996), 219. Subsequent quotations from this work are cited parenthetically in the text.

49. Garry M. Leonard, "'The Woman Is Perfected. Her Dead Body Wears the Smile of Accomplishment': Sylvia Plath and Mademoiselle Magazine," *College Literature* 19, no. 2 (June 1992).

50. Michael Davidson, *Guys Like Us: Citing Masculinity in Cold War Politics* (Chicago: The University of Chicago Press, 2004), 186.

51. Van Dyne, *Revising Life*, 60.

52. Steven Gould Axelrod, *Sylvia Plath: The Wound and the Cure of Words* (Baltimore: The Johns Hopkins University Press, 1990), 145.

53. Rose, *Haunting*, 37.

54. Anne Stevenson, *Bitter Fame: A Life of Sylvia Plath* (Boston: Houghton Mifflin, 1998), 266.

6. Questions of Power

1. Quoted in Lynda K. Bundtzen, *The Other Ariel* (Amherst: University of Massachusetts Press, 2001), 131.

2. In Chapter 3 of her book *The Other Ariel*, Bundtzen provides an excellent analysis of the rich metaphorical possibilities of Plath's bee poem sequence and discusses why Plath might have chosen allegory as her primary "mode of expression" (111). Bundtzen argues that the choice of allegory allows Plath to write within a long tradition of poets from Virgil in *The Georgics* to Emily Dickinson that identifies the poet with the bee or beekeeper; this allegory also provides Plath with an alternative female community to the one she portrays in *The Bell Jar* (118).

3. Many critics have written about the bee poem sequence. The best readings are those attentive to the shifting power relationships in the poem, such as Tim Kendell's analysis in Chapter 7, "A Flying Hedgehog: The Bee Poems," of his *Sylvia Plath: A Critical Study* (London: Faber and Faber, 2001), and Chapter 3 of Lynda Bundtzen's *The Other Ariel* where she describes "authorship and authority" as "distributed" across "sites of power and activity" (108).

4. Foucault, *History of Sexuality*, 103.

5. Erich Fromm, *Escape from Freedom* (New York: Avon, 1965), 37–38.

6. Plath, "The Age of Anxiety and the Escape from Freedom," College Essay for History 38b, May 1954, Box 10, Folder 7, LL, 4.

7. Ibid., 2.

8. Deborah Nelson discusses how the "surveillance" society of the 1950s controlled both public and private spaces and argues that the work of "confessional" poets, such as Plath and Sexton, should be re-evaluated in terms of "the highly charged political debate about privacy in which it arose." She argues that, "Confessional poetry's contribution to public discourse was the dismantling of domestic ideology through the act of exposure itself, through the self-disclosure of that which should have been the subject of surveillance." See Deborah Nelson, "Penetrating Privacy: Confessional Poetry and the Surveillance Society," in *Homemaking: Women Writers and the Politics and Poetics of Home*, ed. Catherine Wiley and Fiona R. Barnes, *Gender & Genre in Literature* 8 (New York: Routledge, 1996), 87, 89.

NOTES TO CHAPTER 6

9. Laura Frost, "'Every Woman Adores a Fascist': Feminist Visions of Fascism from *Three Guineas* to *Fear of Flying*," *Women's Studies* 29 (2000): 46.

10. Ibid., 55.

11. Ibid., 47.

12. Ibid., 46.

13. Ibid., 64.

14. Al Strangeways, *Sylvia Plath: The Shaping of Shadows* (Madison: Farleigh Dickinson University Press, 1998), 15.

15. Several recent studies have discussed Plath's engagement with politics, including Tracy Brain's *The Other Plath* and Robin Peel's *Writing Back*. Brain focuses specifically on Plath's environmentalism, reading her alongside Rachel Carson's *Silent Spring*. See Tracy Brain, *The Other Sylvia Plath* (Harlow, England: Longman, 2001). Peel focuses on Plath's marked turn toward Cold War politics with her move to Britain when she became exposed to the more overtly political environment of nuclear disarmament protest and gained first-hand experience of nationalized medicine. See Robin Peel, *Writing Back: Sylvia Plath and Cold War Politics* (Madison, New Jersey: Fairleigh Dickinson University Press, 2002).

16. Breslin, *From Modern to Contemporary: American Poetry, 1945–1965*.

17. Plath, "The Age of Anxiety," 5.

18. Plath, "Fish in Unruffled Lakes," College Essay, Plath Mss. II, Box 10, Folder 8, LL.

19. Ibid., 3.

20. W. H. Auden, *Collected Poems*, ed. Edward Mendelson (New York: Vintage, 1991), 138–39.

21. Plath, "Age of Anxiety," 3.

22. Ibid., 2.

23. Brain, *The Other Sylvia Plath*, 69.

24. Plath, "The Devil's Advocate," College Essay for Russian 35b, 7, LL.

25. Fromm, *Escape from Freedom*, 208.

26. Plath, "The Age of Anxiety," 2.

27. The Massachusetts law was not overturned by the U. S. Supreme Court until 1972 in Eisenstadt v. Baird. See Claudia Goldin and Lawrence F. Katz, "The Power of the Pill: Oral Contraceptives and Women's Career and Marriage Decisions," *The Journal of Political Economy* 110, no. 4 (August 2002): 732n6.

28. Ted Hughes, *Birthday Letters* (London: Faber and Faber, 1998), 150.

29. Kendall, 141.

30. Ibid., 143.

31. See Frieda Hughes's head notes to Appendix I in Plath, *Ariel: The Restored Edition*, 189.

32. Bundtzen, *The Other Ariel*, 140.

33. Van Dyne's reading of Plath's drafts of this poem show Plath's uncertainty about the poem's ending. Van Dyne, *Revising Life*, 115.

34. Sandra M. Gilbert, "A Fine, White Flying Myth: The Life/Work of Sylvia Plath," in *Shakespeare's Sisters: Feminist Essays on Women Poets*, ed. Susan Gubar (Bloomington: Indiana University Press, 1979), 245.

35. Ibid.

36. Ibid., 246.
37. Ibid.
38. Ibid.

Coda

1. Maxine Kumin, *Nurture: Poems* (New York: Viking, 1989), 41. Subsequent quotations from this work are cited parenthetically in the text.

2. In Adrienne Rich, "Vesuvius at Home: The Power of Emily Dickinson," in *Shakespeare's Sisters: Feminist Essays on Women Poets*, Gilbert and Gubar, 99–121.

3. Adrienne Rich, "The Soul of a Women's College (1984)," in *Blood, Bread, and Poetry: Selected Prose, 1979–1985* (New York: Norton, 1986), 189.

4. Jill Ker Conway, *A Woman's Education* (New York: Alfred A. Knopf, 2001), 121–22.

5. Ibid., 123.
6. Ibid., 124.
7. Ibid.
8. Ibid.
9. Ibid., 134.
10. Ibid., 133.
11. Ibid.

Bibliography

Adams, Katherine H. *A Group of Their Own: College Writing Courses and American Women Writers, 1880–1940.* Albany: State University of New York Press, 2001.

Auden, W. H. *Collected Poems.* Edited by Edward Mendelson. New York: Vintage, 1991.

Axelrod, Steven Gould. *Sylvia Plath: The Wound and the Cure of Words.* Baltimore: The Johns Hopkins University Press, 1990.

Barthes, Roland. *The Pleasure of the Text.* Translated by Richard Miller. New York: The Noonday Press, 1975.

Baym, Nina. "Melodramas of Beset Manhood: How Theories of American Fiction Exclude Women Authors." In *The New Feminist Criticism: Essays on Women, Literature & Theory,* edited by Elaine Showalter, 63–80. New York: Pantheon Books, 1985.

Berger, Charles. "Who Writes the History Book?: Moore's Revisionary Poetics." *Western Humanities Review* 53, no. 3 (Fall 1999): 274–86.

Bishop, Elizabeth. "As We Like It: Miss Moore and Edgar Allan Poe." *Quarterly Review of Literature* 4, no. 2 (1948): 132–34.

———. "Dimensions for a Novel." *Vassar Journal of Undergraduate Studies* 8 (May 1934): 99.

———. *Edgar Allan Poe & the Juke-Box: Uncollected Poems, Drafts, and Fragments.* Edited by Alice Quinn. New York: Farrar, Straus and Giroux, 2006.

———. *Elizabeth Bishop: The Collected Prose.* Edited by Robert Giroux. New York: Farrar, Straus, and Giroux, 1984.

———. *Elizabeth Bishop: The Complete Poems.* New York: Farrar, Straus and Giroux, 1991.

———. Elizabeth Bishop Collection. Vassar College Library. Poughkeepsie, New York.

———. "A Flight of Fancy." *The Blue Pencil* (December 1929): 22–26.

———. "Gerard Manley Hopkins: Notes on Timing in His Poetry." *The Vassar Review* 23 (February 1934): 5–7.

———. "Hymn to the Virgin." *Con Spirito* 1, no. 2 (April 1933): 3.

———. "An Interview with Elizabeth Bishop." In *Elizabeth Bishop and Her Art,* edited by Lloyd Schwartz and Sybil P. Estess, 289–302. Ann Arbor: The University of Michigan Press, 1983.

———. *One Art: Elizabeth Bishop Letters.* Edited by Robert Giroux. New York: Farrar, Straus and Giroux, 1994.

———. "Seven-Days Monologue." *Con Spirito* 1, no. 2 (April 1933): 3–4.

———. "Then Came the Poor." *Con Spirito* 1, no. 1 (February 1933): 2, 4.

———. "Time's Andromedas." *Vassar Journal of Undergraduate Studies* 7 (May 1933): 102–20.

———. "A Word with You." *Con Spirito* 1, no. 2 (April 1933): 2.

Blough, Frani. "The Bacchae, or Revelling Women." *Con Spirito* 1, no. 2 (April 1933): 2.

A Book of Bryn Mawr Stories. Edited by Margaretta Morris and Louise Buffum Congdon. Philadelphia: George W. Jacobs, 1901.

Brain, Tracy. *The Other Sylvia Plath.* Harlow, England: Longman, 2001.

Breslin, James E. B. *From Modern to Contemporary: American Poetry, 1945–1965.* Chicago: University of Chicago Press, 1984.

Bromwich, David. "Elizabeth Bishop's Dream-Houses." In *Modern Critical Views: Elizabeth Bishop*, edited by Harold Bloom, 159–73. New York: Chelsea House, 1985.

Brownstein, Marilyn. "The Archaic Mother and Mother and Mother: The Postmodern Poetry of Marianne Moore." *Contemporary Literature* 30, no. 1 (1989): 13–32.

Bundtzen, Lynda K. *The Other Ariel.* Amherst: University of Massachusetts Press, 2001.

Butler, Judith. *Gender Trouble: Feminism and the Subversion of Identity.* New York: Routledge, 1990.

Conway, Jill Ker. *A Woman's Education.* New York: Alfred A. Knopf, 2001.

Costello, Bonnie. "Attractive Mortality." In *Elizabeth Bishop: The Geography of Gender*, edited by Marilyn May Lombardi, 126–52. Charlottesville: University Press of Virginia, 1993.

Cross, Barbara M., ed. *The Educated Woman in America: Selected Writings of Catharine Beecher, Margaret Fuller, and M. Carey Thomas.* Classics in Education, 25. New York: Teachers College Press, 1965.

Curley, Mary. "President Notes Role of Women." *Sophian,* June 9, 1952, 1, 6.

Damon, Marcia. "College Women Evince Negativistic Attitude." *Scan,* January 15, 1952, 2.

Davidson, Michael. *Guys Like Us: Citing Masculinity in Cold War Politics.* Chicago: The University of Chicago Press, 2004.

Doolittle, Hilda. "Circe." In *H. D.: Collected Poems, 1912–1944*, edited by Louis L. Martz. New York: New Directions, 1983.

Du Plessis, Rachel Blau. "'Corpses of Poesy': Some Modern Poets and Some Gender Ideologies of Lyric." In *Feminist Measures: Soundings in Poetry and Theory*, edited by Lynn Keller and Cristanne Miller, 69–95. Ann Arbor: University of Michigan Press, 1994.

———. "No Moore of the Same: The Feminist Poetics of Marianne Moore." *William Carlos Williams Review* 14, no. 1 (Spring 1988): 6–32.

"Editorial." *Con Spirito* 1, no. 1 (February 1933): 1.

"Editorial." *The American Spectator* 1, no. 3 (January 1933): 1.

Eliot, T. S. *The Complete Poems and Plays, 1909–1950*. San Diego, Harcourt Brace Jovanovich, 1952.

Ellis, Havelock. "The Physician and Sex." *The American Spectator* 1, no. 1 (November 1932): 1.

Emerson, Ralph Waldo. "Friendship." In *Emerson's Essays*. Apollo Editions, 1961.

Erkkila, Betsy. "Elizabeth Bishop, Modernism, and the Left." *American Literary History* 8, no. 2 (Summer 1996): 284–310.

———. *The Wicked Sisters: Women Poets, Literary History & Discord*. New York: Oxford University Press, 1992.

Faderman, Lillian. *Odd Girls and Twilight Lovers: A History of Lesbian Life in Twentieth-Century America*. New York: Penguin, 1991.

Flynn, Richard. "'The Buried Life and the Body of Waking': Muriel Rukeyser and the Politics of Literary History." In *Gendered Modernisms: American Women Poets and Their Readers*, edited by Margaret Dickie and Thomas Travisano, 264–79. Philadelphia: University of Pennsylvania Press, 1996.

Foucault, Michel. *The History of Sexuality, Vol. I: An Introduction*. Translated by Robert Hurley. New York: Vintage Books, 1980.

Fountain, Gary, and Peter Brazeau. *Remembering Elizabeth Bishop: An Oral Biography*. Amherst: University of Massachusetts Press, 1994.

Freud, Sigmund. "Family Romances." In *The Freud Reader*, edited by Peter Gay, 297–300. New York: Norton, 1989.

Fromm, Erich. *Escape from Freedom*. New York: Avon, 1965.

Frost, Laura. "'Every Woman Adores a Fascist': Feminist Visions of Fascism from *Three Guineas* to *Fear of Flying*." *Women's Studies* 29 (2000): 37–69.

Gilbert, Sandra M. "A Fine, White Flying Myth: The Life/Work of Sylvia Plath." In *Shakespeare's Sisters: Feminist Essays on Women Poets*, edited by Susan Gubar, 245–60. Bloomington: Indiana University Press, 1979.

Gilbert, Sandra M., and Susan Gubar. *No Man's Land: The Place of the Woman Writer in the Twentieth Century*. Vol. 1. New Haven, CT: Yale University Press, 1988.

Goldensohn, Lorrie. "The Body's Roses: Race, Sex, and Gender in Elizabeth Bishop's Representations of Self." In *Elizabeth Bishop: The Geography of Gender*, edited by Marilyn May Lombardi, 70–90. Charlottesville: University Press of Virginia, 1993.

———. *Elizabeth Bishop: The Biography of a Poetry*. New York: Columbia University Press, 1992.

Goldin, Claudia, and Lawrence F. Katz. "The Power of the Pill: Oral Contraceptives and Women's Career and Marriage Decisions." *The Journal of Political Economy* 110, no. 4 (August 2002): 730–70.

Gordon, Lynn D. *Gender and Higher Education in the Progressive Era*. New Haven, CT: Yale University Press, 1990.

Gregory, Alyse. "The Dilemma of Marriage." *The New Republic* 4 (July 1923): 151–52.

Griffith, Gabriele. *Heavenly Love? Lesbian Images in Twentieth Century Women's Writing*. Manchester, England: Manchester University Press, 1993.

Hadas, Pamela. "Treading Chasms." In *Modern Critical Views: Marianne Moore*, edited by Harold Bloom, 25–41. New York: Chelsea House, 1987.

Hammer, Langdon. "The New Elizabeth Bishop." *The Yale Review* 82, no. 1 (January 1994): 135–49.

———. "Plath's Lives: Poetry, Professionalism, and the Culture of the School." *Representations* 75 (2001): 61–88.

———. "Useless Concentration: Life and Work in Elizabeth Bishop's Letters and Poems." *American Literary History* 9, no. 1 (Spring 1997): 162–80.

Hawthorne, Nathaniel. "The Intelligence Office." In *Mosses from an Old Manse, Vol. 2, in the Centenary Edition of the Works of Nathaniel Hawthorne Vol. X*. Columbus: The Ohio State University Press, 1974.

Holley, Margaret. *The Poetry of Marianne Moore: A Study in Voice and Value*. Cambridge: Cambridge University Press, 1987.

Horowitz, Helen Lefkowitz. *The Power and Passion of M. Carey Thomas*. New York: Alfred A. Knopf, 1994.

Hotelling, Kirstin. "'The I of Each Is to the I of Each, a Kind of Fretful Speech Which Sets a Limit on Itself': Marianne Moore's Strategic Selfhood." *Modernism/Modernity* 5, no. 1 (1996): 75–96.

Howe, Florence, and Ellen Bass, eds. *No More Masks! An Anthology of Poems by Women*. New York: Anchor, 1973.

Hubbard, Stacy Carson. "Mannerist Moore: Poetry, Painting, Photography." In *Critics and Poets on Marianne Moore: "A Right Good Salvo of Barks,"* edited by Robin G. Schulze, 113–36. Lewisburg, PA: Bucknell University Press, 2005.

Hughes, Ted. *Birthday Letters*. London: Faber and Faber, 1998.

Huyssen, Andreas. "Mass Culture as Woman." In *After the Great Divide: Modernism, Mass Culture, Postmodernism*, 44–62. Bloomington: Indiana University Press, 1986.

Jessup, Eunice Clark. "Memoirs of Literatae and Socialists 1929–1933." *Vassar Quarterly* 55 (1979): 16–17.

Joyce, Elizabeth W. *Cultural Critique and Abstraction: Marianne Moore and the Avant-Garde*. Lewisburg, PA: Bucknell University Press, 1998.

Kaledin, Eugenia. *Mothers and More: American Women in the 1950s*. Boston: Twayne Publishers, 1984.

Kalstone, David. *Becoming a Poet: Elizabeth Bishop with Marianne Moore and Robert Lowell*. Edited by Robert Hemenway. New York: Farrar, Straus and Giroux, 1989.

Keller, Lynn. "'For Inferior Who Is Free?': Liberating the Woman Writer in Marianne Moore's 'Marriage.'" In *Influence and Intertextuality in Literary History*, edited by Jay Clayton and Eric Rothstein. Madison: University of Wisconsin Press, 1991.

Kendall, Tim. *Sylvia Plath: A Critical Study*. London: Faber and Faber, 2001.

Kent, Susan Kingsley. *Sex and Suffrage in Britain, 1860–1914*. Princeton, NJ: Princeton University Press, 1987.

Kumin, Maxine. *Nurture: Poems.* New York: Viking, 1989.

Leavell, Linda. *Marianne Moore and the Visual Arts: Prismatic Color.* Baton Rouge: Louisiana State University Press, 1995.

———. "Marianne Moore, the James Family, and the Politics of Celibacy." *Twentieth-Century Literature* 49, no. 2 (Summer 2003): 219–45.

Leonard, Garry M. "'The Woman Is Perfected. Her Dead Body Wears the Smile of Accomplishment': Sylvia Plath and Mademoiselle Magazine." *College Literature* 19, no. 2 (June 1992): 60–82.

Leonardi, Susan J. *Dangerous by Degrees: Women at Oxford and the Somerville College Novelists.* New Brunswick, NJ: Rutgers University Press, 1989.

Lombardi, Marilyn May, ed. *Elizabeth Bishop: The Geography of Gender.* Charlottesville: University Press of Virginia, 1993.

Longenbach, James. "Elizabeth Bishop's Social Conscience." *English Literary History* 62 (1995): 467–86.

———. *Modern Poetry after Modernism.* New York: Oxford University Press, 1997.

Lowney, John. "'Littered with Old Correspondences': Elizabeth Bishop, Wallace Stevens, and the 1930s." *Arizona Quarterly* 55, no. 2 (Summer 1999): 87–114.

Marchalonis, Shirley. *College Girls: A Century in Fiction.* New Brunswick, NJ: Rutgers University Press, 1995.

McCarthy, Mary. *The Group.* New York: Harcourt, Brace and World, 1963.

———. *How I Grew.* New York: Harcourt Brace Jovanovich, 1987.

———. "In Pace Requiescamus." *Con Spirito* 1, no. 2 (April 1933): 1.

———. "Two Crystal-Gazing Novelists." *Con Spirito* 1, no. 1 (February 1933): 1–2.

McChesney, Nancy. "Coles Discuss Components of True Marriage." *Scan*, April 13, 1951, 1.

McDonald, Gail. *Learning to Be Modern: Pound, Eliot, and the American University.* Oxford: Clarendon Press, 1993.

Merrin, Jeredith. "Elizabeth Bishop: Gaiety, Gayness, and Change." In *Elizabeth Bishop: The Geography of Gender*, edited by Marilyn May Lombardi. Charlottesville: University Press of Virginia, 1993.

———. "Marianne Moore and Elizabeth Bishop." In *Columbia History of American Poetry*, edited by Brett C. Millier and Jay Parini, 343–69. New York: Columbia University Press, 1993.

Meyer, Agnes E. "Women Aren't Men." *Atlantic Monthly* 186.2 (August 1950): 32–36.

Middlebrook, Diane. *Her Husband: Hughes and Plath—a Marriage.* New York: Viking, 2003.

Miller, Cristanne. *Marianne Moore: Questions of Authority.* Cambridge, MA: Harvard University Press, 1995.

———. "Marianne Moore's Black Maternal Hero: A Study in Categorization." *American Literary History* 1, no. 4 (Winter 1989).

Miller, Margaret. "Sur-Realism, the Last Mohican of the Primitives." *Con Spirito* 1, no. 1 (February 1933): 3.

Millier, Brett C. *Elizabeth Bishop: Life and the Memory of It*. Berkeley: University of California Press, 1993.

Milton, John. *The Complete Poetry of John Milton*. Edited by John T. Shawcross. revised ed. New York: Anchor Books, 1971.

Molesworth, Charles. *Marianne Moore: A Literary Life*. Boston: Northeastern University Press, 1991.

Moore, Marianne. *Becoming Marianne Moore: The Early Poems, 1907–1924*. Edited by Robin G. Schulze. Berkeley: University of California Press, 2002.

———. *The Complete Poems of Marianne Moore*. New York: Penguin, 1981.

———. *The Complete Prose of Marianne Moore*. Edited by Patricia C. Willis. New York: Penguin, 1987.

———. "A Jelly-Fish." *The Lantern* 17 (Spring 1909): 110.

———. Marianne Moore Collection. Rosenbach Museum and Library. Philadelphia, Pennsylvania.

———. *The Poems of Marianne Moore*. Edited by Grace Schulman. New York: Viking, 2003.

———. *The Selected Letters of Marianne Moore*. Edited by Bonnie Costello, Celeste Goodridge, and Cristanne Miller. New York: Alfred A. Knopf, 1997.

"Moral Lapse Laid to Kinsey Report." *The New York Times*, October 21, 1950, 14.

Morantz, Regina Markell. "The Scientist as Sex Crusader: Alfred C. Kinsey and American Culture." *American Quarterly* 29, no. 5 (Winter, 1977): 563–89.

Morris, Timothy. *Becoming Canonical in American Poetry*. Urbana: University of Illinois Press, 1995.

"Most of Smith Single: Only 112 Sport Rings." *Scan*, May 15, 1951, 1.

Nathan, George Jean. "The Theatre." *The American Spectator* 1, no. 1 (November 1932): 2.

Neff, Fraiken Wanda. *We Sing Diana*. Boston: Houghton Mifflin, 1928.

Nelson, Deborah. "Penetrating Privacy: Confessional Poetry and the Surveillance Society." In *Homemaking: Women Writers and the Politics and Poetics of Home*, edited by Catherine Wiley and Fiona R. Barnes, *Gender and Genre in Literature* 8, 87–114. New York: Routledge, 1996.

Palatella, John. "'That Sense of Constant Re-Adjustment': The Great Depression and the Provisional Politics of Elizabeth Bishop's *North & South*." *Contemporary Literature* 34, no. 1 (Spring 1993): 18–43.

Palmieri, Patricia Ann. *In Adamless Eden: The Community of Women Faculty at Wellesley*. New Haven, CT: Yale University Press, 1995.

Peel, Robin. *Writing Back: Sylvia Plath and Cold War Politics*. Madison, NJ: Fairleigh Dickinson University Press, 2002.

Pells, Richard H. *Radical Visions and American Dreams: Culture and Social Thought in the Depression Years*. Middletown, CT: Wesleyan University Press, 1973.

Plath, Sylvia. *Ariel: The Restored Edition*. Edited by Frieda Hughes. New York: HarperCollins, 2004.

———. *The Bell Jar*. New York: Perennial, 1996.

———. *The Collected Poems of Sylvia Plath*. Edited by Ted Hughes. New York: Harper-Perennial, 1981.

———. *Letters Home: Correspondence 1950–1963*. Edited by Aurelia Schober Plath. New York: Harper, 1975.

———. Sylvia Plath Collection. Lilly Library, Indiana University. Bloomington.

———. *The Unabridged Journals of Sylvia Plath, 1950–1962*. Edited by Karen V. Kukil. New York: Anchor Books, 2000.

Pondrom, Cyrena N. "Marianne Moore and H. D.: Female Community and Poetic Achievement." In *Marianne Moore: Woman and Poet*, edited by Patricia C. Willis, 371–402. Orono, ME: The National Poetry Foundation, 1990.

Pound, Ezra. *Collected Early Poems of Ezra Pound*. New York: New Directions, 1976.

———. *The Selected Letters of Ezra Pound, 1907–1941*. Edited by D. D. Paige. New York: New Directions, 1971.

Rich, Adrienne. "The Eye of the Outsider: Elizabeth Bishop's Complete Poems, 1927–1979." In *Blood, Bread, and Poetry: Selected Prose 1979–1985*, 124–35. New York: Norton, 1986.

———. "The Soul of a Women's College (1984)." In *Blood, Bread, and Poetry: Selected Prose, 1979–1985*, 188–97. New York: Norton, 1986.

———. "Vesuvius at Home: The Power of Emily Dickinson." In *Shakespeare's Sisters: Feminist Essays on Women Poets*, edited by Sandra M. Gilbert and Susan Gubar, 99–121. Bloomington: Indiana University Press, 1979.

Richardson, Angelique, and Chris Willis, eds. *The New Woman in Fiction and in Fact: Fin-De-Siecle Feminisms*. London: Palgrave Macmillan, 2002.

Rickenbaugh, Ann. "Fear Is Stifling College Liberals." *Scan*, May 11, 1951, 1, 4.

Rose, Jacqueline. *The Haunting of Sylvia Plath. Convergences: Inventories of the Present*, edited by Edward W. Said. Cambridge, MA: Harvard University Press, 1991.

Rotella, Guy. *Castings: Monuments and Monumentality in Poems by Elizabeth Bishop, Robert Lowell, James Merrill, Derek Walcott, and Sean Heaney*. Nashville, TN: Vanderbilt University Press, 2004.

Rukeyser, Muriel. "Lecture by Mr. Eliot." *Con Spirito* 2, no. 1 (November 1933): 2.

———. *Theory of Flight*. New Haven, CT: Yale University Press, 1935.

Russo, Mary. *The Female Grotesque: Risk, Excess and Modernity*. New York: Routledge, 1994.

Schwartz, Lloyd, and Sybil P. Estess, eds. *Elizabeth Bishop and Her Art*. Ann Arbor: University of Michigan Press, 1983.

Scott, Bonnie Kime, ed. *The Gender of Modernism: A Critical Anthology*. Bloomington: Indiana University Press, 1990.

Scott, Joan Wallach. *Gender and the Politics of History*. New York: Columbia University Press, 1988.

Sielke, Sabine. "Snapshots of Marriage, Snares of Mimicry, Snarls of Motherhood: Marianne Moore and Adrienne Rich." *Sagetrieb* 6, no. 3 (Winter 1987): 79–97.

Slatin, John. *The Savage's Romance: The Poetry of Marianne Moore*. University Park: The Pennsylvania State University Press, 1986.

———. "The Town's Assertiveness: Marianne Moore and New York City." In *Marianne Moore: Woman and Poet*, edited by Patricia C. Willis, 61–82. Orono, ME: National Poetry Foundation, 1990.

Smith-Rosenberg, Carroll. *Disorderly Conduct: Visions of Gender in Victorian America*. New York: Oxford University Press, 1985.

Solomon, Barbara Miller. *In the Company of Educated Women: A History of Women and Higher Education in America*. New Haven, CT: Yale University Press, 1985.

Stapleton, Laurence. *Marianne Moore: The Poet's Advance*. Princeton, NJ: Princeton University Press, 1978.

Stevens, Wallace. *The Collected Poems*. New York: Vintage, 1982.

———. *Letters of Wallace Stevens*. Edited by Holly Stevens. Berkeley: University of California Press, 1996.

———. "The Noble Rider and the Sound of Words." In *The Necessary Angel*, 3–36. New York: Vintage, 1951.

Stevenson, Anne. *Bitter Fame: A Life of Sylvia Plath*. Boston: Houghton Mifflin, 1998.

Strangeways, Al. *Sylvia Plath: The Shaping of Shadows*. Madison, NJ: Farleigh Dickinson University Press, 1998.

Suleiman, Susan Rubin. *Subversive Intent: Gender, Politics, and the Avant Garde*. Cambridge, MA: Harvard University Press, 1990.

Tomlinson, Charles, ed. *Marianne Moore: A Collection of Critical Essays*. New York: Prentice Hall, 1969.

Travisano, Thomas. *Elizabeth Bishop: Her Artistic Development*. Charlottesville: University Press of Virginia, 1988.

Untermeyer, Louis. "Daughters of Niobe." *The American Spectator* 1, no. 1 (November 1932): 4.

Van Dyne, Susan R. *Revising Life: Sylvia Plath's Ariel Poems*. Gender and American Culture, edited by Linda K. Kerber and Nell Irvin Painter, Chapel Hill: The University of North Carolina Press, 1993.

Vance, Carole. "Pleasure and Danger: Toward a Politics of Sexuality." In *Pleasure and Danger: Exploring Female Sexuality*, edited by Carole Vance. Boston: Routledge and Kegan Paul, 1984.

Walker, Cheryl. "Antimodern, Modern, and Postmodern Millay: Contexts of Revaluation." In *Gendered Modernisms: American Women Poets and Their Readers*, edited by Margaret Dickie and Thomas Travisano, 170–88. Philadelphia: University of Pennsylvania Press, 1996.

Westcott, Glenway. "Concerning Miss Moore's *Observations*." *The Dial* 78 (January 1925): 1–4.

White, Heather Cass. "Morals, Manners, and 'Marriage': Marianne Moore's Art of Conversation." *Twentieth Century Literature* 45, no. 4 (Winter 1999): 488–510.

Williams, William Carlos. "Marianne Moore." In *Selected Essays*, 121–31. New York: New Directions, 1954.

Willis, Patricia C. "Comment." *Marianne Moore Newsletter* 5, no. 1 (Spring 1981): 2–4.

———. "MM on the Literary Life." *Marianne Moore Newsletter* 5, no. 1 (Spring 1981): 6.

———. *Marianne Moore: Vision into Verse*. Philadelphia: The Rosenbach Museum and Library, 1987.

———. "The Owl and the Lantern: Marianne Moore at Bryn Mawr." *Poesis* 6, no. 3–4 (1985): 84–97.

Wollstonecraft, Mary. *Vindication of the Rights of Woman*. Edited by Carol H. Poston. 2nd ed. *Norton Critical Edition*. New York: Norton, 1988.

Wordsworth, William. "The Prelude, Book I." In *William Wordsworth: Selected Poems*, edited by John O. Hayden. New York: Penguin, 1994.

Wylie, Philip. *Generation of Vipers*. New York: Rinehart, 1946.

Yeats, W. B. *The Poems*. Edited by Richard J. Finneran. Vol. 1, *The Collected Works of W. B. Yeats*. New York: Scribner, 1997.

Zona, Kirstin Hotelling. *Marianne Moore, Elizabeth Bishop, and May Swenson: The Feminist Poetics of Self-Restraint*. Ann Arbor: The University of Michigan Press, 2002.

Index

Numbers in *italics* indicate illustration pages

Adams, Katherine, 24, 110
Addams, Jane, 77
Against this Age (Bodenheim), 77
Aldington, Richard, 96
Alexander, John White: *A Quiet Hour*, 38
Allen, E. Ross, 124, 125, 128
American Academy of Arts and Sciences, 139
American Spectator, The, 22, 25, 86–87, 89, 107–9
"And Shall Life Pass an Old Maid By?," (Moore), 63
"Applicant, The" (Plath), 157, 162
"Ariel" (Plath), 167
Ariel (Plath): 131, 132, 148, 151, 153, 164, 167, 173, 174; "The Jailor," 131, 132; "Lesbos," 131–33, 148, 151–54; "Medusa," 131, 132
"Arrival at Santos" (Bishop), 123
"Arrival of the Bee Box, The" (Plath), 163–64, 167–69
Asquith, Lady Cynthia, 95
Atlantic Monthly, 136
Auden, W. H., 158, 162; and love, 159, 174; "September 1939," 159; *Twelve Songs*, 159
Axelrod, Steven Gould, 151–52

"Babysitters, The" (Plath), 133, 137, 141–43, 145–46, 148, 149, 154
Bacon, Francis, 61, 62, 71
Bakhtin, Mikhail, 75

Barnard College, 23, 135
Barthes, Roland, 26
Baxter, Richard: *The Saints' Everlasting Rest*, 69
Baym, Nina, 88
Becoming a Poet (Kalstone), 119
"Bee God, The" (Hughes), 164
"Bee Meeting, The" (Plath), 160–61, 170
Bee poems (Plath), 156–74; "The Arrival of the Bee Box," 163–64, 167–69; "The Bee Meeting," 160–61, 170; "Stings," 163, 172; "The Swarm," 167–68; 170–71; "Wintering," 171–72
"Beekeeper's Daughter, The" (Plath), 164
Bell Jar, The (Plath), 133, 143, 147, 149–52, 159, 161–63, 172
Berger, Charles, 62, 67
"Bird News, The," 35
birds: as code word for lesbians, 95
Birthday Letters (Hughes), 164
Bishop, Elizabeth: 26, 28, 85, 176; and ART, 120; college essays of, 112–15 (*see also under individual titles*); college life of, 20, 22, 24, 25, 29, 84–106, 134; correspondence with Blough, 116, 125, 126; on Eliot, 110, 113–14; and female community, 97–102, 115–34; and Key West, 95, 114, 116, 124, 126; and Lockwood, 111; on Millay, 107; and Moore, 24,

109, 120, 124–26, 128; post-college life/career, 115–30; sexuality of, 25; socialism of, 96, 108; and Stevens, 119–21; writing experiments of, 25, 109, 116. See also *Con Spirito*
—Works: "Arrival at Santos," 123; "Brazil, January 1, 1502," 128; *A Cold Spring*, 94; `"Chemin de Fer," 119; "Crusoe in England," 25, 102–5; "Dimensions for a Novel,"112–14, 120; "The Fish," 124–25; "A Flight of Fancy," 98; "Florida," 121, 123–26, 128–29; "The Gentleman of Shalott," 112, 116, 119, 121, 123; *Geography III*, 102, 104; "Gerard Manley Hopkins," 114; "Hymn to the Virgin," 85, 113; "In Prison," 100–102; "In the Village," 129; "In the Waiting Room," 129–30; "It is marvelous to wake up together . . . ," 95; "The Man-Moth," 25, 117–19, 121, 130; "The Monument," 119, 121, 123, 130; *North & South*, 109; "Roosters," 125; "The Sea and Its Shore," 116–17;"Seven-Days' Monologue," 90–94, 96, 104, 121, 126; "A Summer's Dream," 94;"Then Came the Poor," 85, 96–99, 105–6; "Time's Andromedas," 106, 114; "A Wordwith You," 89–90, 97
"Blackberrying" (Plath), 147, 150
"Black Earth" (Moore), 30, 50–53, 65
Blough, Frani, 84, 95–100, 107, 108, 115, 124; correspondence with Bishop, 116, 125, 126; on Lawrence, 110–12
Bodenheim, Maxwell: *Against this Age*, 77; *Crazy Man*, 77
Book of Bryn Mawr Stories, A, 58, 59, 67; "Catherine's Career," 59; "Free Among theDead," 59–60; "Her Masterpiece," 61
Boyd, Ernest, 86
Brain, Tracy, 160
Brave New World (Huxley), 112
"Brazil, January 1, 1502" (Bishop), 128
Breslin, James, 113–14, 158–59
Brett, Dorothy, 95

Briscoe, Virginia Wolf, 30
Brooks, Cleanth: *Understanding Poetry* (w. Warren), 135; *The Well Wrought Urn*, 139
Broom, 73, 74
Brown, Marcia, 141–43, *142*, 146, 155
Bryher, 29, 32, 47–48, 64, 71
Bryn Mawr College, 19, 20, 21, 24, 25, 29–56, 58, 59, 61, 82, 132, 135. See also Moore, Marianne; Thomas, M. Carey
Bundtzen, Lynda, 170
Burke, Carolyn, 75
"Burning the Letters" (Plath), 164
Butler, Judith, 87

Cabell, James Branch, 86, 107
Carswell, Catherine, 95
Carter, Pres. Franklin, 57
"Chemin de Fer" (Bishop), 119
Chimaera, The, 48
Christian Science Monitor, 144
Clark, Eleanor, 25, 84, 85, 95, 99, 111
Clark, Eunice, 25, 84, 88, 99
Cold Spring, A (Bishop), 94
Cole, Hubert: *Josephine*, 167
Cole, Mrs. William, 136
Coleridge, S. T.: *Kubla Khan*, 122
Complete Poems (Moore), 42, 54
Collected Poems (Plath), 171
conformity, 138–39, 147. See also homemaker ideal; women: as homemakers
Con Spirito, 22, 25, 84–130
Conway, Jill Kerr, 176–78
Cowley, Malcolm, 85
Crane, Louise, 95, 115, 116, 124, 126
Crazy Man (Bodenheim), 77
Cross, Barbara, 82
"Crusoe in England" (Bishop), 25, 102–5

"Daddy" (Plath), 154, 157, 169, 170
Davidson, Michael, 151
Deanery, the, 21, 35, 46
Defoe, Daniel: *Robinson Crusoe*, 103–4
"Den of Lions" (Plath), 172
"Detective, The" (Plath), 164–66

Dial, 70, 71, 77, 82
Dickinson, Emily, 176
Diehl, Joanne Feit, 105
"Dilemma of Marriage, The" (Gregory), 71–73, 76, 81
"Dimensions for a Novel" (Bishop), 112–14, 120
Doolittle, Hilda. *See* H.D.
Dostoevsky, Fyodor, 158
Draft of XVI Cantos, A (Pound), 30
Dreiser, Theodore, 86
DuPlessis, Rachel Blau, 58, 75

Earhart, Amelia: and stunting, 93
"Education of a Poet" (Moore), 32, 60
Educational Review, 60, 70
"Elfride, Making Epigrams" (Moore), 49, 50
Eliot, Charles, 21–22, 57
Eliot, T. S., 20, 21, 85, 109, 112; "The Hippopotamus," 51; *Prufrock,* 55; "Tradition and the Individual Talent," 113; *The Waste Land,* 30
"Ella Mason and Her Eleven Cats" (Plath), 140
Ellerman, Winifred. *See* Bryher
Emerson, Ralph Waldo: *Essays,* 108; "Friendship," 39–40
"Ennui" (Moore), 44
Erkkila, Betsy, 24, 84, 96
Escape from Freedom (Fromm), 156–60
Essays (Emerson), 108

Faderman, Lillian, 23, 133
Farjeon, Eleanor, 95
Fascism, 156, 157
"Fear is Stifling College Liberals" (Rickenbaugh), 138–39
female community, 115–30, 151, 155, 159, 161, 166
Feminine Mystique, The (Friedan), 173
"Fine, White Flying Myth, A: The Life/Work of Sylvia Plath" (Gilbert), 172
Finnegans Wake (Joyce), 88
"Fish, The" (Bishop), 124–25
"Flight of Fancy, A" (Bishop), 98
"Florida" (Bishop), 123–26, 128–29

Flynn, Richard, 108
Foucault, Michel, 156, 169
"Free Among the Dead" (King), 59–60
Freud, Sigmund, 70–71, 97, 168, 176
Friedan, Betty: *The Feminine Mystique,* 173
"Friendship" (Emerson), 39–40
friendship, 41, 42
Fromm, Erich, 156–60, 162, 168
Frost, Laura, 157
Frost, Robert, 123
Fullerton, William Morton, 37

Garrett, Mary, 75
Gendron, Val, 140–41
Generation of Vipers (Wylie), 137, 145–46
"Gentleman of Shalott, The" (Bishop), 112, 116, 119, 121, 123
Geography III (Bishop), 102, 109
"Geography Lesson" (Plath), 158
"Gerard Manley Hopkins" (Bishop), 114
Gilbert, Sandra: "A Fine, White Flying Myth," 172
Gilman, Charlotte Perkins: *Women and Economics,* 80; "The Yellow Wallpaper," 33
Ginsberg, Allen: *Kaddish,* 159
Godwin, William, 69, 70
Goldensohn, Lorrie, 104, 105
Goldman, Emma, 108
Gordon, Lynn, 21, 22, 29, 60–61
"Goring, The" (Plath), 132
Gregory, Alyse, 70, 71, *72,* 75–76, 81; "The Dilemma of Marriage," 71–73, 75–76, 81; on sex, 73
Griffith, Gabriele, 103
Group, The (McCarthy), 150–51
Gwinn, Mamie, 35

Haldeman, Marcet, 33
Hammer, Langdon, 93, 134–35, 139
Hardy, Thomas: *A Pair of Blue Eyes,* 48, 50
Harmonium (Stevens), 30, 124, 127; "O Florida, Venereal Soil," 127–28; "Stars at Tallapoosa," 120

Hawthorne, Nathaniel, 89; "The Intelligence Office," 100–101
H.D., 19, 64, 82; *Hymen*, 73–75
"Heavy Women" (Plath), 147
Hemingway, Ernest, 124, 125
"Her Masterpiece" (MacIntosh), 61
heteroglossia, 75
"Hippopotamus, The" (Eliot), 51
Hoggart, Richard, 159
Holley, Margaret, 63
homemaker ideal, 20, 22–24, 26, 135–36, 145
homosexuality, 111, 133
Hopkins, Gerard Manley, 113, 114
Horowitz, Helen Lefkowitz, 21
Hound and Horn, 110
Hughes, Frieda, 131, 156
Hughes, Nicholas, 156, 163
Hughes, Ted, 27, 131, 152, 154–56, 163, 164; *Birthday Letters*, 164
Huxley, Aldous, 96, 110; *Brave New World*, 112
Hymen (H.D.), 73–75
"Hymn to the Virgin" (Bishop), 85, 113

Ideas of Order (Stevens), 124, 127
Imitation of Life (Sirk), 143
improvisation: and *Con Spirito*, 109–12
"In Pace Requiescamus" (McCarthy), 109
"In Prison" (Bishop), 100–102
"In the Village" (Bishop), 129
"In the Waiting Room" (Bishop), 129–30
"Insomniac" (Plath), 147
"Intelligence Office, The" (Hawthorne), 100–101
"It is marvelous to wake up together . . ." (Bishop), 95

"Jailor, The" (Plath), 131–32
James, Henry, 36–38, 70
James, Peggy, 35, 36, 38, 39
James, William, 36
"Jelly-Fish, A" (Moore), 42–44
Jones, Howard Mumford, 139
Jong, Erica, 157

Josephine (Cole), 167
Joyce, Elizabeth, 69
Joyce, James, 114, 155; *Finnegans Wake*, 88

Kaddish (Ginsberg), 159
Kaledin, Eugenia, 137
Kalstone, David, 102; *Becoming a Poet*, 119
Kazin, Alfred, 139, 166
Kendall, Tim, 167
Kent, Susan Kingsley: *Sex and Suffrage in Britain, 1860–1914*, 65, 80–81
Kesey, Ken: *One Flew Over the Cuckoo's Nest*, 159
King, Georgiana Goddard: "Free Among the Dead," 59; imitation writing course of, 43, 44, 48–50, 58–59, 67
Kinsey reports, 136–37
Kitchel, Anna, 107, 110
Kluckhohn, Florence, 137
Krafft-Ebing, Richard von, 86
Kreymborg, Alfred, 54, 175
Kristeva, Julia, 152
Kubla Khan (Coleridge), 122
Kukil, Karen, ed.: *Unabridged Journals*, 149
Kuhn, Thomas, 114
Kumin, Maxine: "Marianne, My Mother, and Me," 175–76

Lantern, The, 42, 44, 49
"Lapis Lazuli" (Yeats), 123
Latimer, Ronald Lane, 120
lavender: as lesbian color code, 91, 94
Lawrence, D. H., 110; anti-feminism of, 71, 75–76, 95
Leavell, Linda, 36, 39, 47, 53
Leonard, Garry, 150
lesbianism, 22, 23, 25, 59, 67, 86, 89, 90, 103, 133, 148–54; and Bishop, 85, 91, 94, 95, 101, 106
"Lesbos" (Plath), 131–33, 146, 151–54
Lilly Library, 136, 141
Lockwood, Helen, 111
logopoeia, 75

Longenbach, James, 99, 113
Lowell, Robert, 124; "Skunk Hour," 159
Lowney, John, 120
Loy, Mina, 75, 82
Luhan, Mabel Dodge, 95

MacIntosh, Marian: "Her Masterpiece," 61
Mademoiselle, 135, 139, 172, 173
Magazine, The, 85, 113
"Man with the Blue Guitar, The" (Stevens), 121
"Man-Moth, The" (Bishop), 25, 117–19, 121, 130
Mansfield, Katherine, 95
"Marianne, My Mother, and Me" (Kumin), 175–76
"Marcia" (Plath), 141
"Marriage" (Moore), 40, 43, 48, 58–59, 61–63, 65–66, 68–69, 71, 73–80
marriage, 23, 57–59, 62, 78, 81. See also "Marriage"; Thomas, M. Carey
Mayo family, 143–44
McAlmon, Robert, 64
McCarthy Era, 20, 133
McCarthy, Mary, 25, 84, 85, 87–89, 93, 96, 99, 110; *The Group,* 111, 150–51; onHuxley, 110, 112; on Harold Nicolson, 112; "In Pace Requiescamus," 109; on Vassar, 107, 110–11
McDonald, Gail, 20, 30
McIntosh, Millicent, 23, 125
"Medusa" (Plath), 131–32
Melanchthon, PhilIpp, 53
Merrill, James, 119
Merrin, Jeredith, 94
"Metamorphoses of the Moon" (Plath), 137–38, 155
Meyer, Agnes E.: "Women Aren't Men," 136, 137
Millay, Edna St. Vincent, 19–20, 107
Millier, Brett, 119
Miller, Christanne, 67
Miller, Margaret, 84, 111, 115, 124
Mills College, 135
Milton, John: *Paradise Lost,* 66–67
Mitchell, Dr. S. Weir, 33

modernism (poetic), 30
Molesworth, Charles, 91
"Monument, The" (Bishop), 119, 121, 123, 124
"Moon and the Yew Tree, The" (Plath), 132–33, 149–50, 165, 174
Moore, Marianne, 26, 28, *72,* 108, 114, 115, 139, 175, 176; animal poetry, 25; andBishop, 24, 109, 120, 124–26, 128; and "blameless bachelor," 70; college life of, 19–21, 24, 25, 29–56; on Freud, 187–88 n. 46; on King, 74; letters home, 29, 31–35, 44, 56, 60; and *Hymen* (H.D.), 73–75; on male writers, 76–77, 82; and Mannerist style, 179–80 n. 9; on marriage, 58, 62–65, 69–71, 79–82; and Pound, 44, 51–53; use ofmedieval imagery, 40, 48–50; use of reversals in writing, 61, 65–66, 69; writing experiments of, 24, 40
—Works: "And Shall Life Pass an Old Maid By?," 63; "Black Earth," 30, 50–53, 65;*Complete Poems,* 42, 54; "Education of a Poet," 32, 60; "Elfride, Making Epigrams," 49, 50; "Ennui," 44; "A Jelly-Fish," 42–44; "Marriage," 40, 43, 48, 58–59, 61–63, 65–66, 68–69, 71, 73–80; "My Lantern," 49; "New York," 45; *O to Be aDragon,* 43; *Observations,* 24, 30, 40, 51; "Peter," 30, 50, 53–56, 61; "Piningly," 65, 78; "Progress," 55; "Pym," 36–42; "Radical," 47–48; "Roses Only," 68; "Sea Unicorns and Land Unicorns," 68; "Silence," 44; "SteepleJack, The" (Moore), 66; "The Student," 19, 28; "The Tentative Critic," 49; "Those Various Scalpels," 68, 74; "ToBe Liked by You Would Be a Calamity," 48–50; "To a Screen Maker," 44; "When I Buy Pictures," 40, 41; "Wisdom and Virtue, 45–47, 50, 51, 65–66
Moore, Warner, 31, 32
Morison, Margaret, 46
Morrel, Lady Ottoline, 95

Morris, Timothy, 106
mother-daughter relationships, 31–32
Mount Holyoke College, 82
"Mr. Burnshaw and the Statue" (Stevens), 120
Mummies, 78–79
"Munich Mannequins, The" (Plath), 133
Muser, Frani Blough. *See* Blough, Frani
"My Lantern" (Moore), 49

Nathan, George Jean, 86; "The Theatre," 86
National American Woman Suffrage Association, 77
National College Equal Suffrage League, 77
Nearing, Mary, 75, 76
New Critical perspectives/New Criticism, 113, 139
New Republic, 71, 85
New Statesman, 167
New Woman, The, 24, 30, 39, 45–56, 58, 66, 68, 75
"New York" (Moore), 45
New York Times, 137, 138
Nicolson, Harold: *Public Faces,* 112
Nietzsche, Friedrich, 158, 162
Norcross family, 32, 35, 39
North & South (Bishop), 109
"Notes to a Neophyte" (Plath), 139
Now, Voyager (Prouty), 134

O, to Be a Dragon (Moore), 43
Observations (Moore), 24, 30, 40, 55, 62, 68
"Old Woman and the Statue, The" (Stevens), 120
One Flew Over the Cuckoo's Nest (Kesey), 159
O'Neill, Eugene, 86
Others, 54
Owl's Clover (Stevens), 82, 119–21

Pair of Blue Eyes, A (Hardy), 48, 50
Palmieri, Patricia Ann, 26, 31–32, 82
Paradise Lost (Milton), 66–67

Peebles, Rose, 111, 113
Pells, Richard, 110
Pennock, Dr., 33–34
Personae and Exultations (Pound), 44
"Peter" (Moore), 30, 50, 53–56, 61
physicians: on women's education and health, 23, 33, 34, 70
"Piningly" (Moore), 63, 78
Plank, George, 68
Plath, Otto, 156
Plath, Sylvia, 131–54, *142,* Bee poems, 155–74 (*see also as main entry*); and beekeeping, 156; college courses, 158; college life of, 20, 22–24, 26–28; on freedom, 157–59; on Fromm, 158–60; and initiation, 164–67; and lesbianism, 148–54; on marriage, 135–36; as mother's helper, 143–48; and Napoleon, 167–72; and Nicholas Hughes's birth, 163; on power, 155, 157; rage poems, 131, 151–52; role models of, 139–40; at Smith, 134–43; use of insect metaphor, 162 (*see also* Bee poems)
—Works: "The Applicant," 157, 162; *Ariel,* 131, 132, 148, 151, 153, 164, 167, 173;"The Babysitters," 133, 137, 141, 145–46, 148, 149, 154; *The Bell Jar,* 133, 143, 147, 149–52, 159–63, 172; "Blackberrying," 147, 150; "Burning the Letters," 164; *Collected Poems,* 131; "Daddy," 154, 157, 169, 170; "Den of Lions," 172; "The Detective," 164–66; "Ella Mason and Her Eleven Cats," 140; "Geography Lesson,"158; "The Goring," 132; "Heavy Women," 147; "Insomniac," 147; "Marcia," 141-42;"Metamorphoses of the Moon," 137–38, 155; "The Moon and the Yew Tree," 132–33, 149–50, 165, 174; "The Munich Mannequins," 133; "Notes to a Neophyte," 139; "The Rival," 167; "Two Sisters of Persephone," 140; "Spinster," 140; "The Surgeon at 2a.m.," 164; *Unabridged Journals*

(ed. Kukil), 149; "Virgin in a Tree," 170; "The Zookeeper's Wife," 147
"Poem Out of Childhood" (Rukeyser), 108
Poems of Marianne Moore, The (Schulman), 63
Pondrom, Cyrena, 55
Pope, Alexander: *Rape of the Lock*, 75, 76
Pound, Ezra, 20, 31, 44, 45; *A Draft of XVI Cantos*, 30; and Moore, 51–53, 75, 79; *Personae and Exultations*, 44; "Sestina: Altaforte," 50
"Progress" (Moore), 44
Prelude, The (Wordsworth), 145
Progressive Era, 20–22
Prouty, Olive Higgins, 139–40; *Now, Voyager*, 134; *Stella Dallas*, 134
Prufrock (Eliot), 55
Public Faces (Nicolson), 112
"Pym" (Moore), 36–42

Quiet Hour, A (Alexander), 38
Quinn, Alice, 95

Radcliffe College, 20, 175, 176
"Radical" (Moore), 47–48
Rape of the Lock (Pope), 75, 76
Rich, Adrienne, 89; college life, 20; *Snapshots of a Daughter-in-Law*, 173; "The Soul of a Women's College," 176
Richardson, Angelique, 45
Richardson, Dorothy, 114
Rickenbaugh, Ann: "Fear is Stifling College Liberals," 138–39
"Rival, The" (Plath), 167
Robinson Crusoe (Defoe), 103–4
romance of scholarship, 25, 59–61
Room of One's Own, A (Woolf), 21
"Roosters" (Bishop), 125
Rose, Jacqueline, 152
"Roses Only" (Moore), 68
Rukeyser, Muriel, 84, 86; college life, 20, 25; and Eliot, 110, 112; "Poem Out of Childhood," 108; *Theory of Flight*, 108

Russell, Red and Charlotte, 124
Russo, Mary, 93

Saints' Everlasting Rest, The (Baxter), 69
Sandison, Miss, 111
Sargent, John Singer, 21
Sappho, 86, 108, 151
Scan, 23, 135, 138, 139. See also *Sophian, The*
Schulman, Grace, ed.: *The Poems of Marianne Moore*, 63
Schulze, Robin, ed.: *Becoming Marianne Moore*, 64
Scientific American, 68
Scott, Joan Wallach, 37
Scripps College, 176
"Sea and Its Shore, The" (Bishop), 116–17
"Sea Unicorns and Land Unicorns" (Moore), 68
"September 1939" (Auden), 159
"Sestina: Altaforte" (Pound), 50
"Seven-Days Monologue" (Bishop), 90–94, 96, 104, 122, 126
Seventeen, 172
sex, 71, 73, 81. See also marriage
Sex and Suffrage in Britain: 1860–1914 (Kent), 65, 80–81
sexology, 88, 92; and anti-feminism, 86
Shaw, Anna Howard, 64; and National American Woman Suffrage Association, 77
"Skunk Hour" (Lowell), 159
"Silence" (Moore), 44
Sirk, Douglas: *Imitation of Life*, 143
Sitwell, Edith, 158
Slatin, John, 51
Smith College, 20, 27, 86, 132, 134–43, 156–57, 176–77
Smith-Rosenberg, Carroll, 29, 34, 45, 58, 82, 86
Snapshots of a Daughter-in-Law (Rich), 173
Soares, Lota de Macedo, 104, 105
socialist politics: and Bishop, 96, 108
Solomon, Barbara, 23, 35, 90, 133, 136
Sophian, The, 23, 135. See also *Scan*

"Soul of a Women's College, The" (Rich), 176
"Spinster" (Plath), 140
Spring and All (Williams), 30
Stanford, Donald, 84, 88
"Steeple-Jack, The" (Moore), 66
Stein, Gertrude, 44, 114
Stella Dallas (Prouty), 134
Stevens, Marjorie, 95
Stevens, Wallace, 109, 113, 123, 132; *Harmonium*, 30, 120, 124, 167; *Ideas of Order*, 124, 127; *The Man with the Blue Guitar*, 121; "Mr. Burnshaw and the Statue," 120;"The Old Woman and the Statue," 120; *Owl's Clover*, 82, 119, 121
Stevenson, Anne, 153
Stieglitz, Alfred, 44
"Stings" (Plath), 163, 172
Strangeways, Al, 158
"Student, The" (Moore), 19, 28
suffrage movement, 21, 22, 64, 65, 77–79
"Surgeon at 2 a.m., The" (Plath), 164
"Swarm, The" (Plath), 167–68, 170–71
Swenson, May, 149
"Summer's Dream, A" (Bishop), 94

"Tentative Critic, The" (Moore), 49
"Theatre, The" (Nathan), 86
"Then Came the Poor" (Bishop), 85, 96–99, 105–6
Theory of Flight (Rukeyser), 108
Thomas, M. Carey, 21, 23, 24, 30, 33, 35, 37, 46, 57, 58, 60, 61, 70, 77, 80, 82, 83, 135, 176
"Those Various Scalpels" (Moore), 68, 74
"Time's Andromedas" (Bishop), 114
Tipyn o'Bob, 36, 37, 44, 45
"To Be Liked by You Would Be a Calamity" (Moore), 48–50
"To a Screen-Maker" (Moore), 44
"Tradition and the Individual Talent" (Eliot), 113
Twelve Songs (Auden): "Fish in the Unruffled Lakes," 159

"Two Sisters of Persephone" (Plath), 140

Unabridged Journals (Plath, ed. Kukil), 149
Untermeyer, Louis, 107

Van Dyne, Susan, 131, 151, 152, 161, 172
Vassar College, 20, 22, 23, 83–86, 107, 133, 135; faculty of, 110–11
Vassar Journal of Undergraduate Studies, 109, 113
Vassar Review, The, 84, 87–89, 97, 109
Vindication of the Rights of Woman, A (Wollstonecraft), 80
"Virgin in a Tree" (Plath), 170–71

Walker, Cheryl, 107
Warner, John Riddle, 32
Warren, Robert Penn, and Cleanth Brooks: *Understanding Poetry*, 139
Waste Land, The (Eliot), 30
Watson, J. Sibley, 70
Webster, Daniel, 81, 82
Well Wrought Urn, The: Studies in the Structure of Poetry (Brooks), 139
Wellesley College, 23, 26, 32, 35, 135, 138, 175
Williams College, 138
Wharton, Edith, 37
"When I Buy Pictures" (Moore), 40–41
White, Heather Cass, 76
Whitman, Walt, 88, 108
Williams, William Carlos, 82; *Spring and All*, 30
Willis, Chris, 45
Willis, Patricia, 31, 36–38, 43, 44
Winnicott, D. W., 93
"Wintering" (Plath), 171–72
"Wisdom and Virtue" (Moore), 45–47, 50, 51, 65–66
Wollstonecraft, Mary: *A Vindication of the Rights of Woman*, 80
Woman's Education, A (Conway), 176–77
women: as homemakers/mothers, 20, 22, 23, 34, 86–87, 137, 143, 144;

views of, 35. *See also* homemaker ideal; lesbianism; marriage; physicians: on women's education and health
"Women Aren't Men" (Meyer), 136, 137
Women and Economics (Gilman), 80
women's colleges: 19–20, 23–26, 58, 60, 82–83, 85–87, 89, 132–36, 176. *See also* Bishop, Elizabeth; Moore, Marianne; Plath, Sylvia
Woolf, Virginia, 114, 157; *A Room of One's Own*, 21
"Word With You, A" (Bishop), 89–90, 97

Wordsworth, William, 146; *The Prelude*, 145
Wright, Benjamin, 135
Writer's Digest, 60
Wylie, Philip, 152, 153; *Generation of Vipers*, 137, 145–46

Yeats, W. B.: "Lapis Lazuli," 123
"Yellow Wallpaper, The" (Gilman), 33

Zona, Kirsten Hotelling, 51
"Zookeeper's Wife, The" (Plath), 147